e-Commerce:
Strategy, Technologies and Applications

INFORMATION SYSTEMS SERIES

Consulting Editors

D.E. AVISON
BA, MSc, PhD, FBCS
Professor of Information Systems
Département Systèmes
d' Information et de Décision
ESSEC Business School
France

G. FITZGERALD
BA, MSc, MBCS
Professor of Information Systems
Department of Information Systems and Computing
Brunel University
UK

Editorial Board

This series of student and postgraduate texts covers a wide variety of topics relating to information systems. It is designed to fulfil the needs of the growing number of courses on, and interest in, computing and information systems which do not focus on the purely technological aspects, but seek to relate information systems to their business and organisational contexts.

e-Commerce
Strategy, Technologies and Applications

David Whiteley

Manchester Metropolitan University

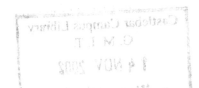
THE McGRAW-HILL COMPANIES

London · Burr Ridge IL · New York · St Louis · San Francisco · Auckland
Bogotá · Caracas · Lisbon · Madrid · Mexico · Milan
Montreal · New Delhi · Panama · Paris · San Juan · São Paulo
Singapore · Sydney · Tokyo · Toronto

658. 05468

Published by
McGraw-Hill Publishing Company
SHOPPENHANGERS ROAD, MAIDENHEAD, BERKSHIRE, SL6 2QL,
ENGLAND
Telephone +44 (0) 1628 502500
Fax: +44 (0) 1628 770224   Web site: http://www.mcgraw-hill.co.uk

British Library Cataloguing in Publication Data

A catalogue record for this book is available from the British Library

ISBN 007 709552 9

Library of Congress Cataloguing-in-Publication Data

The LOC data for this book has been applied for and may be obtained from
the Library of Congress, Washington, D.C.

Further information on this and other McGraw-Hill titles is to be found at
http://www.mcgraw-hill.co.uk
Authors Website address: http://www.mcgraw-hill.co.uk/textbooks/whiteley

Publisher: David Hatter
Produced by: Steven Gardiner Ltd
Cover by: Hybert Design
Printed by Bell & Bain Ltd., Glasgow

Contents

What we call 'Progress' is the exchange of one nuisance for another nuisance.

H. H. Havelock

Acknowledgements

My thanks to the many colleagues in Manchester and throughout the world who contributed to my thinking on e-Commerce. I enjoyed the discussions and the disputes.

Particular thanks go to Professor Andy Bytheway and Pamela Quick. Andy spent much time helping me towards a coherent structure for the book at a time when he was extremely busy making a move from England to the University of the Western Cape. Pam read the whole book, in bits as I got it ready, and suggested corrections and improvements in the sympathetic way that only Pam can.

Thanks are also due to Lena Dominelli, Keith Miller and Ning Zang for their help, encouragement and support

The way I see e-Commerce does not always match the views of my colleagues. The views in this book are my own, as are the errors and omissions that may have survived the reviewing and editing process.

DaveW

Series Foreword

The Information Systems Series is a series of student and postgraduate texts covering a wide variety of topics relating to information systems. The focus of the series is the use of computers and the flow of information in business and large organisations. The series is designed to fill the needs of the growing number of courses on information systems and computing which do not focus on purely technical aspects but which rather seek to relate information systems to their commercial and organisational context.

The term 'information systems' has been defined as the effective design, delivery, use and impact of information technology in organisations and society. Utilising this broad definition it is clear that the subject is interdisciplinary. Thus the series seeks to integrate technological disciplines with management and other disciplines, for example, psychology and sociology. These areas do not have a natural home and were, until comparatively recently, rarely represented by single departments in universities and colleges. To put such books in a purely computer science or management series restricts potential readership and the benefits that such texts can provide. The series on information systems provides such a home.

The titles are mainly for student use, although certain topics will be covered at greater depth and be more research oriented for postgraduate study.

The series includes the following areas, although this is not an exhaustive list: information systems development methodologies, office information systems, management information systems, decision-support systems, information modelling and databases, systems theory, human aspects and the human-computer interface, application systems, technology strategy, planning and control, expert systems, knowledge acquisition and its representation.

A mention of the books so far published in the series gives a 'flavour' of the richness of the information systems world. *Information and Data Modelling, second edition (David Benyon)* concerns itself with one very important aspect, the world of data, in some depth; *Information Systems Development: A Database Approach, second edition (David Avison)* provides a coherent methodology which has been widely used to develop adaptable computer systems using databases; *Multiview: An Exploration in Information Systems Development (David Avison and Trevor Wood-Harper)* looks at an approach to information systems development which combines human and technical considerations; *Relational Database Systems and Relational Database Design (Paul Beynon-Davies)* are two books which offer a comprehensive treatment of relational databases; *Business Management and Systems Analysis (Eddie Moynihan)* explores the areas of overlap between business and IT; *Decision Support Systems (Paul Rhodes)* places management decision making in the perspective of decision theory;

Information Systems: An Emerging Discipline? (John Mingers and Frank Stowell-Editor) debates the practical and philosophical dimensions of the field; *Why Information Systems Fail (Chris Sauer)* looks at the reasons for IS failure and the problems of developing IS in organisations; *Human Computer Factors (Andy Smith)* emphasises user-centred design, usability and the role of the users; *Transforming the Business: the IT Contribution (Robert Moreton and Myrvin Chester)* discusses the role that IS / IT can play in organisational change; and the second edition of *Information Systems Development: Methodologies, Techniques and Tools, (David Avison and Guy Fitzgerald)* provides a comprehensive coverage of the different elements of information systems development. *The Information Systems Life Cycle: A First Course in Information Systems (David Avison and Hanifa Shah)* covers the basic material necessary in a first course in information systems. It can be used as a 'prequel' to Avison and Fitzgerald but can also be used 'stand-alone' where the teaching of IS does not go beyond a first course.

The most recent additions to the series are *Rapid Information Systems Development* by Simon Bell and Trevor Wood-Harper and *Business Information Systems: a process approach* by Brian Warboys, Peter Kawalek, Mark Greenwood and Ian Robertson of the Informatics Process Group (IPG) at the University of Manchester. The first of these books explores rapid applications development in a clear and friendly manner with many examples to help readers in picturing how their real-world problems might be tackled. The second book arises from concern for the effectiveness of organisations and, in particular, the issues around how software support relates to business goals. It believes that modelling the organisational process provides a key to the comprehension of and the effective support of business goals. In doing so the book draws upon systems concepts; understanding organisations as systems highlights the requirements of co-ordination and change, thus providing a refreshing vantage point from which to approach the design of software systems.

We now add David Whiteley's *e-Commerce: Strategy, Technology and Applications* to the series. This is a timely addition from an author with wide experience in the subject. The book covers the three fundamental areas of the subject, Electronic Markets, EDI and Internet e-Commerce and EDI. The coverage ranges from the business use and implications of e-Commerce to the technical requirements. The book is supported by a comprehensive website containing introductory material on e-Commerce, software to support practical e-Commerce projects (an 'e-Commerce Kit') and technical information on HTML and EDI standards.

David Avison and Guy Fitzgerald

Preface

Electronic Commerce, or e-Commerce as we shall refer to it, is a hot topic. The press has just discovered it; governments and boardrooms see it as the essence of business strategy, and stock markets have gone mad for any company with a small turnover, large losses and an Internet connection.

The Internet and e-Commerce need some perspective. The first perspective is that e-Commerce did not just happen in 1998. Car companies and supermarkets have been doing e-Commerce for many years; their e-Commerce technology is called electronic data interchange (EDI). Airline seats have also been sold using e-Commerce systems; that technology is called an electronic market. The French public have also been doing it since 1983, but they do it in French with a system called Télétel.

This book looks at all three of these e-Commerce technologies: EDI, Electronic Markets and Internet e-Commerce. The examination encompasses both the business case for e-Commerce systems and the technology required for their implementation.

Part 1 is a single chapter. It looks at definitions of e-Commerce and introduces the concept of a trade cycle analysis, a model that will be further developed in the remainder of the book.

The business case for e-Commerce is examined in Part 2. Business use of e-Commerce is examined in the context of the value chain and competitive advantage systems. An approach to developing a business strategy for e-Commerce is proposed. The business study is rounded off with an examination of e-Commerce in the passenger air transport industry.

Business to business transactions are characterised by formalised trade exchanges within long-term supplier relationships. Part 3 looks at the use of all three e-Commerce technologies for business to business transactions but concentrates on the use of EDI for regular, repeat trade transactions.

Part 4 examines the use of e-Commerce for business to consumer transactions. Consumer e-Commerce is, for most organisations, the latest element of e-Commerce. The principal technology is the Internet; the web and the use and implementation of e-Shops is examined.

The book is completed in Part 5 by the concluding chapter. The three e-Commerce technologies facilitate an electronically co-ordinated value chain – arguably a pre-requisite for the competitive implementation of e-Commerce systems.

The book is planned for use both by students and business people:

- For the student reader the book covers the full range of topics that might reasonably be expected on an Information Technology / Information Systems, e-Commerce course. The book includes suggestions for exercises and further reading at the end of every chapter.

- For the business reader the book presents the business case but also makes clear the practical implications of implementing e-Commerce systems, a combination not normally available in business books.

The book includes an introduction to EDI Standards and to formatting a web page using HTML.

The book is accompanied by extensive supporting material on the web. The use of the web allows for additional material and examples and it includes an 'e-Commerce kit'. The web material is to be updated on a regular basis and enables us to keep the overall package up-to-date with developments in this fast moving field.

The web site for the book is at: http://www.mcgraw-hill.co.uk/textbooks/whiteley.

Trademarks:

Products and services referred to in this book may be trademark and protected under license. The author and publisher make no claim, express or implied, to these trademarks.

Part 1

Introduction to Electronic Commerce

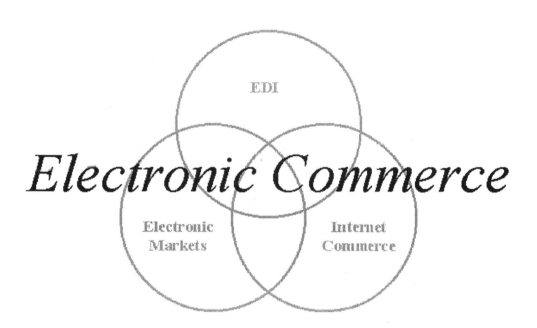

1

Electronic Commerce

Summary

Electronic Commerce (e-Commerce) is a general concept covering any form of business transaction or information exchange executed using information and communication technologies (ICTs). e-Commerce takes place between companies, between companies and their customers, or between companies and public administrations. Electronic Commerce includes electronic trading of goods, services and electronic material (Esprit, 1997).

e-Commerce systems include commercial transactions on the Internet but their scope is much wider than this; they can be classified by application type:

- *Electronic Markets:*
  The principle function of an electronic market is to facilitate the search for the required product or service. Airline booking systems are an example of an electronic market.
- *Electronic Data Interchange (EDI):*
  EDI provides for the efficient transaction of recurrent trade exchanges between commercial organisations. EDI is widely used by, for example, large retail groups and vehicle assemblers when trading with their suppliers.
- *Internet Commerce:*
  The Internet (and similar network facilities) can be used for advertising goods and services and transacting one-off deals. Internet commerce has application for both business to business and business to consumer transactions.

In this chapter, these areas of e-Commerce are outlined in relation to the trading exchanges / trade cycles to which they most appropriately apply. The three areas of e-Commerce are discussed in greater detail in the following chapters.

1.1   The Scope of Electronic Commerce

Electronic Commerce (e-Commerce) is a term popularised by the advent of commercial services on the Internet. Internet e-Commerce is however, only one part of the overall sphere of e-Commerce. The commercial use of the Internet is perhaps typified by once-off sales to consumers. Other types of transactions use other technologies. Electronic Markets (EMs) are in use in a number of trade segments with an emphasis on search facilities and Electronic Data Interchange (EDI) is used for regular and standardised transactions between organisations. The mainstream of e-Commerce consists of these three areas; these are represented as a diagram in Figure 1.1 and outlined in a little more detail below.

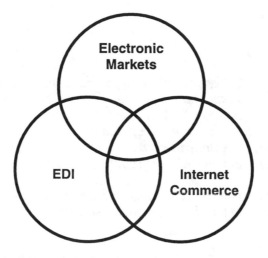

Fig. 1.1 The three categories of e-Commerce.

- Electronic Markets:
  An electronic market is the use of information and communications technology to present a range of offerings available in a market segment so that the purchaser can compare the prices (and other attributes) of the offerings and make a purchase decision. The usual example of an electronic market is an airline booking system.

- Electronic Data Interchange (EDI):
  EDI provides a standardised system for coding trade transactions so that they can be communicated directly from one computer system to another without the need for printed orders and invoices and the delays and errors implicit in paper handling. EDI is used by organisations that make a large number of regular transactions. One sector where EDI is extensively used is the large supermarket chains which use EDI for transactions with their suppliers.

- Internet Commerce:
  Information and communications technologies can also be used to advertise and make once-off sales of a wide range of goods and services. This type of e-Commerce is typified by the commercial use of

the Internet. The Internet can, for example, be used for the purchase of books that are then delivered by post or the booking of tickets that can be picked up by the clients when they arrive at the event. It is to be noted that the Internet is not the only technology used for this type of service and this is not the only use of the Internet in e-Commerce.

1.2   Definition of Electronic Commerce

Electronic commerce is, like so much in the areas of business and information systems, the subject of numerous definitions.

Some authors see e-Commerce as largely or entirely an Internet phenomenon. Seddon (1997) has suggested that 'the world has just entered a third new phase in the evolution of IT capabilities: the Internet era'. The suggestion divides the evolution of information technology (IT) into 20 year periods:

- 1955–1974   The Electronic Data Processing (EDP) era.
- 1975–1994   The Management Information System (MIS) era.
- 1995–2014?   The Internet era.

He goes on to say:

> 'If you accept the proposition that IT capability is dramatically different in each of these 20 year steps, and that the third step is distinguished by world-wide access to the Internet by millions of firms and individuals, the definition of Electronic Commerce is easy:
>> Electronic Commerce is commerce enabled by Internet-era technologies.'

It is the commercialisation and popularisation of the Internet that has put e-Commerce towards the top of the public and political agenda but e-Commerce using electronic markets and EDI have been an established part of the business scene for at least a decade prior to the 'Internet era'. A more general definition of e-Commerce is given by Wigand (1997) as:

> '... the seamless application of information and communication technology from its point of origin to its endpoint along the entire value chain of business processes conducted electronically and designed to enable the accomplishment of a business goal. These processes may be partial or complete and may encompass business to business as well as business to consumer and consumer to business transactions'

This definition introduces the value chain, an important point as e-Commerce technologies can be applied in transactions between manufacturer and supplier, manufacturer and retailer and / or retailer / service supplier and consumer. The definition is, however, possibly a bit all embracing; one is tempted to think of an order processing system of the EDP era as an e-Commerce system with 'partial' e-Commerce processing. A further definition of e-Commerce is provided at a

European Union web site (Esprit, 1997):

> 'Electronic Commerce is a general concept covering any form of business transactions or information exchange executed using information and communication technology, between companies, between companies and their customers, or between companies and public administrations.
>
> Electronic Commerce includes electronic trading of goods, services and electronic material.'

A useful but somewhat broad definition. This book proposes and uses another definition, derived from definitions of telework:

> 'Formulating commercial transactions at a site remote from the trading partner and then using electronic communications to execute that transaction.'

The intention is to exclude the 'conventional' use of information technology (IT) and information systems (IS) such as electronic point of sales (EPOS), order processing and stock control systems; these uses of IT are adequately examined in other information systems literature.

1.3   Electronic Commerce and the Trade Cycle

e-Commerce can be applied to all, or to different phases, of the trade cycle. The trade cycle varies depending on:

- The nature of the organisations (or individuals) involved.
- The frequency of trade between the partners to the exchange.
- The nature of the goods or services being exchanged.

The trade cycle has to support:

- Finding goods or services appropriate to the requirement and agreeing the terms of trade (referred to as search and negotiation).
- Placing the order, taking delivery and making payment (execution and settlement).
- After-sales activities such as warrantee, service, etc.

There are numerous versions of the trade cycles depending on the factors outlined above and, for many transactions, further complicated by the complexities of international trade. That said, three generic trade cycles can be identified:

- Regular, repeat transactions between commercial trading partners (repeat trade cycle).
- Irregular transactions between commercial trading partners where

execution and settlement are separated ('credit' transactions).
- Irregular transactions in once-off trading relationships where execution and settlement are typically combined ('cash' transactions).

The trade cycles for these three categories are shown in Figure 1.2. The applicability of each of the three forms of e-Commerce to these trade cycles is discussed in the following sections.

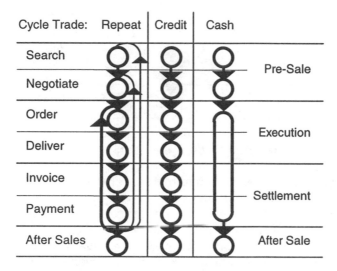

Fig. 1.2 Generic Trade Cycles.

1.4 Electronic Markets

An electronic market is an inter-organisational information system that provides facilities for buyers and sellers to exchange information about price and product offerings (Been, *et al.*, 1995). The electronic market is primarily about the search phase of the trade cycle, see Figure 1.3. The electronic market is most effective in assisting the buyer in a commodity market where products are essentially identical across all sellers. In a differentiated market there is a variety of product offerings and the search problem is more complex. An effective electronic market increases the efficiency of the market, it reduces the search cost for the buyer and makes it more likely that the buyer will continue the search until the 'best buy' is found. The effect for the supplier might be less encouraging:

> 'The effect of an electronic market in a commodity market is a more efficient distribution of information which causes decreasing profit possibilities for sellers.'

(Been, *et al.*, 1995)

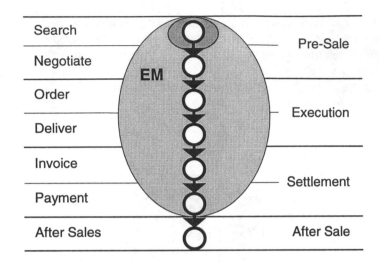

Fig. 1.3 Electronic Markets and Trade Cycle.

Electronic Markets (and electronic information services giving product and price data) exist in commodity exchanges, financial markets and they are also extensively used in the airline industry for passenger seat sales. The use of electronic markets is illustrated by the airline booking system. In this case, the primary use of the electronic markets is to locate an available seat, for the journey the customer wants to make, at a time that is convenient and a price that is acceptable. The electronic market then also allows the deal to be executed and payment to be made. By their nature this, and other electronic markets, conform to one of the Irregular Transaction trade cycles, see Figure 1.3; they may be used only for the pre-sale part of the trade cycle or they may include execution and settlement functions. Electronic markets also tend to be available only to intermediaries – it is the travel agent, not the customer, that uses the airline booking system.

Airline booking systems and a number of other electronic markets have been operational since the 1980's. Malone, *et al.* (1987) predicted that the possibility of using IT to co-ordinate economic activity would lead to a greater use of markets (as opposed to hierarchies) and to more effective competition:

> '... the overall effect of this technology will be to increase the proportion of economic activity co-ordinated by markets.'

In the event this does not seem to be the case. The importance of electronic markets in the sectors where they operate has increased but there has not been any dramatic expansion of the use of electronic markets to additional economic sectors. Part of the difficulty of establishing new electronic markets relates to activities by vendors to gain competitive advantage by product differentiation and techniques to lock-in customers, see Chapter 5 for an examination of the case of the passenger air transport industry. Fundamentally the problem is that the electronic market relies on information provided by the vendors but, as established above, an electronic market is likely to be disadvantageous to (most) vendors in the market place. The Been, *et al.* (1995) paper, referred to above, gives a case study of an attempt by Reuters to establish an electronic information system for the spot market in air cargo space. The initiative did not get the co-operation of the carriers, forwarders or integrators, all of which stood to lose profit margin from greater market transparency, and eventually the initiative failed.

Up to now, this section has been dealing with electronic markets formed to service particular market or product sectors. Alternatively a public access network can be seen as an electronic market and can be used with an index or a search engine to find vendors of the required product or service. The general and non-standardised nature of a service such as the Internet does not provide for an optimised electronic market. Aficionados of the Internet will claim great success for such searchers but, for the average punter, such use of the Internet very often ends in frustration.

It may well be that technical changes in the specification of information, e.g. XML and tags (Wilson, 1997) and in the search engine can improve the situation but it is equally likely that the increased volume of information, disparities in technical standards and the commercial imperatives on indexing services will work the other way. Schofield (1997) quotes Sullivan (Search Engine Watch) as follows:

> '... Sullivan suspects that the major search engines are not keeping pace with the growth of the Web, or with the changes of technology that make the Web a harder place to search.'

The nature and use of electronic markets is further explored in Chapter 7.

1.5   Electronic Data Interchange

EDI is based on a set of standardised messages for the transfer of structured data between computer applications. It can have many applications, e.g. sending test results from the pathology laboratory to the hospital or despatching exam results from the exam boards to schools, but it is principally used for trade exchanges: orders, invoices, payments and the many other transactions that can be used in national and international trade exchanges. Notable users of EDI are vehicle assemblers, ordering components for their production lines, and supermarkets (and other multiple retailers), ordering the goods needed to restock their shelves. EDI allows the stock control / materials management system of the customer to interface with the stock control / production systems of the suppliers without the use of paper documents or the need for human intervention.

EDI is used for regular repeat transactions, see Figure 1.4. It takes quite a lot of work to set up systems to send and retrieve EDI messages and, in general, it is not applicable to one-off exchanges. Also EDI is a formal system and it does not really have a place in the search and negotiation phases (although there have been attempts to formulate messages for this purpose).

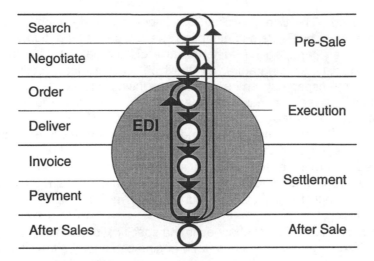

Fig. 1.4 EDI and the Trade Cycle.

EDI, when initially introduced was seen by many as a universal, or at least a generalised, form of trading. In the event its adoption has been limited to a number of trade sectors where the efficiency of the supply chain is of vital importance – the word limited is used above but that limit covers a vast number of transactions.

EDI tends to be limited to (or 'owned by') large organisations which set up their purchasing and logistics systems to utilise EDI and then demand that their immediate suppliers fit in with the arrangement. It is noticeable that while these suppliers will conform with this 'request' there is not necessarily any great enthusiasm from these companies to adopt EDI for trading with their own, second tier suppliers.

EDI is part of schemes for just-in-time manufacture and quick response supply. Mature use of EDI allows for a change in the nature of the product or service being offered – mass customisation is such an example.

EDI, its technical details and its business use is further explored in Chapters 8, 9 and 10.

1.6   Internet Commerce

e-Commerce can be and is used for once-off transactions. This area of trade is typified by the consumer purchasing over the Internet but there are (or have been) other networks:

- Television sales channels are in use in the US;
- The French Minitel is a mature example of an interactive, public access network;

and this type of e-Commerce is also used by organisations to make once-off or infrequent purchases of items such as computer and office supplies.

This form of e-Commerce may give its customers credit facilities but is typified by the 'cash' trade cycle (where a 'cash' payment is taken to include settlement at the time of purchase by a credit card or some form of e-cash), see Figure 1.5.

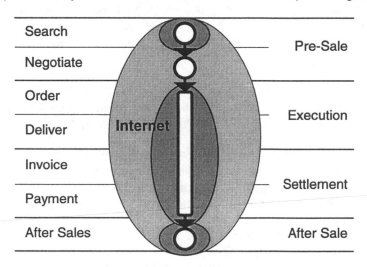

Search		Pre-Sale
Negotiate		
Order		Execution
Deliver	**Internet**	
Invoice		Settlement
Payment		
After Sales		After Sale

Fig. 1.5 Internet and the Trade Cycle.

The Internet can be used for all or part of the trade cycle:

- The first stage of the trade cycle is search and the facilities of the Internet can be used to locate sites offering, or advertising, appropriate goods or services; a function, as already mentioned, that is similar to an electronic market. In many instances, Internet sites offer only information and any further steps down the trade cycle are conducted on the telephone or at a conventional shop outlet.
- An increasing number of sites offer facilities to execute and settle the transaction, or in normal parlance to make a purchase – delivery may be electronic or by a home delivery service depending on the nature of the goods or service being offered. The use of the Internet for on-line purchasing may or may not follow a search – publishing a web site address is an increasingly common feature on conventional advertising.
- The final use of Internet e-Commerce is for after-sales service. Many IT providers now offer on-line support and on-line services such a banking are, arguably, a special case of the use of after-sales transactions. Again the use of the Internet for after-sales may or may not be a follow-on to an earlier on-line transaction.

Some of the hype about Internet commerce would seem to suggest that it will displace most or all other forms of retailing. The hype constantly predicts the 'breakthrough' a couple of years ahead or once the next piece of technical 'gee-wizery' is in place. The reality is somewhat different. Some sites, arguably niche traders, are doing very well (amazon.com is the most frequently quoted example) but other sites have produced very little by way of direct sales.

Internet trade is not suited to all goods or to all people. Marketing strategy is popularly enshrined in the concept of the four Ps: product, price, promotion and place (Needle, 1994). The Internet as a marketing and sales channel can be examined in this context:

- Product: Some products are more suited than others to selling over the Internet. Existing mail order operations give an indication and technical products, that would appeal to an Internet audience, could be added to the list.
- Price: The Internet can have a price advantage. There is no need for a retail outlet and the business facilities needed by an Internet vendor could be relatively cheap. Set against this is the cost of delivering goods and the premium rate currently being charged by credit card companies to some Internet vendors.
- Promotion: The Internet provides a very cheap way of promoting a company and a product. That said, promotion on the Internet, unlike almost any other form of advertising, relies an the customer having the facility to access the Internet and then using it to find the promotional material.
- Place: Internet purchases have to be delivered to the client. Information services can be delivered electronically but tangible goods require costly physical delivery (and for bulky items, someone available to accept the delivery).

Bloch *et al.* (1996) in their paper 'Leveraging Electronic Commerce for Competitive Advantage: a Business Value Framework' provides an intelligent assessment of the possibilities and uncertainties of e-Commerce on the Internet. They, somewhat graphically, sum up the overall uncertainty thus:

> 'Some, for instance, think the Internet is like the Gold Rush in the 1900s, where only Levi's selling jeans and pick sellers were making money. Others believe the World Wide Web is like China, i.e. that people investing now are there for the future but don't get much or any value today.'

Or as a first year student put it in an essay on e-Commerce:

> 'You would not buy an ice-cream cone over the Internet.'

The Cats-Baril and Jelassi case study on Minitel usage (1994) is perhaps relevant here with statistics suggesting that, as the novelty wears off, people get down to efficiently using the services they know about and that they find useful.

1.7   e-Commerce in Perspective

e-Commerce is not appropriate to all business transactions and, within e-Commerce there is no one technology that can or should be appropriate to all requirements.

e-Commerce is not a new phenomenon; electronic markets, EDI and consumer e-Commerce on the Minitel have been around for many years. Predictions in the past have included:

- The expansion of electronic markets into a significantly greater number of trade sectors than has been the case.
- The use of EDI as a universal and non-proprietary way of doing business.

The suggestion of this book, supported by an examination of Internet commerce and the evolution of other forms of e-Commerce, is that Internet commerce will similarly settle down as just one, albeit an important one, of many ways of doing business. Figure 1.6 merges the Venn diagram showing three categories of e-Commerce (Figure 1.1) with the three generic trade cycles (Figure 1.2) to suggest, in general terms, how differing business requirements are most likely to match onto the available e-Commerce technologies.

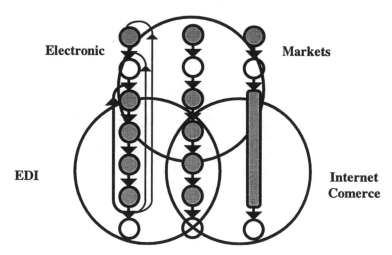

Fig. 1.6 e-Commerce Technologies and Generic Trade Cycles.

The business background to e-Commerce is further discussed in Part 2 followed by business to business e-Commerce (principally EDI) in Part 3 and business to consumer e-Commerce (Internet commerce) in Part 4. The book aims to set out the business opportunities presented by e-Commerce and to explain the technology that will support these developments. e-Commerce is a developing technology that presents many exciting opportunities – its successful implementation requires realistic evaluation and careful planning.

Further Reading

A useful paper discussing the definition and scope of e-Commerce is:

Wigand, R. T. (1997) 'Electronic Commerce: Definition, Theory and Context', *The Information Society*, Vol. 13, No. 1, pp. 1–16.

Further papers covering this area are available on the Internet; the relevant url's are available from the book's web page.

Part 2

Business Strategy in an Electronic Age

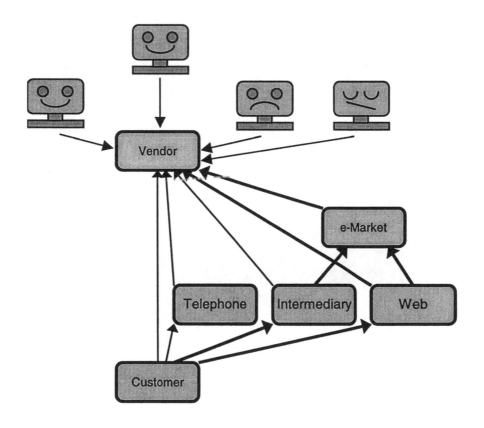

2

The Value Chain

Summary

Chapter 2 introduces the concepts of the supply chain, value chain and the value system.

The production of goods and services is the result of the efforts of many organisations – a complex web of contracts and co-operation known as the supply chain or the value system. The structure of the value system varies greatly between business sectors and sometimes between different organisations within a sector.

Each stage in the supply chain adds value, the interfaces between the stages require the exchange of information and e-Commerce technologies can be utilised for many of these interfaces.

2.1 Supply Chains

The products sold in shops and purchased for use in organisations are the result of a complex web of relationships between manufacturers, component suppliers, wholesalers, retailers and the logistic infrastructure that links them together. Superimposed on this web of co-operating trading partners is a further layer of organisations that provide services such as the machinery used by manufacturers, advertising for the product and so on. Most organisations have a large number of trade relationships. For large retailers and manufacturers of complex products the number of supplier organisations will be hundreds and possibly thousands.

The web of trade relationships is referred to as the supply chain or the value chain (as each stage adds value to the product before passing it on). Value chains differ between trade sectors and some of these differences are brought out in later chapters in this book. An overall value chain for a manufactured product, in a very simple form, is shown in Figure 2.1.

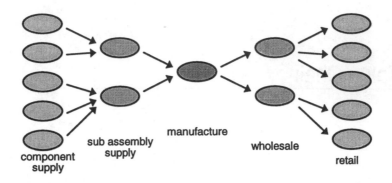

Fig. 2.1 Manufacturing Value Chain.

Each trade exchange in the supply chain is a transaction that adds cost without adding intrinsic value. e-Commerce is, borrowing from Wigland's definition (see Chapter 1), the application of information and communications technology to the value chain to enable the accomplishment of a business goal. The business goal can be to reduce costs, improve service or to tap into a new market. The form of e-Commerce that is appropriate is dependant on the circumstances of the party to the exchange and the nature of the trade relationship.

2.2   Porter's Value Chain Model

Porter (1985) introduced his model of the Generic Value Chain in his book *Competitive Advantage: Creating and Sustaining Superior Performance*. This followed on from his more famous model of Competitive Forces that will be used in Chapter 3.

Porter's model was essentially concerned with the internal activities of the company. The three (basic) primary activities of a product process are:

- Inbound Logistics: Handling goods that are bought into the company, storing them and making them available to operations as required.
- Operations: The production process, in many cases a series of sub-activities that can be represented on a detailed value chain analysis.
- Outbound Logistics: Taking the products of the company, storing them if necessary and distributing them to the customer in a timely manner.

To these basic primary activities Porter adds two further primary activities:

- Marketing and Sales: Finding out the requirements of potential customers and letting them know of the products and services that can be offered.
- Service: Any requirement for installation or advice before delivery and then after-sales service once the transaction is completed.

To support these primary functions there will be a company infrastructure that performs a number of support activities. Porter classifies these activities as:

- Procurement: The function of finding suppliers of the materials required as inputs to the operations of the organisation. Procurement is responsible for negotiating quality supplies at an acceptable price and with reliable delivery.
- Technology Development: The organisation needs to update its production processes, train staff and to manage innovation to ensure that its products and its overall range of goods and services remain competitive.
- Human Resources Management: The recruitment, training and personnel management of the people who work for the organisation.
- Firm Infrastructure: The overall management of the company including planning and accountancy.

Porter's diagram of the generic value chain is reproduced at Figure 2.2.

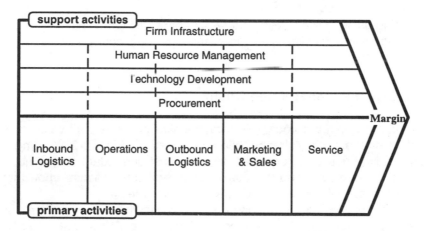

Fig. 2.2 Porter's Generic Value Chain.

The generic value chain is just the starting point to constructing a specific value chain for a company or division of a company. Having identified the component activities and linkages each element can be analysed in terms of cost and value added so that the overall efficiency of the value chain can be established. Once analysed any performance deficits can be addressed to improve product quality, customer service and / or price competitiveness.

The efficiency of the linkages may be enhanced by the use of information and communications technologies (ICTs). Internal linkages can be co-ordinated using e-Commerce technologies but they are more likely to be embedded in point-of-sale / stock control systems or production / materials requirement planning systems. The internal systems, in turn, need to interface with suppliers and customers. The production planning and control process can inform the inbound logistics system of the quantity and timing of components / stock requirements. The marketing and sales system can be interfaced with production and outbound logistics to improve the quality of service delivery, see Figure 2.3.

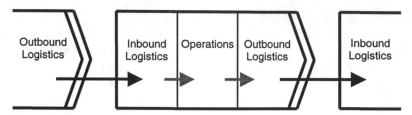

Fig. 2.3 Value Chain Linkages.

ICTs can also be used in other value chain activities; possible applications are:

- Human Resources Management using electronic media to advertise vacancies in the organisation;
- Procurement using online searches to identify appropriate sources of supply;
- Marketing using online advertising or portable sales terminals;
- Servicing providing online assistance and / or fault diagnosis.

2.3 Inter Organisational Value Chain

The value chain within a company is a microcosm of the overall value chain; the nature of that chain has already been indicated in Figure 2.1. The overall competitive advantage of an organisation is not just dependant on the quality and efficiency of the company and the quality of its products but also upon that of its suppliers and of any wholesalers and retailers it may use.

The analysis of the overall supply chain is called the *value system*; the term introduced by Porter (1985) in the book *Competitive Advantage: Creating and Sustaining Superior Performance*, see Figure 2.4

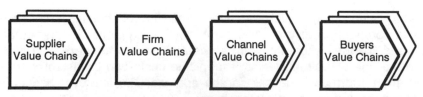

(The Channel refers to intermediaries such as wholesalers.)

Fig. 2.4 Porter's Value System (Single Firm).

Value chains differ considerably across trade sectors and between different organisations within a trade sector. Value systems in automobile assembly, food supermarkets and the insurance sector are summarised as follows:

- Automobile assembly uses a vast number of components; the making of a car is a component assembly job. Some of the components, such as engines and body panels, may be produced by the company (possibly in other plants), whereas most of the parts: lights, brakes, wheels, tyres, etc. are bought in from suppliers. Components are delivered to the production line on a just-in-time basis; larger components might be 'sequenced delivery' with their arrival synchronised to match the order of the vehicles on the assembly line.

  The sales channel is the dealer network; each vehicle assembler sells through a chain of dealers tied by contract to that marque. Each dealer is assigned a sales territory and the cars are not normally available through any other sales channel (although that is argued to be anticompetitive and changes may be forced upon the industry). Vehicle supply to the network is a mixture of the carmaker instructing the dealers what to stock and the dealers ordering to meet demand. The dealer network also has a system of swapping vehicles so that the specific requirements of a customer can be met.

  The automobile assembly value system is summarised in Figure 2.5.

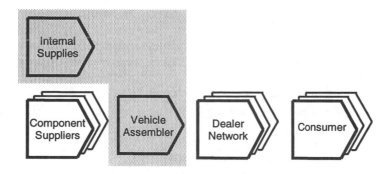

Fig. 2.5 Value System for Automobile Assembly.

- Food retailers divide into those, such as the large supermarket chains, who deal direct with the manufacturers and the small retailers who need to deal with a wholesaler.

  The supermarket supply chain is from the food manufacturer. Produce is either delivered to a regional distribution depot or direct to the shop. Items that are relatively small or are sold in modest quantities can be delivered by the manufacturer to the regional depot where the load can be split up and sent on to the shops where they are needed.   Items required in large quantities or that need to be very fresh can be delivered direct from the supplier to the supermarket, obviating the need to 'double handle' the goods at the regional warehouse. The supermarket sells directly to the consumer; there is no requirement for any intermediary or 'channel'.

The supply chains of the supermarkets differ from smaller retailers who get much of their produce from a wholesaler rather than direct from the manufacturer.

The supermarket value system is summarised in Figure 2.6.

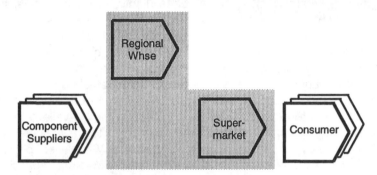

Fig. 2.6 Value System of the Supermarkets.

- Insurance is a service industry and, unlike the manufacture and retail value systems outlined above, it is not directly reliant on its suppliers. Its value system is therefore focused on sales. Insurance policies to the public can be:
  - Sold by an agent employed by the Insurance Company;
  - Sold by a intermediary (the 'channel'), typically an insurance broker;
  - Direct sales using telesales or the Internet.

The value system for the insurance company is represented in Figure 2.7.

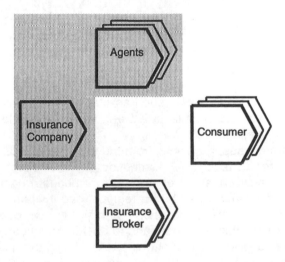

Fig. 2.7 Value System for Insurance.

In each of these three cases the buyer is the consumer, an ordinary member of the public as opposed to an organisation, and as such there is not a buyer value chain to analyse.

As already discussed, an organisation needs to analyse its own value chain and it should apply similar techniques to its overall value system. The organisation needs to establish which of its inter-organisational relationships add to its competitive advantage and which fail to achieve appropriate levels of quality and price. As illustrated in the summaries above, value chains do differ between organisations in the same trade sector and those organisations can usefully benchmark their practices against those of competitors to see if they are achieving industry best practice.

The linkages in the value system have to be managed. These linkages do not add intrinsic value and their efficiency relative to competitor organisations can be a source of competitive advantage. The physical linkages involve goods handling, transport and warehousing. These are complimented by administrative linkages that are summarised by the trade cycle, introduced in Chapter 1. The essential stages are:

- Pre-sale: finding a supplier ad agreeing terms;
- Execution: placing an order and taking delivery of the goods;
- Settlement: requesting and receiving payment;
- After-sales: any subsequent support actions.

These stages can also be co-ordinated using e-Commerce techniques. The use of e-Commerce alters the time frame and cost structure of the administration of the value chain. It can be used to re-engineer the linkages in terms of:

- Just-in-time manufacture or quick response supply. Techniques that reduce materials handling, investment in stock and the need for warehousing facilities.
- Efficient document processing; removing the need for paper documents and facilitating the efficient machine matching of the exchanges from each stage of the trade cycle.

The efficient organisation of the supply or value chain is an important source of competitive advantage. Competitive advantage is the subject of the next chapter.

Exercises

The exercises for this chapter concentrate on the value system; some knowledge of the operation of business is assumed.

- Consider the value system of the insurance industry, for sales to the public, and comment on the advantages and disadvantages of the three sales channels that are outlined.

- Outline the value system of an organisation you know. Identify linkages where e-Commerce might be usefully applied.

Further Reading

The basic source text on the value chain is:

Porter, M. E. (1985) *Competitive Advantage: Creating and Sustaining Superior Performance*, Free Press, New York.

This material has subsequently been reproduced and discussed in many subsequent business / IS texts. Examples of texts that include this material are:

Morton, R. and Chester, M. (1997) *Transforming the Business: the IT contribution*, McGraw Hill, Maidenhead, UK.
Lynch, R. (1997) *Corporate Strategy*, Pitman, London.

3

Competitive Advantage

Summary

Commercial organisations only survive if they are competitive; they prosper if they achieve a competitive advantage. The two generic competitive strategies are price leadership and product differentiation. The threats to a competitive position are explained using Porter's model.

The use of e-Commerce to achieve competitive price advantage, differentiation and to combat competitive threats is illustrated with case study examples.

3.1 Competitive Strategy

The ability of an organisation to prosper arises from its competitive advantage over the other organisations operating within its market sector. The ability of the organisation to survive requires that its competitive position is not significantly less than the other firms operating within the market sector.

The three basic strategies for competitive advantage are cost leadership, differentiation and focus (Porter, 1980). Cost leadership is simply to be able to sell the goods or provide the service at a price that is lower than that of the competition. Differentiation is where the goods or services provided have some quality that makes them more attractive than competing products even though the competition may have a somewhat lower price. Focus is concentration on a single aspect of the market, a product niche.

Information and communications technologies (ICTs) can have a considerable part to play in a competitive strategy. The appropriate use of IS and IT can lower the administrative costs of the organisation and the use of ICTs, in the logistics supply chain, can add to that advantage. The use of ICTs, in addition to cost reductions, can also differentiate a product in terms of quality of service and responsiveness to customer requirements. For the niche player, ICTs can be used to target information on the selected segment and to gather customer data from that segment. Eventually quick response supply and just-in-time manufacture, enabled by ICTs, can provide the capability to evolve new products and services and to facilitate customisation.

The classic cases of competitive advantages facilitated by ICTs include:

- American Hospital Supplies (AHS, latterly Baxter Health Care) who provided their customers (the hospitals) with online terminal access to their order processing systems. The hospitals found online ordering convenient and, in many cases, switched an increasing amount of their business to AHS. Additional the AHS system provided a stock control function, a value added service which had a 'lock-in' effect on the customers of their service.

- Airline booking systems, such as American Airline's Sabre system and United's Apollo system, that were initially developed as competitive weapons with the flights of their owning airlines displayed more prominently than those of their rivals. After anti-trust cases they were required to act as unbiased markets but continued to make substantial profits for their owning airlines.

- Federal Express which launched a web site allowing customers to track the progress of their packages whilst in transit. The facility was quickly copied by UPS, one of FedEx's major competitors but the third major player in the market, DHL, was a couple of years later in launching a matching service.

Each of these cases is an example of the use of e-Commerce and it is that area of the application of IS and IT that is, in the current technology and trading environment, most likely to produce competitive advantage for an organisation.

3.2 Porter's Model

The basis of much of the thinking on competitive advantage has been the writing of Michael Porter. Porter, in his book *Competitive Strategy: Techniques for Analysing Industries and Competitors* (1980) introduced his model of competitive rivalry; a model that is still widely used in business and academic papers.

Porter's model helps a firm identify threats to its competitive position and to lay plans, that may include IT and e-Commerce, to protect or enhance that position. The model, see Figure 3.1, shows five forces of competitive rivalry:

- Competitive rivalry among existing firms in the trade sector;
- Threat of potential new entrants to the sector;
- Threat of a substitute product or service to the existing trade;
- The bargaining power of the buyers;
- The bargaining power of the suppliers.

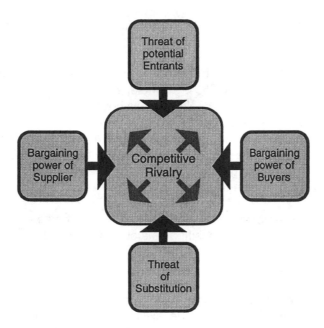

Fig. 3.1 Porter's Model of Competitive Forces.

Typically one or two of these forces dominate in an analysis of the competitive position of an organisation in a trade sector.   Each of these threats is further examined below.

- **Threat of New Entrants**

The threat of new entrants relates to the ease with which a new company, or a company in a different product area can enter a given trade sector. Barrier to entry into a particular market include the need for capital, knowledge and skills.   The barriers to entry, for example, to the vehicle assembly sector are massive; to start building cars there is the need to develop a new model range, build a car assembly plant, contract a large number of component suppliers and sign up a dealer network. Getting into business in building personal computers is, in contrast, much easier; the components are readily available and there is not the same need for investment in product development or large-scale production facilities before the company makes a start.

   IT can be a barrier to entry to a given market place. Existing players in the sector may well have a substantial investment in IS / IT, including for instance the use of EDI to co-ordinate their supply chain. This experience and investment can be difficult for a new entrant to match. The converse is that developments in IT and e-Commerce may leave existing players with a heavy investment in expensive, obsolescent technologies giving the new entrant the opportunity to enter the market with fresh ideas and a business plan facilitated by a new generation of IT provision. Internet e-Commerce is a technology that can facilitate new entrants to existing markets without the need to match the IT and infrastructure investment of the existing players. Recent developments in Internet e-Commerce have facilitated the entry of new players into a number of market segments; examples are:

- The advent of Internet bookshops where new operators, with amazon.com being the obvious example, have been able to set-up in competition with traditional bookshops without the need to invest in a chain of high street bookstores.
- Internet banks where setting up online has, like the bookstores, avoided the need to invest in a branch network and the use of commercially available banking packages has avoided the need to match the major IS development costs of the traditional banks.

Arguably, in some segments, the use of Internet e-Commerce changes the nature of the product sufficiently to be classified as a substitute product.

- **Threat of Substitution**

Substitution is a threat to existing players where a new product becomes available that supplies the same function as the existing product or service. The classic examples are the (partial) substitution of natural fibres such as cotton and wool by synthetic fibres or the replacement of glass bottles by a plastic alternative in some sectors of the packaging industry. Existing players can protect themselves by keeping their product up-to-date or alternatively, in some instances, have become major players in the business of supplying the substitute product.

The IT industry has itself substituted many products previously used in business with the replacement of the typewriter by the word processor being but one example. Of the e-Commerce technologies, Internet e-Commerce has the potential to make significant inroads into traditional retail sectors with online banking or down-loadable music from the artist's web site, being substitute distribution channels for conventional retailing and, arguably, constituting substitute products.

- **Bargaining power of Buyers**

For a business to be profitable the cost of producing and distributing its product has to be less than the price it can fetch in the market place. Where there are a number of competitors in the market or a surplus of supply the buyer is in a strong position to bargain for a low price and for other favourable conditions of trade. Over recent years the large retail chains have developed a strong bargaining position vis-a-vis their suppliers. For many, or most, products sold in supermarkets or department stores there are several sources of supply and the buyer has been able to dictate the price paid (and other terms of trade) to the supplier; the threat is that if you do not accept our terms then there are other suppliers that will.

The bargaining strength of the buyer is of least threat to the low cost producer; that organisation can agree to tight terms of trade that competitor firms could not profitably match. The other defence is to have a branded product that the store will feel obliged to stock because their customers expect it. Branded goods that food stores feel obliged to carry are many of the products from, for example, Kellogg's or Heinz; these brands have been able to maintain a competitive position whereas in other lines of merchandise the store's own brand has taken a much bigger market share.

The use of IS / IT may help companies achieve efficiencies that enable them to meet the price requirements of the powerful buyer. Another approach is to use ICTs to facilitate a level of service that will keep the customer loyal. Short cycle times, quick response supply and reliable service are features that can be enabled by e-Commerce technology. Value added services such as stock control and accountancy facilities available from the suppliers are also features that can lock the customer in.

e-Commerce can also be used to reshape the supply chain. Intermediaries such as wholesalers and agents can become unnecessary when an organisation can efficiently deal directly with small traders and members of the public using e-Commerce systems. Competitive advantage, in all three categories, can be achieved using e-Commerce for direct sales. This process of dis-intermediarisation can save costs of distribution, allow an organisation to differentiate its products and services and / or focus its attention on selected segments of the market.

- **Bargaining power of Suppliers**

The organisation, whilst trying to get an adequate price from its buyers, will be looking to get favourable terms from its own suppliers at the next stage along the value chain. The organisation's ability to get a good deal is the mirror image of its position with its buyers. If the supply is plentiful and / or there are several suppliers it should get a good price. If the product is scarce or the number of suppliers that are able to meet its needs is limited then the supplier is in a more favourable position.

For the supplier, the strategies of price advantage and differentiation such a branding or quality of service give a stronger competitive position. The ability to trade electronically is a factor in the quality of service and may be a requirement of trade from the buying organisation.

- **Competition between Existing Players**

The final force is the competition between existing players in the market. The competition is to get the buyers and to trade at a price that produces an acceptable profit. That competition is won on the basis of the generic competitive advantage of price, differentiation or focus. The competitive position of each organisation is determined, in part at least, by the deal it is able to make with its suppliers. The competitive position of each organisation is not absolute; in most markets the factors that lead to a successful deal in one place at a given time will not necessarily be replicated in the next bargain that is to be struck.

e-Commerce is a factor in competition between existing players. The use of e-Commerce can:

- Reduce the administrative costs of trading (transaction costs);
- Increase the logistic efficiency of the supply chain and hence facilitate reduced stockholding and greater reliability of supply;
- Meet the requirements of a trading partners that trade is conducted electronically;
- Differentiate the product or service that is offered from that of competitor organisations;
- Cut out intermediaries in the supply chain, e.g. replacing ticket sales through an agent with direct sales to the public;
- Provide a new marketing and servicing channel.

3.3 First Mover Advantage

The ability to gain advantage from the innovative use of IS / IT can owe a lot to timing. The first organisation to implement a new type of ICT system will, if the system is successful, gain the price advantage or the differentiation while competitors are still operating with traditional methods and systems. The examples of AHS, American / United and FedEx quoted in Section 3.1 are all cases of first mover advantage; amazon.com and eBay are similarly cases of first movers establishing a lead in their chosen market, in these two cases using Internet e-Commerce.

The first mover can gain advantage but it is a risky business. New technologies and new ways of using them are expensive to develop and are often not successful. There are advantages to being a late mover: the idea has been tried, its effectiveness can be assessed and the late mover can implement an improved version of the system. In terms of the technology, the advantages are that it has been tested and will be cheaper and easier to implement the second time round; it may be that standard components have been developed or that packaged solutions are available, advantages that were not available to the first mover. Newcomers to the e-Commerce scene, using EDI or Internet e-Commerce, have the advantages of being able to benefit from the work of the pioneers without the need to contribute to the development effort. The late mover does not, however, have the ability to surprise competitors or the market; it is essentially a catching up operation.

3.4 Sustainable Competitive Advantage

Having gained competitive advantage the problem is then to exploit and sustain it. The problem for the originator, and for the competitors, is illustrated by the case of the FedEx parcel tracking system. The idea of giving the customer access to tracking information via the Internet was a new one that had considerable appeal to the customer. The use of the system also had considerable advantage to FedEx who no longer had to deal with a vast number of calls checking up on progress of consignments; the customers could now access the system themselves.   The development and implementation of the idea, as with many e-Commerce systems, could not be entirely private – customers had to become involved at some stage. The competition was quick to catch on to the idea and UPS was soon able to make available a similar system built onto their internal IT infrastructure for tracking packages.   DHL, on the other hand, were unable to react as quickly because of technical difficulties in implementing and integrating a competitive system.

To gain competitive advantage using IS and IT usually needs an element of surprise; the system needs to be out in the market place before competitors make a start in copying the idea.   Sustaining that competitive advantage requires either that the technical advantage is converted into brand advantage, e.g. amazon.com, or that the technical lead is sustained by continuous product and service development.

Sustainable competitive advantage from EDI systems has been rare.   Most EDI systems have been implemented in trade sectors where all competitors have a mature use of IT and IS and hence the use of EDI by one player is readily emulated by the competition.   One notable case of competitive advantage using EDI (and Minitel) systems is that of Brun Passot in France (Jelassi, 1994).   Brun Passot made EDI ordering of office supplies available to its corporate customers, a service that proved popular with existing customers and gained a number of large new accounts; the competition was not able to mobilise to match the service because it was fragmented and did not have the IT infrastructure that was needed as the basis of such a service (a similar case to that of AHS reported earlier in this chapter).   Whilst sustainable competitive advantage using EDI has been rare, there is the opposite case of lost competitiveness from not having implemented supply chain improvements to match competitors.   In sectors where EDI is appropriate and where it has become the standard way of doing business, organisations that don't follow sector best practice are left at a competitive disadvantage with their outdated supply chain practices reflected in higher costs, decreased service levels and lower profit.

Sustainable competitive advantage appears to be more common with Internet e-Commerce; probably to be expected with a new technology where the element of surprise can be greater.   The notable names in Internet e-Commerce, have entered existing markets or created new markets using web technologies at a time when the entry costs to those markets were low and the element of surprise was greatest.   In producing technologically sophisticated sites and developing their supply chain logistics, they have considerably raised the entry costs for newcomers to those market.   They need to continue to develop their sites and their service to keep ahead of the competition but their most precious asset is the brand name that they, as first movers, have established for themselves.

And with electronic markets it can be argued, given the market acts in a unbiased way, that the advantage lies with the customer as opposed to the supplier – more of that story later in the book.

3.5 Competitive Advantage using e-Commerce

The discussion of competitive advantage in this chapter has been illustrated with a number of examples including e-Commerce systems. The possible competitive use of e-Commerce, together with these examples are summarised in Figure 3.2.

Force	System	Competitive Advantage
New Entrants / Substitution	Internet e-Commerce	• Reduced entry costs • New sales channel • New service opportunities
Suppliers (& Trade Buyers)	e-Commerce Logistics (EDI / IeC)	• Cost reductions • Quick response • Lockin
Buyers (Consumers)	Internet e-Commerce	• New sales channel • dis-intermediarisation • Customer Information
Competitive Rivalry	e-Commerce	• Cost leadership • Differentiation • Focus

Fig. 3.2 e-Commerce for Competitive Advantage.

Exercises

The exercises require that the competition models set out in the chapter are used to assess the competitive position of well known traders. It is presumed that students will have a reasonable understanding of the suggested trade segment but if assumptions are required then they should be made explicit. The two exercises are:

1. Use Porter's model to assess the competitive position of a large online trader. It is suggested that the assessment is of amazon.com (as a online bookstore) against its online and conventional competitors. The external forces are:
    *   Suppliers, principally the publishers;
    *   Buyers, the book buying public;
    *   New Entrants, the possibility of new (large scale) online bookshops being set up;
    *   Substitution, that there would be a new sales channel for books or that the book itself would be replaced by an alternative media.
    Consider all five forces separately, making notes on amazon's competitive position in each case.

2. Continuing with the online bookshop theme, consider ways that a bookshop could seek to achieve cost leadership, differentiation and focus. Make notes suggesting the strategy that could be applied in each case. Note that simple discounting is not to be considered a satisfactory strategy if the result is that the bookshop ends up in bankruptcy.

Further Reading

Michael Porter introduced his model of competitive rivalry in the book:

> Porter M. (1980) *Competitive Strategy: Techniques for Analysing Industries and Competitors*, The Free Press, New York.

This book is a precursor to his book on Competitive Advantage that was introduced in the previous chapter.

Porter's model of competitive rivalry is extensively used in the business and IS literature. One book that successfully applies this and other theoretical work to the IS arena is:

> Earl M. (1989) *Management Strategies for Information Technology*, Prentice Hall, Hemel Hempstead, UK

This book is still relevant and extensively used despite its age. Other more modern work that contain material relevant to this area are:

> Robson W. (1996) *Strategic Management Information Systems: an Integrated Approach*, 2nd ed., Pitman.
> Ward J. and Griffiths P. (1996) *Strategic Planning for Information Systems*, 2nd ed., Wiley.

4

Business Strategy

Summary

Chapter 4 looks at the strategic implications of e-Commerce and suggests that, unlike most other IS and IT facilities, it has the potential to redefine corporate strategy as opposed to being a component within the implementation of that overall strategy.

The chapter discusses the components of strategy formulation and proposes an e-Commerce strategy model.

4.1   Introduction to Business Strategy

Many or most organisations have a business strategy. The strategy can be a formal plan, be implied by the mission statement and / or be evident from the way the organisation goes about its business.   Andrews (1971) in his book *The Concept of Corporate Strategy* defined it as:

> 'Corporate strategy is the pattern of major objectives, purpose or goals and essential policies or plans for achieving those goals, stated in such a way as to define what business the company is in or is to be in and the kind of company it is or is to be.'

Needle (1994) in his book *Business in Context* suggests a four stage process of strategy formulation:

- Consideration of environmental changes which bring about new opportunities and pose new threats.
- Assessment of the internal strengths and weaknesses of the institution and in particular its ability to respond to those opportunities and threats.
- A decision-making process influenced by the values, preferences and power of interested parties.
- A strategy generating process concerned with generating options and evaluating them.

The process of strategy formulation, as can be seen from the above, is a mixture of the rational and the non-rational.   Two organisations faced with the same environmental circumstances and with similar business capabilities may well develop entirely opposite strategies.   In the car market, for example, one vehicle assembler may go for volume production that competes on price whilst another aims for higher margins in quality and niche markets. Similarly a vendor seeing the environmental changes brought about by the popularisation of e-Commerce might switch its strategy to online selling whereas another organisation might seek to further develop its agent network or its retail outlets.

Strategy formation is an ongoing process. As the environment changes and the capabilities of the business evolve the strategy needs to evolve; not as a knee-jerk reaction to short-term changes but as a considered process over time.   The strategy also needs to become part of the fabric of an organisation. A strategy that is ignored or is at odds with the behaviour of the business is hardly relevant. To be effective the strategy needs to be accepted throughout the business and to pervade the tactical decision-making process. Research evidence suggests that organisations with clear strategic input, over time, do better than those without such guidance.

The overall business strategy can lead to, and be supported by, a structure of departmental or functional strategies including an IS / IT strategy.   This IS / IT strategy is a way of ensuring a rational development of the organisations computing infrastructure within the context of the overall corporate strategy.

This chapter looks at the development of a strategy for e-Commerce within an organisation. Historically the development of an e-Commerce strategy might be seen as an element in the IS / IT strategy.   However, for many organisations, e-Commerce has wider implications than just another IT system – e-Commerce is a technology for strategic IS and may well be an essential component in the formulation of the overall business strategy.

4.2   Strategic Implications of IT

Each development in computer technology has presented new opportunities for business, opportunities that took many years to be fully evaluated and adopted. The early data processing systems were little more than manual or punched card accounting systems transferred directly into computer systems. Many of the first uses of networks were for direct data entry, a useful development but not as significant as using the network to distribute information round the organisation and directly, in a timely manner, to those who had need of it. In both cases these systems gave significant business value but they did not impact on the strategy of the business.

The extension of the network outside the company gave birth to the inter-organisational system and the use of EDI. The development of EDI was a slow process, evolving over many years, and one that is still going on (although some of the gains achieved from standardisation of EDI formats are arguably in danger of being lost). Some inter-organisational systems had a significance that was greater than the automation of existing business processes; American Hospital Supply and the airline booking systems of United and American Airlines are frequently quoted cases of early strategic IS.

The evolution of the network from an intra-organisational and inter-organisational facility to one that reaches out to almost any member of the public (but only in the 'developed nations') sets new horizons in many areas and e-Commerce is one of these. The development of public access networks is typified by personal computer access on the Internet but it is a developing story that includes interactive facilities integrated with digital TV and logic functions available on the move with mobile telephones.

Taking advantage of the opportunities offered by new technology requires imagination and flair. Inter-organisational e-Commerce was, in the main, the domain of the large organisation; it was for many organisations a way of automating and increasing the efficiency of existing trading arrangements (but often with small, start-up companies providing the new software facilities required to support the operation). Internet e-Commerce has been, in contrast, in its initial phases, the province of the individual entrepreneur with a bright idea and often without any investment in current sales channels. Following on from initial e-Commerce sensations the big companies are moving to join the Internet e-Commerce act. Some of them have been hurt by new entrants into their business sector, some see a genuine business opportunity and others are just scared of being left out. The use of Internet e-Commerce can have far reaching effects for the company that uses it and for the way it does business. For many organisations the e-Commerce implementation is a strategic information system.

4.3   Technology

Technology, it is generally agreed, is not the place to start developing a systems strategy or a system design; methodologies usually start with the business requirement, 'the problem' and move through design onto the technology, 'the solution'.

e-Commerce applications, however, are not necessarily like other systems. In some cases it is a technological solution to a business problem:

- EDI used to process large numbers of invoices, reduce queries and speed payments;
- Internet e-Commerce used to replace telesales as a way of taking orders from business customers;

but for many new entrants to e-Business it is the technology that is the opportunity, the catalyst that changes an existing market or creates a new type of business.

The business strategist intending to develop e-Commerce systems must know the technologies and what they can do. The three technologies, as outlined in Chapter 1 are:

- EDI: A technology that helped streamline supply logistics and facilitated dramatic decreases in trade cycle times between businesses. Now a standard solution to inter-organisational business requirements but also a possible component to facilitate small batch production, quick response supply and new e-Commerce systems.

- Electronic Markets: An opportunity to redefine the way that a market operates but a system that requires co-operation between rivals within a trade sector.

- Internet e-Commerce: The new technology of business to consumer direct trade but also applicable to numerous business to business applications. A rapidly developing technology that reaches out from the vendor to the office PC and the home computer but also includes a number of emerging interactive and multimedia technologies. Internet e-Commerce has many applications for direct sales, an online mail order catalogue or a telesales outfit without the telesales staff; the use of this technology can broaden and expand the sector of direct sales (although many of the issues that have always limited the scope of this sector still remain). Internet e-Commerce has the capability to create new trade sectors or to create a step change in the way business is done.

Bloch *et al.* (1996), in their paper *Leveraging Electronic Commerce for Competitive Advantage* propose that the web can be used to improve, transform and redefine business value. They propose ten components of business value, see Figure 4.1.

The organisation	Source of business value
• Improve it	• product promotion
	• new direct sales channel
	• direct savings
	• time to market
	• customer service
	• brand image
• Transform it	• technological and organisational learning
	• customer relations
• Redefine it	• new product capabilities
	• new business models

Fig. 4.1 The Components of Business Value of e-Commerce (Bloch *et al.*, 1996).

These elements indicate the scope of e-Commerce as a technology. Taking the elements in turn, e-Commerce can be used as:

- Product Promotion: The web is a new medium of advertising that escapes from the fixed format of paper and the limited time slot of broadcast media. It is available at any time, it is interactive, it can be changed for the individual customer and it can take input from the customer.

- New Sales Channel: Internet e-Commerce is a new form of direct selling. It does not require retail premises (although there are interesting possibilities for combining e-Commerce and retail premises). It combines many of the advantages of catalogue selling and telesales and it can extend the applicability of direct sales to new markets, products and services.
- Direct Savings: Selling online cuts out the costs of retail premises and potentially reduces the staff requirement. Using a public access network cuts the cost of network facilities. Order entry is by the customer straight into the system. Information (such as bank statements) can be made available without the paperwork, postage and handling costs. Savings on the other aspects of the trade cycle can be more problematic, it depends on what is being sold.
- Time to Market: New products can be put online as soon as they are ready. Time can be saved on many aspects of conventional product launch and promotion cycle. Some information and investment products have a limited lifecycle and online they can be delivered direct to market.
- Customer Service: Customer service differs greatly between conventional and direct retail sales.   Internet e-Commerce, as an information rich environment, gives new opportunities for direct retailers to excel in many areas of customer information and customer support.
- Brand Image: It is new, it is cool, it gives an up-to-date image to be on the web.   The aura gained from being online can give charisma to conventional operations irrespective of online sales.
- Technological and Organisational Learning: Companies taking part in e-Commerce markets, using evolving technologies, need to be flexible and agile. An organisation at the forefront of e-Commerce learns new capabilities that can be potentially exploited in the future.
- Customer Relations: e-Commerce allows an organisation to develop a closer relationship with the customer. The organisation can learn the customer's needs and evolve its product or service options to meet that requirement.
- New Product Capabilities: Information from customers can be used to customise products or could be the spark that inspires new products or services. Examples could be an insurance policy or a car with features that the customer selected as opposed to accepting the package the supplier determined.
- New Business Models: The online entrepreneur is not limited by time and geography in the way that existing businesses have been. The use of networking gives opportunities to develop new business models and networked organisational structures.

4.4   Business Environment

All businesses operate within an external environment. They can influence that environment but their activities are also enabled or constrained by that environment. Needle (1994) identifies the environmental factors as the economy, the state, technology, labour and cultural factors. All of these factors need consideration in developing a business strategy; some of the ways they might be relevant to an e-Commerce strategy are:

- The Economy in general and as it affects the relevant market sectors are obvious factors in strategy formulation; the view taken of the economy needs to focus on long-term trends as opposed to immediate problems. e-Commerce can give an organisation the opportunity to spread its reach and hence the spread of any economic analysis needs to be broader.
- The State influences the economy and sets the regulatory framework within which businesses operate. e-Commerce has (or can have) a global spread and the applicability of the regulation of any individual state to this activity is often ambiguous; this can and does cause problems but is also seen as an opportunity by some less scrupulous online operations. e-Commerce is generally seen as a positive development by governments and there can be initiatives to assist companies in its adoption.
- Technology was the topic of the previous section.
- The Labour market will determine if an organisation can get the people and skills it needs for its operations. The regulation of the labour market and the strength of trade unions can also be a determinant in restructuring a company. For e-Commerce the availability of people with the requisite technical skills can be an issue. Also an issue is trade union reaction to any restructuring or downsizing resulting from e-Commerce implementation.
- Culture varies in different countries and an appropriate way to operate in one country would not necessarily be successful in another; the differences between Japanese and western business cultures is a frequently quoted example of this. For an organisation wishing to use Internet e-Commerce the availability of home computers and the acceptance of their use for e-Commerce, within a society, are important factors.

Analysing the environment is no easy task. Some organisations will carry out a study generating masses of data, not all of which will be accurate or readily applied. Other organisations work on a hunch, possibly the hunch of one person and amazon.com is arguably a case in point. For some aspects of the environmental analysis a model or method can be used and Porter's model (Chapter 3) to analyse the competitive environment is one such example.

Given that e-Commerce operates on a global basis the environment and cultural factors in each target market are important factors.

4.5   Business Capability

A business idea, backed up by the imaginative use of technology, will only work if the business has the skills and infrastructure to operate it. Before any business goes into a new market, or massively expands in an existing market it needs to make sure it can do the job:

> 'A knowledge of the resources and organisation possesses, and what can be done with them, is a prerequisite for future plans and establishes whether a gap exists between what management would like to do and what they can do.'

(Needle, 1994)

This analysis is often referred to as gap analysis. At the basic level the need is to check that existing capacity can cope with the expected demand or can be expanded to do so. Any requirement for expansion requires capital, people with appropriate skills and a management structure that can make a success of the larger organisation; the expansion may force a change in the organisational culture.

The introduction of e-Commerce needs new skills and, in all probability, alters the way that business is done. The organisation needs to be sure that it can make a success of the new sales channel and also that its administration and production capacity can respond in a timely manner to the demands of an electronic sales channel.

4.6 Existing Business Strategy

Very possibly the organisation already has a business strategy and this can and should be part of the evaluation of the e-Commerce strategy. A simple model for evolving a corporate business strategy has already been outlined in the first section of this chapter.

The adoption of e-Commerce by an organisation may be in a marginal activity or may involve the automation of an existing process, part of the normal evolution of business practice. Alternatively the adoption of e-Commerce may imply a major change in the infrastructure of a business or the way that it conducts business. Examples of where e-Commerce strategy could radically affect business strategy might be:

- A decision to close down retail outlets and serve customers online.
- Expansion into new geographical markets where the company previously did not operate.
- A move from selling through local agents to selling direct.

In all cases the corporate business strategy needs to be an input to the e-Commerce strategy. In cases where e-Commerce is seen as a strategic system the business strategy will be modified or reshaped by the adoption of the e-Commerce strategy making the business strategy an output from the process.

4.7 Strategy Formulation and Implementation Planning

The inputs to the strategy formulation process are the results of evaluating e-Commerce technology, the business environment, the capabilities of the organisation plus the existing business strategy.   These inputs to the strategy formulation process, together with the subsequent steps of implementation and evaluation are shown in Figure 4.2 (implementation and evaluation are further discussed in Sections 4.7 and 4.8).

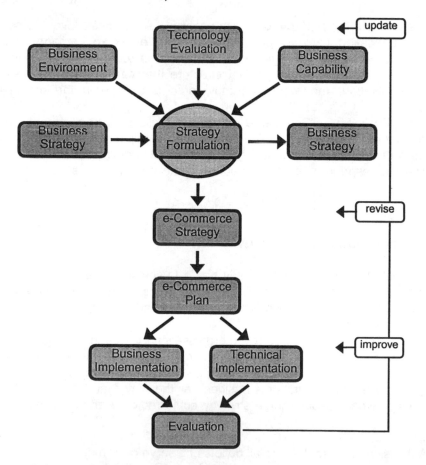

Fig. 4.2 e-Commerce Strategy Formulation.

The strategy formulation stage can be a somewhat unstructured process with interest groups lobbying for their favoured options and alliances forming and reforming.   There is no set pattern to the process as it is so dependant on the personalities involved.   Some organisations will hire consultants to give advice or to gather the evidence in an impartial manner. The process is liable to include stages of identifying options, evaluating options and then selecting the strategy that is to be adopted.

The strategy once adopted then needs to be translated into a plan for implementation. This needs to include a timetable for jobs to be done and the commitment of resources to enable the jobs to be done.

4.8 e-Commerce Implementation

The strategy once devised then needs to be implemented and the use of e-Commerce in business is the subject of the remaining chapters of this book. The strategy diagram divides implementation into the technical and the business aspects and these are briefly considered below:

- **Technical Implementation**

The approach to technical implementation of an e-Commerce system depends on the business objectives, business requirements and the technologies that have been selected. It is noted that many Internet e-Commerce systems are cobbled together rather than designed and that is often apparent. It is important that the design process considers:

- The ease of use of the system by the intended end users; always an important factor in system design but crucial if the end users are to be members of the public with perhaps limited computer literacy and the option to switch to an alternative web site if not satisfied.
- The functionality that the users need; this has to be what the users want rather than what the organisation thinks they need. Users of e-Commerce are not a captive audience that can be interviewed and evaluated like the users of a traditional IS development.
- The back office systems: Customers of an online service quite reasonably expect a rapid response and the back office systems need to be able to meet this requirement. For a volume e-Commerce system this requires that the customer front end integrates with the IS systems.

The approach to design for an Internet e-Commerce system would sensibly be based on a prototyping lifecycle as the design of the user interface is crucial to the success of the overall project. That said the use of prototyping is not intended to be an excuse for the absence of design. A thorough evaluation of each stage of the transaction lifecycle is a good starting point to make sure that the full requirements are included.

- **Business Implementation**

As well as building its e-Shop (or other e-Commerce facility) the organisation needs to:

- Put in place the business infrastructure to support the new e-Commerce facility.
- Market the new e-Commerce facility to the intended users.

Most organisations moving into e-Commerce will take a staged approach. Initial implementations may have limited functionality and be offered to a limited audience. As already indicated, full implementation of e-Commerce can have a considerable effect on the shape of the business and the way it does business.

4.9 e-Commerce Evaluation

All new IS systems should be properly evaluated after implementation and this is particularly important for a system that is used by people outside the company. Evaluating an e-Commerce system will include the internal stakeholders but crucially there needs to be a way of assessing customer reaction to the system (and potential customers who gave up before completing a transaction are particularly inaccessible). Chapter 15 (Section 15.8) includes an evaluation model for Internet e-Commerce sites.
   Loopback from the evaluation is shown at three levels:

- Improve it: Implementing an e-Commerce site remains an inexact science (if there is much science to it at all). Feedback from customers and testing using people not involved in the site development can indicate where changes are needed; the site can be improved.
- Revise it: Business results from the use of e-Commerce may indicate the need to change the e-Commerce strategy and the implementation plan; the planning can be revised.
- Update it: Developments in the competitive position, changes in the company or the emergence of new e-Commerce technologies may indicate the need to re-visit the strategic process.; the strategy can be updated.

Exercises

For this chapter, the exercises concern both corporate and e-Commerce strategy. The exercises are:

1. Suggest three advantages and three disadvantages for an organisation in devising and implementing a corporate strategy.

2. Using the corporate strategy formulation process outlined in Section 4.1:
   - List environmental changes which bring about new opportunities or pose new threats to the college or university at which you are studying;
   - Assess the strengths and weaknesses of the institution and its ability to respond to the environmental changes;
   - Suggest some strategic initiatives that your college or university might take to improve its position in the education market place.

3. Moving onto e-Commerce, review Bloch's ten points of business value and suggest how each might apply to the promotion of your college or university.

4. Using the material from the proceeding exercises, suggest how the college or university might further promote itself using the Internet (note that the institution probably already has a web page and the requirement is for imaginative new initiatives over and above this provision).

If appropriate an alternative trade sector can be selected as the subject of the study, possible organisations include the student union, the local bus company or any other organisation with which the student has familiarity. It is appreciated that students will not, at this stage of the course, have all the background necessary to fully answer these questions; however with appropriate use of general knowledge and imagination a useful answer can be given that will help reinforce the understanding of the strategic process.

Further Reading

For a concise general description of the strategic process the reader is recommended to use:

Needle D. (1994) *Business in Context* (2nd ed.) Thomson Business Press, London.

The whole book is excellent and the fourth chapter on Management Strategy is up to the standard of the rest of the text.
   A general text on business strategy is:

Lynch R. (1997) *Corporate Strategy*, Pitman, London.

5

Case Study: e-Commerce in Passenger Air Transport

Summary

Passenger air transport was one of the early users of e-Commerce, in this case electronic markets. Early innovations of airline booking systems, such as United and American Airlines, gained competitive advantage from the deployment of their systems and, even after the elimination of various anti-competitive features, continued to gain significant business value. The use of airline booking systems by travel agents gave access to a wealth of information and was an important element in creating what is now a fiercely competitive market in air travel.

With the advent of Internet e-Commerce, the air transport industry is again at the forefront of e-Commerce developments with each of the larger airlines providing for on-line bookings and, in many cases, linking this into their frequent flyer programs and electronic check-in facilities at the airport.

The Internet e-Commerce developments have the potential to, once again, restructure the market. A move away from the direct use of airline booking systems could de-emphasise price competition. A shift to direct on-line booking also threatens the role of the travel agent as an intermediary but possibly opens the market for a new breed of on-line intermediaries.

5.1   Choices

For anyone wanting to travel across the Atlantic: London to New York, Washington to Paris or Toronto to Frankfurt; what is the choice? At one level there is a lot of choice. That is the choice between British Airways (BA), United, Air France, American Airways (AA), Lufthansa, etc. and each of these airlines would like you to see them as a superior product, your preferred option. However, whatever the airline's name the offering is much the same – a cramped seat, plastic food and a cut-down movie in a standard metal tube with wings on it (or if one pays four times as much for first class, a big seat, plastic food served on china and a choice of cut-down movies). For many customers, the real choice between airlines is price and, as the supply of airline seats has increased and the customers have become increasingly price conscious, this has not been good for profitability in the airline industry.

5.2   Airline Booking Systems

For any airline other than a very small point-to-point operator, selling tickets is a complex operation. Sales take place through several channels and a multiplicity of vendors and the airline needs to know what seats are sold and which are available at any time. Sell too many seats and there will be a group of very cross passengers left behind, sell too few seats and a tight margin quickly turns into a loss. The solution to this complexity is a computerised seat reservation system and airlines have been developing and using such systems since the 1960s.

In the late 1970s, the development of computer networks facilitated the access of computer systems from remote terminals and a number of airlines, notably United and AA, took the opportunity to provide terminal access to their airline booking systems for use by travel agents. Initially both United, with its Apollo system, and AA, with Sabre, used their systems as competitive weapons. United Airlines had moved to Denver and were in direct competition with Frontier Air. United made Apollo available to local travel agents but Frontier had no comparable offering available. Frontier sought to include their flights in the Apollo system but the operation of the booking system favoured sales of United's tickets and Frontier were quickly in financial difficulty. AA adopted similar tactics with their Sabre system. Sabre was installed in a significant number of travel agents and other airlines were forced into listing their flights in the system. AA used Sabre to give prominence to its own flights, integrated Sabre with its customer database and for any sales by competitor airlines had access to their sales data. The advantage gained by United and AA was challenged in the courts using anti-trust legislation. The courts ruled in favour of the plaintiffs and the operators of the airline booking systems were forced to run the systems as an unbiased market and respect the privacy of their competitor's sales data. For some airlines the ruling was too late, Frontier, for example, was in financial difficulty, it merged with People Express but when that airline also got into difficulty, Frontier was wound up.

Following on from the anti-trust ruling the two large American seat reservation systems became profitable businesses for their owning airlines; they make a charge for each seat sold. In 1984, AA made an overall return of 7.5% on sales revenue but the return from Sabre was an extremely healthy 50% of its reservation revenue. The cases of United and AA's booking systems are covered in numerous texts, Earl (1989) has been used in the preparation of this material.

Over the years there have been a number of mergers between airline booking systems, including European players who also developed airline booking systems but which are not extensively discussed in the literature. At the time of writing the three large booking systems are Amadeus, Galileo and Sabre. The airline booking systems are principally used by travel agents; these systems enable them to advise their clients on the best buy to suit their requirements (although incentives offered by the airlines may mean that advice is less objective than it could be). World-wide there are some 115,000 travel agents linked to one or other of the booking systems (1997 figures); in the US nearly all travel agents are linked in whereas in Europe (where the business is more about packaged holidays than flight only bookings) the figure is less than half of all agents.

The development of these three major systems is summarised below:

TM

Sabre was started by AA in the early 1960s, installed its first terminal in a travel agency in 1976 and provided for direct consumer access in 1985. Sabre runs booking systems and other applications for numerous airlines; US Airways recently became a stakeholder and migrated its main IT functions to Sabre.

At the time of writing Sabre is processing over 400 million bookings a year for over 440 airlines giving it about 40% of the world market. The Sabre system links more than 210,000 terminals to 30 mainframe computers based in the US. At peak periods the system processes in excess of 7,450 messages a second.

In addition to the traditional terminal based system Sabre has a web based offering for use by the travel trade and its own web based retail outlet, branded as Tavelocity.com.

(Information for this summary is taken from Sabre's web site at www.sabre.com.)

TM

Galileo started in 1971 as a partnership between the United's Apollo system and the Galileo system that had been developed by a number of European airlines.

At the time of writing Galileo has about 30% of the world market and processes 250 million tickets on more than 530 airlines. Galileo services some 160,500 terminals on 21 mainframes based in the US and the UK; peak message rate is 5,000 per second.

Galileo has produced a net based product but not for the retail trade, its view is that:

'The last thing we want to do is compete with our travel agency subscribers or travel vendors. ... it would be very hard to have a healthy relationship with your vendors and subscribers if you are in competition with them'.

(Information for this summary is taken from Galileo's web site at www.galilieo.com.)

Amadeus was founded in 1987 by four European airlines, one of which is no longer a shareholder. In 1995 the US carrier Continental migrated its systems to Amadeus.

At the time of writing Amadeus provides bookings on 469 airlines. Its system, based in Germany, hosts in excess of 190,000 terminals. Internet based travel agency products are available.

(Information for this summary is taken from Amadeus' web site at www.amadeus.net.)

5.3 Competition and Customer Loyalty

The outcome of the introduction of airline booking systems, a process intended to give first mover competitive advantage to their owners, has been to make air transport into a commodity product with relatively easy access for the customer to price comparisons. The airlines have tried to distance themselves from this process. To persuade passengers to use their airline and to stay loyal to their brand they have:

- Advertised their airline suggesting that it is distinctive and in some way superior to the competition. Thus there is United with 'the friendly skies' and BA as 'the world's favourite airline'.
- Set up hub operations to facilitate easy connections and hence more journey opportunities. The development of hubs has been particularly prevalent in the US but it is being emulated by the major European carriers.
- Instigated loyalty programs, referred to as frequent flyer programs. Each flight taken earns points and sufficient points can mean priority treatment at airports and the possibility of a free flight or an upgrade to business class.
- Formed alliances. The two biggest alliances are the Star Alliance, led by United in partnership with Lufthansa and Our World led by BA and AA. Both these alliances include a number of other airlines and offer extensive coverage across the world. These and other alliances facilitate code sharing and through routing, using the network of the partner airlines.

All of these developments have doubtless had some effect. Hub operations and alliances can make through routing easier but in many cases, to be competitive, the airline has had to offer a through price that is less than the sum of the parts, and that has not helped the profit margin. There are customers for whom the loyalty card works, they are sticking with one airline to save up for their free flight, but there are also a great number of customers who belong to several loyalty schemes with the accumulation of points very much a secondary consideration to finding the cheapest available fare.

Counter developments have been the opening up of routes, once restricted to a couple of carriers, to increased competition (a process referred to as de-regulation or 'open skies') and the development of low cost, no frills, carriers such as SouthWest in the US and EasyJet in the UK.

Overall the attempts to brand airlines and create customer loyalty have not been a great success. Customers still look for convenience and, most of all, price. Worse than that, the search for a good price has spread from the leisure market to the corporate market with businesses increasingly looking for value for money from their corporate travel budgets. The search cost of finding the cheapest seat is kept to a minimum by the airline booking system; a system that is paid for by the airlines.

5.4   Web Booking Systems

The Internet offers the airlines a new sales channel but also, it is suggested, a way to escape from the current price competitive system. A customer using the airline's own web site does not (in most cases) see the available range of prices from competing airlines; they are presented with only the flights of the airline providing the web page (and any of its code share partners that it wants to include). The airline also attempts to make its web site attractive to the user, 'sticky' in the jargon of web marketing. Added value features that the web service may include are:

- Online presentation of the customer's frequent flyers account;
- Facility for the customer to pre-allocate their seat and select meal options;
- Additional travel services such as hotel booking and car rentals;
- Travel and airport information;
- Access to bargain offers and auctions of airline seats (some auctions are paid for with frequent flyer points);
- Personalisation of the web site to suit the customer's expected travel requirements (a profile is developed from the flight booking information stored on the airline's customer information database).

A research exercise conducted by Hersey and Whiteley in 1999, investigated the use of web sites by airlines world-wide. The start point of the research was the World Airline Directory (Flight International, 1999a, b and c). The directory lists all airlines with one or more airplanes with 19 or more seats, a total of some 1,350 airlines. A one in four sample was taken and the web site (if any) of each airline was visited. The survey found that 33% of airlines had web sites and 10% of the web sites provided online booking, see Figure 5.1.

The survey also found that, of the sample, all the largest airlines and 45% of the second tier (on a five point size classification) had online booking facilities.

	with web site	with online booking
North America	58%	22%
South America	33%	8%
Western Europe	42%	12%
Eastern Europe	7%	1%
Pacific	44%	9%
Asia	23%	3%
Africa	26%	3%
Average	33%	10%

Fig. 5.1 Incidence of Airline Web Sites by Continent.

The quantitive analysis was followed up by case studies of eighteen European and North American airlines, see Figure 5.2. Note that all these airlines had e-Commerce enabled web sites.

	Western Europe	North America
Major International Airlines	Air France British Airways (BA) Lufthansa	American Airlines (AA) Delta United Airlines
Other International Airlines	Iberia Virgin	US Airlines Canadian Airlines
Regional Airlines	EasyJet Ryanair KLM UK Crossair	Alaskan Atlantic Coast Sky West SouthWest

Fig. 5.2 Airlines Selected for Case Study Analysis.

Using a web assessment model (shown in Chapter 13) the following features of airline web sites were noted:

- Company Information:
  A number of authors have advocated that an e-Commerce web site should provide comprehensive company information; one reason for this is that it can reassure customers as to the bona-fides of the organisation they are about to do business with.

  All the airlines surveyed provided company information; in most cases it was extensive and in some cases the annual report was available to be downloaded. One nice touch, on a couple of sites, was the facility to see the current share price in real time (for those who are interested in such things).

- Customer Details:
  An important issue with e-Commerce sites is customer registration. To make an online purchase the customer has to supply a delivery address and payment details. e-Commerce vendors see an advantage in taking these details before the customer uses the site but such a requirement, for prior registration, is unwelcome to many customers; they may not in the end wish to make a purchase. e-Commerce vendors may also wish to retain customer details after the transaction but again customers can be concerned with this practice; they can be concerned about the use / abuse of their details and they may not be intending to use the site again.

  The airlines in the study adopted differing practices in this area. Some, such as AA, required prior registration before the site could be used whereas comparable airlines, such as BA, did not.

- Product Information:
  Product information is clearly essential on an e-Commerce enabled web site. In most cases, to find details of flights, the customer inputs their requirement in terms of departure point, destination and date of travel and the system would come back with details of suitable flights. This enquiry process was not always reassuring. The departure points were either specified as a city or an airport code; sometimes these were typed in and on other sites there were look-up lists to select from. The process is OK if you know exactly what you are looking for but can be a problem if a city has several airports, the nearest airport is in an adjacent city or the user is unsure of the spelling of the code or name. The error messages can also be unhelpful: 'no flights available' might mean that the airline does not fly that route, the flights were full or the query had been incorrectly specified. The system is also not ideal for a customer whose schedule is flexible and who is looking for a cheap flight; in general the systems do not indicate the fare structure and whether a better price might be available on another day.

  Many sites did contain other product information. This included facilities to search for and book travel requirements such as car hire and hotels and information on airports, the aeroplanes and tourist attractions. Some sites had esoteric features such as flight simulators, weather information for the destination (Delta) and language tuition (United).

- Negotiation:
  In most western societies and for most products the price is fixed and the customer wanting a better deal only has the option of shopping around; this is generally true of airline seats and certainly true of airline e-Commerce sites. The one exception to this is sites that include seat auctions; Canadian was one such example where loyalty scheme members can bid for seats on selected flights using their frequent flyer points.

- Order:
  The product information phase, where flight details can be found, leads onto the order phase where the purchase is made. To order a ticket the customer selects the flight and fills in their details (if they had not been previously registered with the site). A few sites (Lufthansa and SouthWest) provided mock orders and help facilities but in general the users were left to find their own way through the order form.

  Some airlines limit online sales to specific markets; generally this was done by limiting sales to credit card holders from certain countries, usually this was North American airlines restricting online sales to their own domestic market. These limitations could be to do with restrictions on accepting overseas payments or could be an attempt to carry forward differential sales and pricing policies into an electronic age.

- Payment:
  Payment is generally only by credit card; the details could be entered online or, in most cases, rung through to a telesales office. Not many of the airlines gave security information (a practice that is common, for instance, with online bookshops).

- Delivery:
  Once the online purchase is completed the customer needs a ticket (or something that substitutes for the ticket). The European airlines tend still to use traditional tickets and these could be posted to the customer or, in some instances and for late purchases, be picked up at the airport. A growing trend, led by the North American airlines, is the e-Ticket where the customer gets a booking number online and uses that as a proof of purchase at the airport (some airlines are now installing ticket dispensers at the airport that link in with their loyalty scheme cards and their e-Ticket provision).

- After Sales:
  Most airlines encourage customer feedback (or they say they do) – in some instances this is by e-Mail and in others the expectation is that the customer will use the telesales facilities if they have any queries. United in an edition of their flight magazine reported on the thousands of e-Mails they get from their customers; the issue of coping with all this electronic correspondence and replying appropriately was one they were too polite to discuss.

  Many airlines, particularly the major carriers, have extensive frequently answered question (FAQs) facilities on their web pages.

- Community:
  Attempts to foster a sense of community on airline sites, over and above the incorporation of the loyalty scheme, were limited. Possibly the nature of the product does not lend itself to such treatment.

- Performance:
  Some sites were noticeably quicker than others and a few had dead links and / or produced error messages. In some cases the error messages were unhelpful and on a couple of sites they reoccurred on a return visit. Not a good way to attract and keep online customers.

- Ease of Use:
  Not all airline sites are easy to use. Generally it was found that regional carriers with limited point-to-point networks were easier to use than the sites of the major airlines with more complex route structures. One exception to the rule that complexity made the site difficult to use was Lufthansa which is a large airline, with an extensive site, but the site was still very easy to navigate and understand.

- Aesthetic Effect:
  Most airline sites that offer online bookings are for medium to large airlines and are well designed. Four airlines in the survey were deemed to be poor with lurid backgrounds, inconsistent fonts or poorly prepared images (hopefully these sites will be improved by the time this book is read and hence the sites are not named).

- Innovation:
  As with many categories of e-Commerce sites, there seems to be a standard pattern emerging for airline sites. Features that were a bit different were videoclips (BA and SouthWest), a booking assistant (Lufthansa and Delta) and a Java seat mapper (United and US).

The two best web sites, based on an assessment of each of the factors outlined above, were found to be:

- Lufthansa: Comprehensive web site that is also quick, responsive, useable and attractive. Good payment information and options;
- SouthWest: Beautifully designed, very quick, incredibly useable and provides excellent information.

Fuller details of the research are available in Whiteley, *et al.* (1999a) (also available online, see the book web page for access details). It is noted that the airlines are continually updating their web sites and features noted in the research will not necessarily be present in the version currently in use.

As found in the above study, using an airline site is not always easy. There are regular airline customers who know how to work their chosen sites and make good use of the facility. For the new user the sites are not necessarily as easy to handle. In a study, where a group of 24 students were asked to purchase airline tickets for a round trip from the UK to New York, only ten of the students found the process relatively easy with seven having medium difficulty and a further seven considerable difficulty. One student comment reflects the feeling of a number of participants:

> 'As a solution to the complete lack of definite data I have managed to find I would get a phone book, look up British Airways, etc. and ask them (for free) to find the information for you – a process that would take less time than it would to get through the initial search on the web.'

This contrasted with a similar exercise to use an online bookshop where 34 students found their shopping task to be relatively easy and only one had any real difficulty. Arguably the bookshop sites are more mature than those of the airlines but it is also noted that travel is a more complex product and that making a booking without expert assistance is, perhaps, inevitably more difficult. It is noted that the prices obtained in the exercise ranged from about £250 to £888.50; an inexperienced user who eventually finds they paid over three times the going rate is unlikely to be pleased. Note that the flight was eventually booked through a travel agent for £199. Details of the study are available from Whiteley (1999b) (see the book web page for access details).

5.5   Competitive Outcomes

The intending passenger now has a number of channels to choose from when booking an airline seat. They can:

- Go direct to the airline. This can be:
  - At an airline's sales counter (typically at the airport);
  - Using the airline''s direct telesales office;
  - Via the airlines web page.
- Use an intermediary:
  - A high street travel agent;
  - An online travel intermediary;
  The intermediary may then go direct to the airline or interface using a airline booking system (and possibly a consolidator).

These options are summarised in Figure 5.3.

For many years the normal way of buying an airline seat has been through a travel agent. The travel agent is an intermediary. For most members of the travelling public they offer a degree of expertise and seemingly impartial advice (although in many instances they fall short of the ideal on both counts). For the airline they provide a retail channel that has traditionally been cheaper than other ways of reaching the general public. That said, selling through a travel agent is not that cheap; commission rates are typically 8% to 10% of the purchase price of the ticket with overall cost of sales running at about 15% of revenue. As margins are becoming tighter the paying of commission to travel agents is being questioned. A number of airlines have cut commission and there is talk of airlines selling at net price. Travel agents have responded to cuts in commission by threatening to charge their customers a booking fee, a threat that most agents have not dared to carry out. For the airlines the paying of commission to the travel agent has its ironies; the agent has very possibly advised the client to buy the cheapest available seat whereas the airline's balance sheet is best served by the sale of its more costly fares.

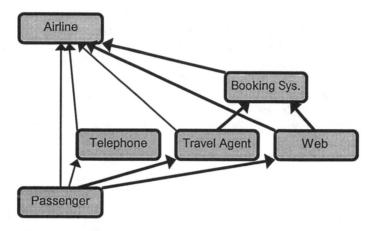

Fig. 5.3 Options for booking Airline Seats.

The airlines do make direct sales but these as a proportion of overall sales have been relatively low. Direct sales have been transacted at airports, as telesales, and in some instances through high street shops owned by the airlines. Running a direct sales outlet is not cheap, particularly for a large airline where overheads and staff costs would tend to be higher than would be the case for a travel agent.

The advent of the web alters the cost structure of direct sales. Airline web sites do not come cheap but once installed and linked to the booking system they can be run at a fraction of the cost of traditional direct sales or of the commission plus overrides paid to travel agents. A further advantage of direct sales is that the airline determines the offers shown to the customer. The opportunities for price comparisons, whilst still there for the determined user, are less accessible than through a travel agent.

The alternative to the traditional travel agent and the airline web site is the online travel agent. These web sites can link into the airline booking system and display the alternatives direct to the client. One of these online travel agents is offered by one of the booking systems, see Sabre above.

The outcome of the competition between traditional travel agents, airline web direct booking and online travel agents remain to be seen. The airlines are clearly pushing for direct booking through their own web sites. A number of American airlines are claiming considerable success (at least on their projected figures!) and

BA has also stated its policy of fostering this sales channel:

> 'BA sells 2% of tickets online and intends to increase that to 50% over the next 5 years.'

(Doward, 1999)

The airlines have much to gain from direct online selling but they also need to work out the implications; differential pricing where ticket prices vary depending on which country the ticket is sold in is one practice that is unlikely to survive exposure on the web. The traditional travel agent is under threat, particularly if the airlines get tough on commissions, but the market is difficult and the individual airlines may be reluctant to alienate a major sales channel. The online travel agents have the potential to undermine any plans of the airlines to use the web to reduce price transparency; there is, however, some evidence that consumers have a preference to use the web site of the airline they intend to travel with (and that could be an issue of trust). Overall the future shape of airline retailing is dependant on the number of consumers who take to e-Commerce in general and then choose to use that channel to buy their airline tickets. The predictions are that they will but most of these predictions come from organisations that have a vested interest.

Exercises

The exercise for this chapter is to check out booking of airline seats online. Factors to be looked at are how easy is it to find appropriate web sites, how easy are they to use and how easy is it to find a best price. The following sequence of steps is recommended:

1. Select a trip and some dates. The trip should be substantial, trans Atlantic or trans Pacific and should be from one major airline hub to another (so that there will be several competing carriers); examples could be London or Frankfurt to New York or San Francisco to Tokyo. The dates should be two or three months hence for, say, Friday to Monday at Easter or 23 December to 02 January.

2. Use the web to find out a list of carriers that fly the required route.

3. Use the web sites of two or three selected airlines to find the cheapest available return flight.

4. Find an online travel agent and find the cheapest price from that agent for the requirements.

For all stages of the exercise make notes on the ease of use of the web sites. Note the price comparisons between the airlines and, in particular any price differential between the airline site and the online travel agent. Compare notes on your bookings and of any fellow students doing the same exercise.

Further Reading

A useful paper on the use of IT and its impact on airline ticket sales is:

Morrell P. (1998) 'Airline sales and distribution channels: the impact of new technology', *Tourism Economics*, Vol. 4, No. 1, pp. 5– 9.

For further information on airline booking systems the reader can visit the web sites of the three major operators in this field, the url's are given in the text.   Further research papers on web site useability, including the two referenced in this chapter, are available online, see the book web page for links.

Part 3

Business to Business Electronic Commerce

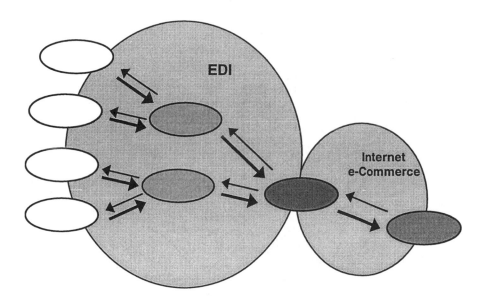

6

Inter-organisational Transactions

Summary

Business to business transactions cover a variety of situations. They vary from the regular repeat transactions typified by a retailer restocking shelves or a manufacturer buying in standard components to irregular transactions such as an organisation buying a new PC or office stationery. These purchases conform to differing trade cycles and are amenable to differing e-Commerce solutions:

- *Electronic Markets;*
- *Electronic Data interchange;*
- *Inter-organisational e-Commerce.*

These e-Commerce 'technologies' are explained in the remaining chapters of the section.

The use of these 'technologies' is illustrated by a (theoretical) case study of a stationery company: Pens and Things.

6.1   Inter-organisational Transactions

Organisations, particularly business organisations, are constantly buying and selling goods and services. Shops buy produce in bulk from their suppliers and sell those goods in small quantities to their customers. Manufacturers buy raw materials or components from their suppliers, assemble them into new products and sell them, in turn, to their customers. Retailers and vehicle assemblers, for example, make a great number of transactions and the whole operation of their business is dependent on their efficient execution. The scale of these operations is instanced by Bhs, a UK and European multiple clothing store:

> 'Bhs regularly deal with 400 suppliers and place 6,000 contracts per season. For the mechandising systems this can mean 4.5 million replenishment decisions each working week'.

(Bhs, 1994)

Other business service sector organisations such as solicitors and accountants, may be less dependant on a constant flow of goods but they still need supplies and they are careful to account for the transactions with their customers. For all businesses there is a web of inter-organisational transactions. This web of transactions forms the value chain, discussed in Chapter 2, and is illustrated as the Logistics Network at Figure 6.1.

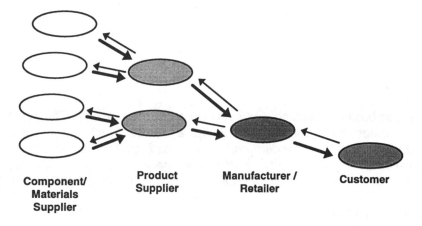

| Component/
Materials
Supplier | Product
Supplier | Manufacturer /
Retailer | Customer |

Fig. 6.1 The Logistics Network.

6.2 The Credit Transaction Trade Cycle

Most inter-organisational trade transactions take place as part of an established, ongoing trade relationship. Retail sales take place with someone walking in off the street (literally or electronically), selecting the goods they need, paying cash and disappearing – that is not the way that Safeway buy cornflakes for their supermarkets or Ford buy wheels to fit onto their new cars.

The trade cycle for inter-organisational transactions is generally a credit trade cycle. The stages in the trade cycle are:

- Pre-Sales:
  Before trading starts, the two organisations need to make contact (search) and agree trading terms (negotiate). The customer organisation may go out to tender or simply contact a firm it knows. The supplying firm may want to run credit checks on the customer. Both organisations will need to agree the price of the goods, conditions of delivery and terms of payment. Many supply contracts are part of a just-in-time manufacture or quick response supply arrangement and are specified in very exacting detail; for example, for vehicle assemblers the components may have to be delivered in the sequence of the cars on the production line and lead times from order to delivery may be as short as one hour.

- Execution:
  Execution consists of requesting the goods (order) and then collecting or receiving them (delivery). For most supplies, certainly those of significant value or purchased on a regular basis, firms will have formal purchasing procedures – orders originate from a purchasing department and often from a purchasing or stock replenishment computer application. The delivery of the goods is also formalised – goods come with a delivery note that is cross checked, manually or electronically, with the original purchase order to complete the execution stage.

- Settlement:
  The supplier of the goods has to be paid and with inter-organisational transaction this usually takes place after delivery. The supplier requests payment, say at the end of the month, (invoice) and the customer, at some stage, settles the account (payment).

- After-Sales:
  In any transaction there can be problems, damaged or faulty goods, and these issues are sorted out after the execution phase. For items such as machinery there can be an on-going process of warrantee or maintenance (after sales).

The stages of this trade cycle are shown in Figure 6.2. Many inter-organisational transactions will be repeated on a regular basis, for example the produce purchases of the retailer and the component orders of the vehicle assembler – this

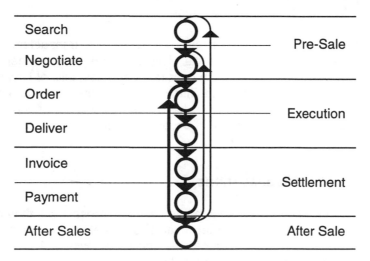

Fig. 6.2 The Credit Trade Cycle.

is shown by the loop of the execution and settlement stages.   Additionally, customers and suppliers will re-visit price and other conditions of the contract on a periodic basis or the customer will switch to an alternative supplier, shown as a loop back to the negotiate and search phases respectively.

Each stage of the inter-organisational trade cycle is documented and both the customer and the supplier have systems to trace the progress of the transaction. The customer will check for delivery of the goods and will not want to pay before that delivery is recorded in their system. The supplier, very possibly, integrates the order entry system with stock control or production control and certainly needs to check payment against the invoices that are issued. The exchange of documents for the trade cycle is shown in Figure 6.3.

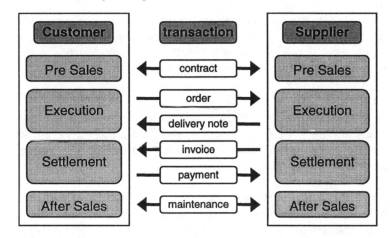

Fig. 6.3 Trade Cycle Document Exchange.

The document exchanges shown are for a simple transaction and lots of transactions are more complex than this. This is particularly true where transport is in the hands of a third party (requiring consignment notes, bills of lading, etc.) and / or the transaction is for export (requiring customs declarations and the like); an export transaction is likely to require the exchange of forty or more documents between the several organisations that become involved.

6.3   A Variety of Transactions

Organisations are many and various and so are the transactions they make. They range from the large supermarket chains and vehicle assemblers (already mentioned) down to the local corner store, where the owner will get supplies from the cash-and-carry in a slack period mid-afternoon.

The type of transaction that takes place and how it is executed depends on the size of the business involved, the nature of the business and the norms of the particular trade sector. This variety of transactions can be typified by three classifications:

- Discrete transactions of commodity items.
- Repeat transactions for commodity items.
- Discrete transactions of non commodity items.

These differing transaction may be done electronically and can be mapped onto the three e-Commerce technologies outlined in Chapter 1:

- Electronic Markets:
  Electronic Markets provide an efficient search mechanism to compare commodity product offerings and find a suitable supplier; the most obvious example is the airline booking system. Electronic Markets are further discussed in Chapter 7.

- Electronic Data Interchange (EDI):
  EDI comes into its own once the supplier has been located and terms of trade arranged; it provides for the automation of regular repeat orders, and other standardised exchanges, on a weekly, daily or even hourly basis. EDI is examined in detail in Chapters 8, 9 and 10.

- Internet Commerce:
  In addition to the large and / or regular purchases, organisations will be making once off, consumer style purchases; stationery purchases may well come into this category. These more informal purchases are not the subject of electronic markets and probably do not justify an EDI system but they can be undertaken using e-Commerce facilities on the Internet (or similar network facilities).

All three e-Commerce technologies could well be used by a single company. Pens and Things is such a company and the case study given below is used in the following chapters to illustrate the use of e-Commerce.

6.4   Pens and Things

The use and diversity of inter-organisational transactions can be illustrated by a case study, in this instance a study of a fictional company called Pens and Things Ltd:

Pens and Things

Pens and Things was established in 1894 by Earnest Barker as a small business making the then new invention, the fountain pen (invented ten years earlier by the American Lewis Waterman). For many years the company was known as Barker and Sons but it has recently diversified into selling other specialist stationery items and in 1997 took the new name Pens and Things.

Pens and Things has retained the original Barker name for its prestige fountain pens.   Over the years the Barker Pen has established a world-wide reputation – most sales are now of gift box sets that contain a Barker Fountain Pen and a Matching Barker Ball-point Pen.

Pens and Things manufactures its Barker Pens in a small factory in the English Lake District. The factory makes the pen cases, nibs, etc. but the gift boxes, ink cartridges and ball-point refills are bought in from other manufacturers.

Pens and Things also sells a number of other stationery items such as letter openers and pen holders, some of these marked with the 'Barker' brand. All of these items are bought in from other manufacturers.

The Barker Pen is sold on a world-wide basis. Sales in the UK are direct to selected wholesalers or the major department stores and jewellery shop chains. For the export market, sales are typically through a local agency that buys in bulk from Pens and Things and then sells onto the stores in that country. A catalogue that specifies the full product range is produced once a year and distributed to all trade customers and agencies.   Changes to the product range, between issues of the catalogue, are documented in leaflets and sent out to all recipients of the catalogue.

The case study of Pens and Things is used in subsequent chapters to illustrate the requirement for and use of e-Commerce.

Exercises

The following exercise is suggested by way of preparation for the use of the Pens and Things case study in the remaining chapters in this section.

1. Draw a system diagram of Pens and Things using any diagramming convention you deem appropriate (or as directed by the tutor). The diagram to include trade exchanges with customer and supplier organisations.

Further exercises, including suggestions for assignments, are given at the end of the later chapters of Part 3.

Further Reading

A number of important papers on e-Commerce appeared in the late 1980's and early 1990's. The seminal paper in this area is:

Malone T., Yates J. and Benjamin R. (1987) 'Electronic Markets and Electronic Hierarchies', *Communication of the ACM*, Vol. 30, No. 6, pp. 484–97.

Other relevant papers from that era are:

Benjamin R., de Long D., Morton M. S. (1990) 'Electronic Data Interchange: How much Competitive Advantage', *Long Range Planning*, Vol. 23, No. 1, pp. 29–40.

Johnston H. R. and Vitale M. (1988) 'Creating Competitive Advantage with Interorganizational Information Systems', MIS Quarterly, June 1988.

More recent writing in this area has included a number of interesting case studies. One such example is:

Jelassi T. (1994a) 'Binding the Customer through IT', European Case Book on Competing through Information Technology, Prentice Hall, Hemel Hempstead.

A number of additional case studies are available on the Internet; the relevant url's are available from the web page.

7

Electronic Markets

Summary

The topic of this chapter is the first of the three e-Commerce 'technologies', the electronic market. The application of this technology is relatively limited and the coverage of the topic has been similarly restricted (with most of the material on business to business transactions being concentrated on EDI).

Electronic markets are used for passenger ticket reservations and in various financial and commodity markets. These markets give the customer (or the customer's intermediary) easy access to comparative data on price, and other attributes, of the goods or services on offer. Access to this information is advantageous for the consumer but making the information available is not necessarily beneficial to the supplier.

This chapter looks at electric markets, their benefits in terms of reducing search costs and the conflicts of interest that have limited the spread of this e-Commerce technology.

7.1   Markets

Market theory has a strong place in economic theory. The market economy has been the world's predominate economic model (since the break up of the Soviet Block and the 'reform' of the economic systems in its constituent countries).

The base line model or analogy for market economy is the produce sale in a rural market town. The model is one of supply and demand. If there has been a good potato harvest and supply outstrips demand then prices will go down until some suppliers withdraw from the market and an equilibrium is reached. If there has been a poor harvest and potatoes are in short supply, the price will go up until the number of customers willing to pay the higher price matches the available supply of potatoes.

For a market to work effectively there are three conditions (from McAfee and McMillan, 1997):

- There are as many buyers as sellers and none of these buyers and sellers represent a significant fraction of total demand or supply;
- The goods or service to be transacted is homogeneous or standardised, that is, does not have idiosyncratic or differentiated features across distinct units;
- Buyers and sellers are well informed about the quantity and characteristics of the goods as well as the transaction price.

Whether the market mechanism ever operated in pure form is a matter of conjecture. The development of the modern industrial, and post-industrial, economy challenges the simple concepts of markets. The market is no longer local, many goods and services have become more complex (and hence less homogeneous), large organisations operate in the market with the power to distort market mechanisms and, as a consequence of all these factors, it becomes harder to be 'be well informed about the quality and characteristics of the goods as well as the transaction price'.

7.2   Electronic Markets

An electronic market is an attempt to use information and communication technologies to provide geographically dispersed traders with the information necessary for the fair operation of the market. The electronic market can bring together product, price and service information from many or most suppliers of a particular class of goods or in a specific trade sector. Easy access to information on a range of competing product offerings reduces the search cost of finding the supplier that best meets the purchase requirement. An electronic market place can be defined as:

> 'An inter-organisational information system that allows participating buyers and sellers to exchange information about price and product offerings'.

(quoted in Been, et al., 1995)

The electronic market is, in effect, a brokering service to bring together suppliers and customers in a specific market segment. The area of operation of an electronic market in respect of the trade cycle is shown in Figure 7.1.

The particular strength of an electronic market is that it facilitates the search phase of the trade cycle; it is about finding the best buy (on whatever criteria the customer may wish to apply). Having found an appropriate offering the electronic market will then, normally, include facilities for the execution and settlement of the transaction.

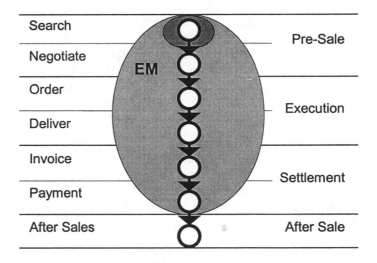

Fig. 7.1 Electronic Markets and Trade Cycle.

7.3   Usage of Electronic Markets

Electronic markets are exampled by the airline booking systems. Currently there are three airline booking systems that list most scheduled flights available world-wide. The three systems are Amadeus, Galileo and Sabre; they have been discussed in Chapter 5. The use of these systems has typically been via an intermediary, in this case the customer wishing to purchase a ticket does so via a travel agent.

Electronic markets are also used in the financial and commodity markets and again the dealing is done via intermediaries; to buy stocks and shares a member of the public uses the services of a stockbroker.

Arguably the use of electronic markets has served the customer well. With the assistance of a good travel agent the airline customer can be informed of all the flights available for an intended journey and then select, on the basis of price, convenience, loyalty scheme, etc. the flight that they wish to book.

7.4   Advantages and Disadvantages of Electronic Markets

The advantages of an electronic market to the customer are self-evident. Using an airline booking system, for example, there is a screen that shows all the flights from (say) New York to Los Angeles and the consumer can make an informed choice without having to spend time and effort finding out which airlines fly that route and then contacting each of the airlines to obtain flight times, price and availability details. Once a flight is selected the system facilitates the booking of that flight, paying the fare and printing the ticket.

For the seller the advantages are less evident. The seller that is the most competitive may do well, the electronic market makes available information on their product and the advantage of that offering should be apparent. Less competitive suppliers are likely to be forced into price reductions and the competitive effect may force all suppliers to cut prices, possibly below the level at which it is possible to make a profit (as is the case on some air transport routes). The situation is summed up by Bean, *et al.* (1995) as follows:

> 'The effect of an electronic market in a commodity market is the more efficient distribution of information which decreases the profit possibility for sellers. By the introduction of an electronic market search costs can be lowered. If buyers face lower search costs it will be more difficult for sellers to maintain high price levels.'

The paper from which this quote was taken is a case study of Reuters' attempt to setup an electronic market, at Schiphol in the Netherlands, for the sale of air-cargo space. The system encountered opposition from the freight forwarders and the carriers. The freight forwarders feared that prices would be forced down and that their role as an intermediary would be reduced or eliminated. The carriers were similarly reluctant to become involved arguing, among other points, that the system treated air-cargo as a commodity and did not take into account the service element of business. In the end the operation of the system had to be suspended. The system relied on the carriers providing and updating information on their space availability and on the freight forwarders using the system; since neither of these classes of players were prepared to participate the system could not function.

7.5   Future of Electronic Markets

Malone, Yates and Benjamin (1987), in their seminal paper 'Electronic Markets and Electronic Hierarchies' predicted a move to electronic markets (from electronic heirachies), a move that has not occurred. The operation of electronic markets is not, in general, to the advantage of the vendors and it is they who have to provide the information (the computerisation of pre-existing financial and commodity markets is a somewhat different case).

The advent of the Internet has, however, given the opportunity for a new class of intermediary to set up which do offer a service analogous to the electronic market. Examples of this are:

- Online travel agents that provide an interface for clients to access airline booking systems.
- Shopbots that search the Internet for the best deal. An example is the services that search the online bookshops to find the one with the lowest price for a specific title.
- Online auction sites that facilitate person-to-person trading.

These web-based facilities are covered in Chapter 5 (travel agents) and in the chapters on business to consumer e-Commerce. These sites do not have the ease of use of the purpose made electronic market but they do have the effect of encouraging price competition and presumably the capacity to worry the online company that would rather the customer came straight to their home site.

Exercises

In general, electronic markets are not accessible by members of the general public. Chapter 5 has already suggested that students should access the airline booking systems via an appropriate Internet travel agent; this should have given some idea about the operation of an electronic market.

Further Reading

The Malone, *et al.* paper recommended in Chapter 6 should be seen as baseline reading for this Chapter:

> Malone T., Yates J. and Benjamin R. (1987) 'Electronic Markets and Electronic Hierarchies', *Communication of the ACM*, Vol. 30, No.6, pp. 484–97.

After the early 1990's writers tended to concentrate on EDI systems and there was not a lot of material on electronic markets; possibly the story had already been told on airline booking systems and electronic markets in the financial sector were a 'challenging' topic. An excellent paper on a failed attempt to establish an electronic market is:

> Been J., Christiaanse E., O'Callaghan R. and Van Diepen T. (1995) 'Electronic Markets in the Air Cargo Community', *Third European Conference on Information Systems*, Athens.

An alternative perspective on electronic markets is provided by:

> McAfee R. P. and McMillan J. (1997) 'Electronic Markets', in Kalakota R. and Whinston A. (eds.) *Readings in Electronic Commerce*, Addison Wesley, pp. 293–309.

The authors of the above chapter see electronic markets much more as auction systems and instance a number of cases where bidding systems have been used in an attempt to introduce market forces into monopoly markets; auctions of US Treasury Bills and the UK wholesale electricity supply market are among the examples discussed.

8

Electronic Data Interchange (EDI)

Summary

This chapter outlines the second of the three EC 'technologies', electronic data interchange (EDI).

EDI is used in a number of trade sectors for inter-organisation, regular, repeat transactions. EDI systems require EDI standards, EDI software, an EDI network and a trading community. Organisations that use EDI can gain important operational and strategic advantages.

This chapter introduces EDI as a replacement for paperwork using the Pens and Things case study as an example. The material is introductory, EDI is explained in more detail in Chapter 9 and its business use is further explored in Chapter 10.

8.1   Introduction to EDI

Electronic Data Interchange (EDI) is used by organisations for transactions that occur on a regular basis to a pre-determined format. For the most part it is used for purchase transactions and Chapter 6 has already instanced supermarkets buying supplies of cornflakes and a vehicle assembler purchasing wheels to fit to the cars on the production line. The area of application of EDI to the trade cycle is shown in Figure 8.1.

EDI is most commonly applied in the Execution and Settlement phases of the trade cycle. In execution of a simple trade exchange, the customer's order can be sent by EDI and the delivery notification from the supplier can also be electronic. For settlement the supplier can use EDI to send the invoice and the customer can finish the cycle with an electronic funds transfer via the bank and an EDI payment notification to the supplier. This whole cycle may be more complex and other electronic messages can be included. The cycle can be repeated many times, as often as the supermarket wants to buy cornflakes or the vehicle assembler needs new supplies of wheels.

EDI can be used for Pre-Sales transactions; there have been EDI messages developed for transactions such as contract but they are not widely implemented. Finding an appropriate trading partner and negotiating conditions of trade is likely to be undertaken by a member of staff in the buying department (or a manager on the golf course). The Pre-Sales phase could also involve the use of an electronic market, see Chapter 7, or an open access network such as the Internet, see Chapter 11.

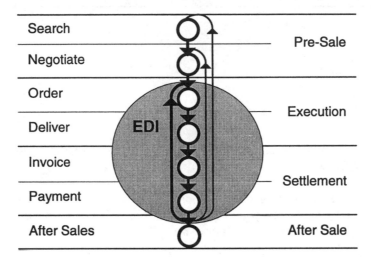

Fig. 8.1 The Credit Trade Cycle.

EDI could be used for after-sale transactions but only if they were in a standardised format and frequent enough to justify the system costs; transactions such as a dealer claiming payment for warrantee work could be a possible application.

EDI can also be used for standardised and repeated transactions that do not fall within the usual definition of trade exchanges. Examples are:

- In the UK, many National Health Service Dentists keep dental records on a computer system and treatment details are sent, by EDI, to the Dental Practice Board. The board then pays the dentists for its proportion of the treatment cost and again this transaction is electronic, using the national bank clearing system (BACS) (Willmott 1995).

- British Telecom has also started using EDI, in this case for its bills from the gas, electricity and heating oil utilities. With 9,000 telephone exchanges computer centres and offices up and down the country it was processing about 120,000 bills a year from the various utilities. In 1996 it started a programme of switching these invoices to EDI starting with the 250 bills from Scottish Power – the 250 bills, processed manually, took up two days work, much of which can be saved using EDI (Electronic Commerce. 1996).

Both these applications of EDI facilitate the passing of data between the computer applications of trading / co-operating organisations without the delays, inaccuracies and inefficiencies associated with the exchange of data on paper.

8.2   EDI Definition

EDI is often summed up as Paperless Trading. More formally EDI is defined, by the International Data Exchange Association (IDEA), as:

> 'The transfer of structured data, by agreed message standards, from one computer system to another, by electronic means.'

This definition of EDI has four elements, each of them essential to an EDI system:

1. Structured Data:
   EDI transactions are composed of codes, values and (if necessary) short pieces of text; each element with a strictly defined purpose.   For example, an order has codes for the customer and product and values such as quantity ordered.

2. Agreed Message Standards:
   The EDI transaction has to have a standard format. The standard is not just agreed between the trading partners but is a general standard agreed at national or international level. A Purchase Order will be one of a number of agreed message standards.

3. From One Computer System To Another:
   The EDI message sent is between two computer applications. There is no requirement for people to read the message or re-key it into a computer system. For example, the message is directly between the customer's Purchasing System and the supplier's Order Processing System.

4. By Electronic Means:
   Usually this is by data communications but the physical transfer of magnetic tape or floppy disc would be within the definition of EDI. Often networks specifically designed for EDI will be used.

There are many further definitions of EDI; most of them include the same four points. The definition presented by Sokol (1989) is one further example:

> 'the INTER-COMPANY COMPUTER-TO-COMPUTER communication of STANDARD BUSINESS TRANSACTIONS in a STANDARD FORMAT that permits the receiver to perform the intended transaction.'

This definition emphasises the point that the normal application of EDI is in business transactions between companies but, contrary to this definition, there are also applications of EDI for information exchange and for intra-company transactions.

8.3   The Benefits of EDI

EDI can bring a number of advantages to the organisations that use it. It should save considerable time on the exchange of business transactions and has the potential for considerable savings in costs.

EDI can be simply used to replace paper transactions with electronic transactions – this is the normal route taken in the initial installation of EDI. The full advantage of EDI is only realised when business practices are restructured to make full use of the potential of EDI; when EDI is used as an enabling technology to change the way the business operates – just-in-time (JIT) manufacture and quick response supply being prime examples of where EDI is used as an enabling technology to gain competitive advantage.

The direct advantages of EDI include:

- Shortened Ordering Time:
  Paper orders have to be printed, enveloped and sent out by the customer's post room, passed through the postal service, received by the supplier's post room and input to the supplier's order processing system. To achieve all this, reliably, in under three days would be to do very well. EDI orders are sent straight into the network and the only delay is how often the supplier retrieves messages from the system. Orders can be in the supplier's system within a day, or if there is urgency the messages can be retrieved more frequently, for example every hour.

- Cost Cutting:
  The use of EDI can cut costs. These include the costs of stationery and postage but these will probably be fully matched by the costs of running the EDI service. The principle saving from the use of EDI is the potential to save staff costs. The obvious example of this is that if the orders are directly input to the system there is no need for an order entry clerk. Note also that seasonal peaks, staff holidays, etc. no longer create a backlog in the order entry area. The cost savings need to be offset against the system development and network costs.

- Elimination of Errors:
  Keying any information into a computer system is a source of errors and keying paper orders into the order processing system is no exception. EDI eliminates this source of errors. On the down side, there is no order entry clerk who might have spotted errors made by the customer – the customer will get what the customer asked for.

- Fast Response:
  With paper orders it would be several days before the customer was informed of any supply difficulty, such as the product is out of stock. With EDI the customer can be informed straightaway giving time for an alternative product to be ordered or an alternative supplier to be used.

- Accurate Invoicing:
  Just like orders, invoices can be sent electronically. EDI invoices have similar advantages to EDI orders in saved time and avoided errors. However, the major advantage in EDI invoices is that they can be automatically matched against the original order and cleared for payment without the sort of queries that arise when paper invoices are matched to orders.

- EDI Payment:
  Payment can also be made by EDI. The EDI payment system can also generate an EDI payment advice that can be electronically matched against the relevant invoices, again avoiding query and delay.

Indirect advantages of the use of EDI can be:

- Reduced Stock Holding:
  The ability to order regularly and quickly reduces the amount of goods that need to be kept in a store room or warehouse at the shop or the factory. For many JIT manufacture and quick response supply systems stockholding is eliminated altogether with goods being delivered only as they are needed. Reduced stock holding cuts the cost of warehousing, the double handling goods (into store and then out again onto the factory or shop) and the capital requirement to pay for the goods that are just sitting in store.

- Cash Flow:
  Speeding up the trade cycle by getting invoices out quickly, and directly matched to the corresponding orders and deliveries, can and should speed up payments and hence improve cash flow. Elimination of most invoice queries can be particularly significant in reducing delays in payments.

- Business Opportunities:
  There is a steady increase in the number of customers, particularly large, powerful customers, that will only trade with suppliers that do business via EDI. Supermarkets and vehicle assemblers are prime examples. Being ready and able to trade electronically can be an advantage when competing for new business.

- Customer Lock-in:
  An established EDI system should be of considerable advantage to both customer and supplier. Switching to a new supplier requires that the electronic trading system and trading relationship be redeveloped, a problem to be avoided if a switch of supplier is not essential.

To gain these advantages EDI has to be seen as an investment – there are costs upfront and the payback is longer term. The costs is the set up of the EDI system (hardware, software and network) and the time required to establish agreements with trading partners. The savings only start when there is a significant volume of business transacted using EDI, a point that is called the 'critical mass' in the jargon of EDI.

8.4   EDI Example

The nature and use of EDI is best illustrated by an example. At the simplest level EDI can be a direct replacement for the paper transactions and this, using the Pens and Things case study (see Chapter 6), is what this example shows.

Pens and Things plans its production on a monthly basis. Each month the details of orders and sales are reviewed and sales forecasts for the coming month are made. The sales forecast is then compared with the goods in stock and a production plan is devised. The production plan is, in turn, correlated with the stocks of raw materials, components and packaging and orders are placed with the suppliers. The monthly production plan does, however, need to be flexible – any significant new order can require that the plan is modified and that new materials be ordered at short notice, if they are not available from the factory store.

Most of Pens and Things production materials are easily held in store. The range of materials is limited, the items are relatively small, not easily damaged and the materials are applicable across a range of products; Pens and Things can keep two or three months supplies in stock without any great disadvantage. The exception to this is the packaging. The packaging is bulky, easily damaged and whereas, for example, all pens use the same ink cartridge or ball-point refills, there is a considerable range of packaging varying in colour, quality and style. The requirement for packaging is also very dependent upon the customer order and is the item most vulnerable to short notice changes in the production schedule.

Pens and Things has been talking to its packaging supplier on how the situation might be improved. Pens and Things wants to cut down on its stock of packaging and its supplier would like to improve its processing of orders, particularly urgent orders. The packaging supplier uses EDI with other customers, EDI is an option in Pens and Things production control system and it is EDI that is to be used for this requirement.

Assume, for example, Pens and Things need, at short notice, more packaging for their Executive Elite fountain pen and ball-point pen set.

Before the EDI system went in:

> The production controller would have typed out an order and posted or, more probably, faxed it. A copy of the order would be retained and be entered into the stock control system 'to keep the records straight'. The order is shown at Figure 8.2.

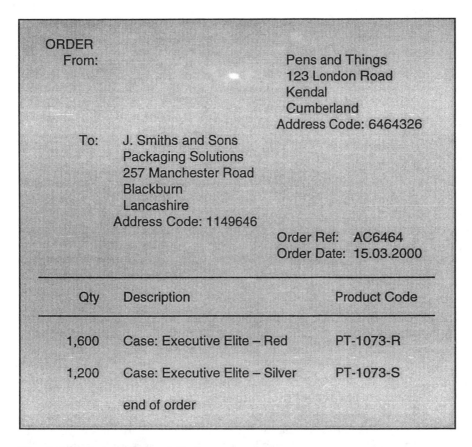

Fig. 8.2 Example (Paper) Order.

When the order arrived with the packaging company it had to be keyed into their order processing system / production control system. Hopefully the order would be recognised as urgent and would be keyed in correctly, but that would not always be the case.

Following the introduction of the EDI system:

The amendment of the schedule on the production control system reviews the materials requirements and the order is automatically generated. The order is now coded in an EDI standard format (in this case EDIFACT) and is sent electronically overnight. The order is shown at Figure 8.3 (and will be further explained in Chapter 9).

```
UNH+000001+ORDERS:2:932:UN'
BGM+220+AC6464'
DTM+4:20000305:102'
NAD+BY+6464326::91'
NAD+SU+1149646::91'
UNS+D'
LIN+1++PT-1073-R:VP'
QTY+21:1600'
LIN+2++PT-1073-S:VP'
QTY+21:1200'
UNT+11+000001'
```

Fig. 8.3 Example EDI Order.

The order is picked up electronically by the packaging company and is straightaway ready for processing by their order processing / production control system.

The EDI order is not in a format that is readily read by the staff at either company but then they do not need to read it. The advantages are that:

- The order is sent automatically once the production schedule is updated.
- The order will be promptly available in the suppliers production control system.
- There will be no errors made in keying in the order.

The system does cost money to set-up, particularly for Pens and Things for who it is the first EDI application. Running the system does have a small saving in office costs as the order does not need to be manually processed (although there needs to be quite a volume of orders for this saving to have any real significance).

Exercise

The following exercises are suggested for class discussion or as an aid to students using the text for self study.

1. List the four elements of an EDI system.

2. List the transaction types that take place between trading partners that seem suitable for EDI implementation. Suggest some communications that would not be suitable for this technology.

3. Review the advantages of EDI given in Section 8.3 and evaluate how each applies to the EDI implementation proposed in the example in Section 8.4.

4. The advantages of EDI given in Section 8 compare EDI to paper orders; if the orders were sent by fax, which of the advantages would still apply.

Exercises more suitable to be set as an assignment are given at the end or Chapters 9 and 10.

Further Reading

There have been a number of texts printed on EDI but most of these date from late 1980 / early 1990 and are now out of print. A good introductory text on EDI is:

> Parfett M. (1992) *What is EDI? A guide to Electronic Data Interchange*, (2nd ed). NCC Blackwell.

This text remains relevant to EDI usage today; it should be available from the library.

Texts on specific aspects of EDI and EDI case studies are specified for further reading in Chapters 9 and 10. See also the web site for details of sources on the Internet.

9

EDI: the Nuts and Bolts

Summary

This chapter gives further details of the technical elements of an EDI system:

- *EDI Standards*
- *EDI Networks*
- *EDI Implementation*
- *EDI Agreements*

Details of the elements of EDI are important for the understanding of EDI. Also these details can be used, in conjunction with the material provided on the web pages, to set up a practical student exercise.

9.1   EDI Technology

EDI is defined by its technology: the EDI standards, the EDI networks and the EDI software that interfaces these two elements and the business applications. These elements together with the EDI Agreement are covered in depth in this chapter.

The technology is, however, only a small part of the story. It is often said that '*EDI is 90% business and 10% technology*'. The business aspects of EDI are examined in Chapter 10.

9.2   EDI Standards

At the heart of any EDI application is the EDI standard. The essence of EDI is the coding and structuring of the data into a common and generally accepted format – anything less is nothing more than a system of file-transfers.

Coding and structuring the documents for business transactions is no easy matter. There have been a number of EDI standards developed in various industry sectors or within a specific country and there are complex committee structures and procedures to support them.

Following on from the various sectorial and national EDI standards is the United Nations (UN) EDI Standard: EDIFACT. This is the standard that was used in the example in Chapter 8 and it is the standard that should be adopted for any new EDI application. Examples of the EDIFACT standard are included in the text; full details of selected segments and messages are included on the web pages that support this book.

9.2.1 The Need for EDI Standards

EDI provides an electronic linkage between two trading partners. Business transactions are output from the sending computer system, transmitted or transported in electronic format and input into the second, receiving computer system.

The computer systems that exchange data need a common format; without a common format the data is meaningless. Two organisations that exchange data can, with relative ease, agree a format that meets their mutual needs. As the network of exchanges develops then the number of organisations needing to be party to the agreement grows. To illustrate this, assume a network of three customers (say supermarkets) ordering goods from four suppliers (food manufacturers), see Figure 9.1.

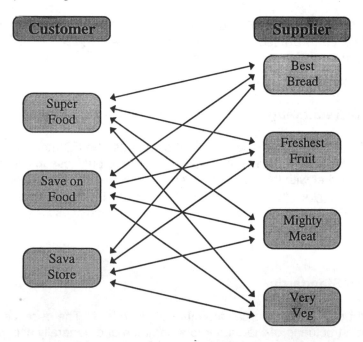

Fig. 9.1 Interchanges between Customers and Suppliers.

The network in Figure 9.1 has 12 separate interchanges. It is unlikely that each of these exchanges would have its own format but it is perfectly possible that each customer would have developed its own standards (giving each supplier three separate standards to cope with). It is also possible that new exchanges added to the system will have requirements not envisaged when the data formats were originally agreed; this would require a change to the existing standard or the introduction of an additional standard. The overall picture is one of unnecessary complexity and incompatibility.

EDI standards overcome these difficulties. The EDI standard provides, or attempts to provide, a standard for data interchange that is:

- Ready formulated and available for use;
- Comprehensive in its coverage of the data requirements for any given transaction;
- Independent of hardware and software;
- Independent of the special interest of any party in the trading network.

EDI Standards provide a common language for the interchange of standard transactions.

Most of the work on EDI standards has been concerned with the interchange of trade documentation and financial transactions but the principle applies to any interchange where the data can be systematised and codified. EDI standards are used for the interchange of information as diverse as weather station readings and school exam results.

9.2.2 National and Sectorial Standards

- **Evolution of EDI Standards**

The first EDI standards evolved from the formats used for file transfer of data between computer applications. The evolution of EDI standards can be seen as having three stages (although in practice it was and is somewhat more complex than that):

1. The first formats that might properly be called EDI were developed by organisations that had to process data from a large number of customer organisations. The data recipients set the standard and the customers conformed to it.

2. The concept of EDI as an application independent interchange standard evolved and several industry sector and / or national standards bodies developed EDI standards to meet the needs of a specific user community.

3. The requirements of international and cross sector trade meant that the sector and national standards were becoming an impediment to the further development of electronic trading. EDIFACT was developed, under the auspices of the United Nations (UN), as a universal standard for commercial EDI.

- **Early EDI Applications**

An example of an early EDI application in the UK was the BACS system:

> BACS was and is a consortium of the major banks that provides an automated clearing service for the transfer of money between bank accounts.   Many organisations that made a significant number of payments (including the pay-roll) use this service.
>
> Users of the BACS system recorded the information they would have printed as cheques on a computer file in accordance with the format required by BACS.   The data was then sent to BACS where the payments were processed without the delay, expense and risk of paper documents and manual data input. The use of the system was made much easier by the availability, for most types of computer, of standard software that output the payment data in the required format.
>
> In the early days the computer file would be recorded on a magnetic tape and couriered to the BACS headquarters. Subsequently an online submission facility was added to the service.

Other early examples of the early use of EDI or EDI-like systems were:

> LACES:
> A freight clearance system used at London Heathrow Airport from 1971–1981 (Preston, 1988).

> World Meteorological Office (WMO) System:
> A system of structured messages that is used on a world-wide basis to exchange weather information, weather reports and weather forecasts (Metzgen, 1990).

These applications and their data interchange formats were widely used but for only one purpose with one specific application.

- **Sector and National EDI Standards**

The use of EDI on systems such as BACS and the more general use of online systems demonstrated the potential of EDI for the exchange of general business documents. A number of trade sector organisations understood this potential and developed EDI formats for use in their sector. Some of the more notable examples are:

> ODETTE:
> An EDI format developed for, and widely used in, the European motor industry. ODETTE stands for the Organisation for Data Exchange by Teletransmission in Europe. ODETTE was predated by VGA, a standard developed, and still used, by the German motor industry. The motor industry is planning to move from VGA and ODETTE to EDIFACT when

the standards are stable and their requirements are fully met.   One problem they have is that the EDIFACT standard, with its wider application and more bureaucratic procedures, is slower to react to evolving needs than is the case with the sector based ODETTE standard.

TRADACOMS:
A UK EDI standard for general trade developed by the ANA (Article Numbering Association) in 1982.   TRADACOMS evolved to become the predominate UK EDI standard with widespread application in the retail and catering trades (this was in the late 1980's / early 1990's when Britain accounted for half the European EDI activity).   Other European countries also developed their own standards for retail / general trade; examples of such standards are SEDAS in Germany and GENCOD in France.   TRADACOMS and the other national standards mentioned here are looking to evolve to, or convert to EDIFACT – a slow process given the investment in the existing standards.

   (The ANA is the body responsible for the allocation and administration of the product codes used for the bar codes on grocery and other items – product coding has an important role to play in EDI systems).

ANSI X12:
EDI in North America developed with differing standards in the various business sectors.   Examples of such standards are UCS for the grocery industry and ORDERNET for the pharmaceutical trade (Sokol, 1989). Electronic trade had developed rapidly in North America and the problems of cross sector trade were becoming apparent.   The problem was taken up by the American National Standards Institute (ANSI) and X12 was developed as a national standard with the aim of replacing the various sector standards.

- **The International EDI Standard**

As already outlined, EDI developed in closed user communities within trade sectors and / or national boundaries.   The use of sector and national standards for this type of trade was satisfactory.   However, as electronic trade developed to cover wider trading relationships there is a growing problem of trade between organisations using different EDI standards.

   In addition to the problem of cross sector trade there is a desire to use EDI for international trade.   This (sensibly) requires a common format for the exchange of the standard business forms (order, invoice, etc.) between organisations in differing countries.   International trade also requires a great deal of additional documentation for shipping, customs authorities, international credit arrangements, etc. – all of this is potentially electronic and obviously a common format is very desirable.

   To facilitate this cross sector and international development of EDI the EDIFACT standard has been, and is being, developed.   EDIFACT is the United Nations standard of **E**lectronic **D**ata **I**nterchange for **A**dministration, **C**ommerce and

Transport.   The EDIFACT standard was born, in the mid-1980s out of a United Nations Economic Commission for Europe (UNECE) committee and is supported by the Commission of the European Union.

Underlying the EDIFACT initiative are various UN attempts to standardise on trade documentation. These specify, for example, standards for the layouts of invoices (a provision of some importance for organisations processing many hundreds of invoices from numerous sources). Notable amongst the standards documentation is the UN Trade Data Element Directory, a subset of which forms the EDIFACT Data Element Directory.

EDIFACT effectively assumed a world role when the Americans accepted it as the world standard (while retaining their own ANSI X12 standard for domestic use in the short term):

> '... members of the American National Standards Institute (ANSI) voted to stop work on their domestic X12 EDI messages after 1997 and switch all their efforts to the international EDIFACT standards within the United Nations framework.'

> (TEDIS, 1992)

The acceptance by the North Americans of EDIFACT as the international standard was somewhat surprising. ANSI had done a lot of development work on the X12 standard and EDIFACT was, at that time, essentially a European standard.

Since 1988 the use of EDI has been vigorously promoted by the European Union (EU) through its TEDIS programme. TEDIS has promoted EDI through sectorial organisations but has also emphasised intersectorial trade. EDIFACT is seen as the common standard and as vital for electronic trade within the 'single market' – funds have been made available for industry sectors to change from their existing EDI standard to EDIFACT.

EDIFACT has been adopted as the EDI standard of choice by countries and sectors new to EDI. In Europe, countries such as the Netherlands, Denmark and Norway have been noted for their recent development of EDI with EDIFACT as the predominate standard. Electronic trade is also developing outside Europe and North America; Australia and Singapore have been much written about with EDIFACT being the standard of choice.

The importance of a single international standard has been recognised by many sectors currently using their own EDI standards. Many sector and national standards are been replaced or are 'evolving' towards the EDIFACT standard – included in this process are ODETTE, TRADACOMS and ANSI X12, a development already mentioned above.

9.2.3 The EDIFACT Standard

The EDIFACT standard, like all other EDI standards, is about the exchange of (electronic) documents – for EDIFACT each document type is referred to as a message.   For trade purposes the documents include order, despatch advice, invoice, payment order and remittance advice.   Other sectors will have their own documentation requirements, sectors using EDIFACT include:

- Transport
- Customs
- Finance
- Construction
- Statistics
- Insurance
- Tourism
- Healthcare
- Social Administration
- Public Administration
- Public Procurement

(The above, together with 'Trade', are the 12 message development groups of the Western Europe EDIFACT board).

For transmission purposes EDIFACT messages are sent in an electronic envelope known as an interchange.   Note this is the data standard and is separately defined from any enveloping requirement of the transmission protocol.

Within that interchange there may well be a number of messages.   Messages equate to the trade documents and order and invoice are prime examples.   The order that was shown in Chapter 7 is one such message and Pens and Things could have sent it as the only message in an interchange or they could have included further messages within that interchange.

The messages themselves are made up of a series of data segments.   Data segments encode a single aspect of the trade document, for instance the order date or the buyers name and address.   Each EDIFACT message specifies a great number of data segments and individual data segments may be components of a number of messages.   The users of the message select the data segments that are applicable to their particular needs.

Data segments are, in turn, made up of tag and a number of data items.   The tag identifies the data segment and the data elements give the codes and / or values required in the document (message).   The data elements include the codes and values for items such as date and address code but they are frequently used in combination with type or qualifier data items to specify the format of the data and its use; for instance a date could be the order date and be in eight digit century format.   The requirement to use data elements together forms a composite data element.

This structure of the EDIFACT message is shown in Figure 9.2.   The function groups have been omitted; these are an intermediary level between the interchange and the message but they are not normally implemented.

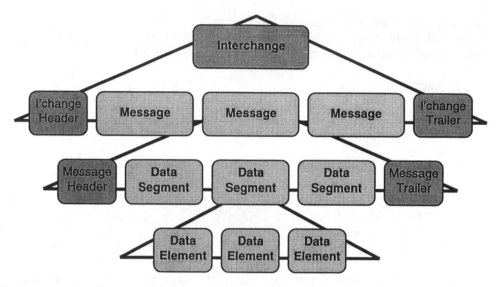

Fig. 9.2 EDIFACT Structure Chart (Simplified).

The application or the EDIFACT standard can be illustrated by further examining the example order that was given in Chapter 8. The order is shown again in Figure 9.3 with the addition of the interchange header and trailer and the (partial) inclusion of a second order.

```
UNB+UNOA:1+6464:xx+1141:xx+      Interchange   Header
BEN0273'
UNH+000001+ORDERS:2:932:UN'      Message 1     Header
BGM+220+AC6464'                                   •
DTM+4:20000315:102'                              • Data
NAD+BY+6464326::91'                              • Segments
NAD+SU+1149646::91'                               •
UNS+D'                                            •
LIN+1++PT-1073-R:VP'                              •
QTY+21:1600'                                      •
LIN+2++PT-1073-S:VP'                              •
QTY+21:1200'                                      •
UNT+13+000001'                                   Trailer
UNH                              Message 2
::::::::::
UNT
UNZ+1+BEN0273'                                 Trailer
```

Fig. 9.3 Example EDIFACT Interchange.

The EDIFACT order encodes the example order shown in Chapter 8, Figure 8.2. The interpretation of the EDIFACT order is as follows:

- **Interchange Header**

  - **UNB**   Interchange Header

    ```
    UNB+UNOA:1+6464:xx+1141:xx+BEN0273
    ```

Control Agency	UNOA	i.e. UN Level A
Version	2	
Sender Code	6464	
Code Qualifier		
Recipient Code	1141149	
Code Qualifier		
Date of Transmission	20000305	
Time of Transmission	1233	
Control Reference	BEN0273	

Order Message

- **UNH**   Message Header

  ```
  UNH+000001+ORDERS:2:911:UN'
  ```

Message Number	000001
Message Type	ORDERS
Version	2
Release	932
Control Agency	UN

- **BGM**   Beginning of Message

  ```
  BGM+220+AC6464'
  ```

Message Name Code	220	i.e. order
Document Number	AC6464	i.e. order number

- **DTM**   Date / Time / Period

  ```
  DTM+4:20000305:102'
  ```

Qualifier	4	i.e. order date
Date	20000305	
Format Qualifier	102	i.e. century date

- **NAD**   Name and Address

  ```
  NAD+BY+6464326::91'
  NAD+SU+1149646::91'
  ```

Party qualifier	BY	i.e. buyer
	SU	i.e. supplier
Address code	6464326 and 1149646	
Code list agency	91	i.e. user defined

- **UNS**   Section Control

  ```
  UNS+D'
  ```

  Section Identification   D   i.e. detail segment

- **LIN**   Line Item

  ```
  LIN+1++PT-1073-R:VP'
  LIN+2++PT-1073-S:VP'
  ```

  Line item number   1 and 2
  Item number   PT-1073-R and PT-1073-S
  Item number type   VP   i.e. vendor part number

- **QTY**   Quantity

  ```
  QTY+21:1600'
  QTY+21:1200'
  ```

  Quantity qualifier   21   i.e. ordered quantity
  Quantity   1600 and 1200

- **UNT**   Message Trailer

  ```
  UNT+11+000001'
  ```

  Control Count   11   i.e. eleven segments
  Message Number   000001

Interchange Trailer

- **UNZ**   Interchange Trailer

  ```
  UNZ+1+BEN0273
  ```

  Control Count   1   i.e. one message
  Control Reference   BEN0273

- **Formatting Characters**

  Data element separator   +
  Component data element separator   :
       (within a composite data element)
  Segment terminator   '

Decoded, this is the following order:

The order identification is:
- Order Number   AC6464
- Order Date   15.03.2000
From Pens and Things:
- Customer (Buyer) Address Code: 6464326
To Packaging Solutions:
- Supplier Address Code   1149646

For 'Executive Elite' gift cases in red and silver:

	Qty	Product
• Line 1 (Red Cases)	1,600	PT-1073-R
• Line 1 (Silver Cases)	1,200	PT-1073-S

See Chapter 8, Figure 8.2.

The EDIFACT coding of the order provides a machine independent, unambiguous specification of the requirement that can be sent / accepted by any system with the appropriate EDI software.

9.2.4 Coding Standards

The EDI standard provides the common format for the message but just as important is the ability to correctly interpret the data held within that format.

Data in computer systems normally has a code as a key. Computer systems have codes for customers, suppliers, products and so on. For EDI it is preferable to send the codes rather than the associated names, addresses and descriptions. The use of codes cuts down the size of the transmitted message and, provided the codes are mutually agreed, they can be used to match the appropriate records in the receiving computer system.

* **EAN / UPC Codes**

For the grocery and general retail trade there are standard systems of coding. These are used for bar codes on merchandise and to identify address points within the participating organisations; they are also used in EDI messages. The two main systems are:

* EAN   European Article Number
* UPC   Universal Product Code (American)

The coding systems are administered by the national Article Numbering Associations (ANA). These organisations have also been closely involved in the development of EDI; the British ANA developed the Tradacom EDI standard that was discussed earlier in this chapter.

The EAN and the UPC systems are similar. The EAN is a 13 digit code with a two digit country code whereas the UPC is a 12 digit code with only a single digit for the country. The makeup of the EAN code is shown in Figure 9.4.

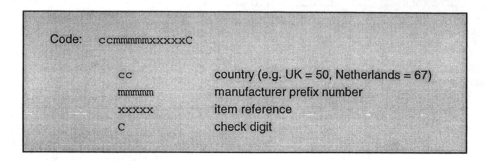

Fig. 9.4 EAN Coding System.

The check digit calculation, for the product code, uses a modulus 10 algorithm. This is calculated by multiplying alternative digits, of the code, by 1 and 3 respectively. The results of these multiplications are summed and the check digit is the difference between that sum and the next highest multiple of 10, see Figure 9.5.

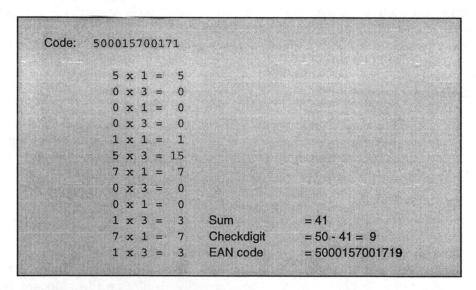

Fig. 9.5 EAN Checkdigit Calculation.

For very small items, eight digit (EAN-8) codes can be allocated. This is so that the smaller bar code can be printed on individual items.

The EAN code in the example above is a product code for a 420 gram tin of Heinz Baked Beans. Each Heinz product has the same manufacturers' prefix but a different item code allocated by the company, for example:

Baked Beans – 420 gram tin: 50 00157 00171 9
Cream of Tomato Soup – 300 gram tin: 50 00157 00207 5
Baked Beans – 205 gram tin: 50 00157 00023 1

In the EDI Order message these codes can be used in the order line, e.g. the line:

LIN+1++5000157001719:EN'

EAN address point codes are used in EDI messages to identify the sender and receiver of the message. Address point codes are simular to the product code; the country and manufacturer's prefix are the same as for the companies products but the check digit calculation differs for the two usages. The sender of the order may wish to specify a number of locations, for instance an order, in addition to the buyer and supplier, might identify:

The Delivery Point – the warehouse where the goods will be delivered;
The Invoice Point   – the head office where the invoice is to be sent.

The EDIFACT order message provides for up to 20 name and address segments (NAD) to be sent in an order.

- **Generic Products**

EAN codes are appropriate for ordering branded products. They are not applicable where the requirement is for a generic product. This circumstance may not arise when baked beans are ordered (we all tend to have our preferences for a particular brand) but the order might be for:

- A generic product, e.g. red biros (any old red biros), or
- A commodity product, e.g. sheet steel or paper.

Product coding in these circumstances is either agreed between customer and supplier or there is an agreement on an industry sector basis. The paper and board trade is one such industry where coding conventions have been agreed to specify grams / sq. cm, direction of fibre, size of sheet, etc. Coupled with such a convention is the need for an understanding of the 'pack quantity'. It is unfortunate if an order for 1,000 sheets of paper is interpreted as an order for 1,000 reams (and it has happened!).

9.3   EDI Communications

The EDI standard specifies the syntax for the coding of the electronic document, it does not specify the method of transmission. The transmission of the electronic document can be:

- A magnetic tape or diskette that is posted or despatched using a courier service.
- A direct data communications link.
- A value added data service (VADS), also known as a value added network (VAN).

The physical transfer of magnetic tape or diskette is one way of transmitting EDI messages. This method used to be standard with the Bankers Automated Clearing Service (BACS) payment service. It has also been used by some retail chains where collection of the disks can be tied in with daily deliveries of stock – this has been particularly prevalent in Germany (Parfit, 1992). However, one of the advantages of EDI is speed of transmission and this is hardly facilitated by the physical transportation of the diskette or tape. For this, and other reasons, this way of transmitting EDI is declining in popularity.

The use of direct data communications links is the second possibility. It can be appropriate for trading relationships where there are large data volumes or where there are only one or two trading partners involved. It does, however, have a number of complications. It presumes that the trading partners agree transmission times, protocols and linespeeds – requirements that become complex when there are several trading partners, some of them involved in a number of trading relationships.

The final possibility is the use of a VADS. These can provide a number of facilities but the essential is the use of postboxes and mailboxes to provide 'time independence' and 'protocol independence'. The facilities of a VADS are further discussed in the following sections.

9.3.1 Postboxes and Mailboxes

The basic facility of a VADS is a post and forward network. This network is centred on a computer system with communications facilities. For each user of the system there are two files:

- The postbox – where outgoing messages are placed.
- The mailbox – where incoming messages can be picked up.

Taking the trading network shown at Figure 9.1, the postbox and mailbox arrangement of the VADS would be as shown at Figure 9.6.

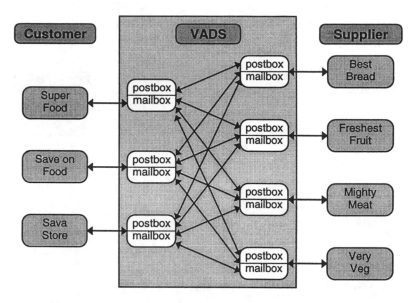

Fig. 9.6 VADS – Postbox and Mailbox Files.

If Sava Store, for example, needed to place orders for bread, meat and vegetables then it formats an EDI interchange containing a number of orders for those three suppliers. The sequence of events would then be:

• Sava Store establishes a communications link to the VADS system. Sava Store makes extensive use of the system and has a leased line communications link.

• Sava Store then transmits the EDI interchange and it is temporarily stored in its postbox.

• The VADS computer system inspects postboxes, unpacks the interchanges, moves any available messages (orders in this case) to the mailboxs of the intended recipients and repackages them as new interchanges. The inspection of postboxes is frequent and, to all intents and purposes, the interchanges are immediately available to the recipient.

• The users of the system establishes a communication link to the VADS system at their convenience. Best Bread is the first user of the system to come online, in this case the communications link is a dial-up line.

• Best Bread inspects its mailboxes for new interchanges. On finding the order from Sava Store (and possibly further interchanges from other customers) it causes them to be transmitted to its own order processing system.

The EDI interchange is then available for processing in the user's application. See Figure 9.7 for a diagram of this interchange taking place.

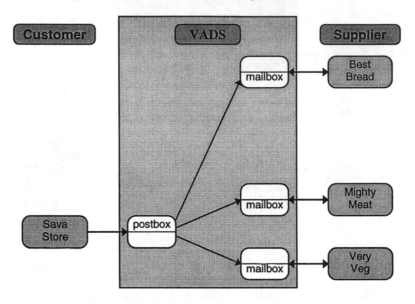

Fig. 9.7 VADS – Example Interchange.

The post-box / mailbox system is also referred to as a 'store and forward' system. The two principle advantages of such a system are:

- Time Independence:
  The sending and receipt of the interchange are asynchronous. The two processes can be carried out at the convenience of the users involved. The first user may send all its EDI transmissions, to all its trading partners, in a single batch, at the end of its overnight processing run. The individual interchange can then be picked up by the trading partners, at their individual convenience.

- Protocol Independence
  The type of communications link to be used is an option available to each user of the VADS system. Low volume users will probably opt for a dial-up modem link whereas high volume users may well use a leased line or a packet switching network. The VADS supplier makes available a wide variety of communications facilities and has the ability to handle a range of protocols. The transmission protocol envelope is stripped off incoming interchanges leaving just the EDI interchange. Interchanges are then re-enveloped with the transmission protocol appropriate to the recipient when they are retrieved from the mailbox.

9.3.2 Value Added Data Services

A number of organisations have set out to provide VADS. Two such services that are extensively used are the IBM network and GEIS (General Electric Information Services).

The basic and most important facility of the VADS is the postbox / mailbox provision. There are, however, a number of further facilities that can be made available; some or all of them may be provided by any particular VADS provider.

- Trading Community:
  An established EDI VADS will have a large number of clients all with an interest in electronic trade. There is a tendency for organisations in a particular trade sector to concentrate on one particular VADS (there are instances of formal agreements between a trade sector organisation and a VADS). Joining the appropriate VADS can ease access to new electronic trading partners.

- Inter-network Connections:
  A VADS facilitates trade between partners that subscribe to the same VADS but not between partners that might be using different VADS services – not infrequently organisations have joined more than one VADS to overcome this problem. A number of the VADS have made inter-network agreements that provide for the passing of interchanges between them.

- International Connections:
  Many VADS are nationally based with a single computer service providing the switching service – a set-up that is appropriate for domestic trade. A number of the VADS's are part of international organisations or have alliances with VADS's in other countries thus facilitating international trade.

- Privacy, Security and Reliability:
  A commonly expressed concern by EDI users is the privacy of the system and the security of their messages (a concern that can seem exaggerated given the relative insecurity of the postal system that EDI might be replacing).
  Privacy provisions will normally include user-id / password protection of postboxes and mailboxes. The setting up of a trading relationship can also be under user control with both users required to enter the appropriate control message before the exchange of message can take place. The EDI message can also be encrypted or can include an electronic signature (provisions that are not dependant on the VADS).
  Security will be built into the VADS system – it is important to the users and to the reputation of the VADS that messages are not lost.

The service must also be reliable – the VADS should have an appropriate hardware and software configuration so that it can ensure the continuous availability of its service.

- Message Storage and Logging:
  Users of the VADS would normally have control over the retrieval and retention of messages in their mailbox. New messages can be called off selectively or in total. Once a message has been called off it will be marked as no longer new but it can still be retained in the mailbox (and it is worthwhile making use of this facility until the message is secure in the users system).

  As part of its service provision the VADS may well have a message logging facilities. This provides an audit trail of when the message arrived in the VADS, when the recipient retrieved it and when it was eventually deleted. A useful provision should messages be lost – the result of an enquiry is normally to prove a fault in one of the users systems / procedures rather than any fault in the operation of the VADS.

- Message Validation:
  A number of VADS will provide a service that validates EDI messages for conformance with the chosen EDI standard and returns an invalid interchange. This service is optional and normally incurs an extra charge.

- Local Access:
  VADS, despite their alternative name of Value Added Network are message switching services, not network services. The cost of the connection from the user to the VADS can be reduced by using a local access node or a packet switching service. The time independence provided by the VADS gives the user the option of accessing the service when cheap rate telephone charges apply.

- Charges:
  The VADS is a commercial organisation and charges for its services. The charges tend to be a combination of:

  - Subscription: A monthly or annual subscription.
  - Usage charge: A charge for the number of characters transmitted.

  Differing VADS apply these charges in differing combinations – in theory a user could select the VADS with the charging structure that gave it most advantage – in practice users choose the VADS already used by their trading partners. For the Pens and Things example, the VADS that is most likely to be adopted is that already used by Packaging Solutions.

- Software and Consultancy:
  Network providers tend to have considerable experience in EDI and an interest in promoting its widespread adoption. Most VADS providers supply (or sell) EDI software that provides for easy access to their own network. These VADS providers will also provide consultancy and training – the basic provision concerns the use of the software and the network but there can also be consultancy on the business use of EDI within the organisation.

9.3.3 EDI in the Internet

Recently a number of organisations have started using the Internet as an EDI VADS. Using the Internet provides the basic store and forward facilities but not necessarily the other features of a VADS service that are listed above. Security and reliability are two of the major concerns, unlike the traditional VADS, the Internet does not guarantee the safe delivery of any data you send into it. The plus side of using the Internet is that it is cheaper than any of the commercial networks that provide specific EDI VADS services.

9.4   EDI Implementation

The final technical element of the EDI system is the EDI software. If Pens and Things is to send an order from its production control system to Packaging Solutions it needs to code that order into the agreed EDI standard and 'squirt' it into the chosen VADS. To pick up the order at the other end, Packaging Solutions has a similar need to extract the data from the network and to decode the data from the EDI message into its order processing system. The coding / decoding of the EDI message and the interfacing with the VADS is normally achieved using EDI Software. The overall picture is summarised in Figure 9.8.

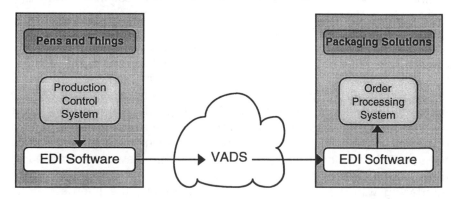

Fig. 9.8 Sending an order using EDI Software.

9.4.1 EDI Software

The EDI software is normally bought in from a specialist supplier. There are a number of software houses supplying EDI solutions or the EDI software may come from:

- A major trading partner – the trading partner may supply the software or recommend a third party supplier.
- The VADS supplier.
- As part of application package, e.g. packaged software for production control, order processing or accounting may include EDI software as an integral feature or as an optional module.
- A third party. An example of this is that a number of banks provide EDI solutions that include the collection of and accounting for electronic payments.

Obtaining EDI software from an 'interested' party has both advantages and disadvantages. If the software is, for example, bought from the VADS supplier then, hopefully, there would not be any problem interfacing with the chosen network but using an additional VADS or switching to a new network supplier may be more problematic. Suppliers that link EDI Software with other interests are good examples of 'customer lock-in' strategies that were discussed in Section 1.

The basic functions of the EDI Software are the two already outlined, namely:

- Coding business transactions into the chosen EDI Standard;
- Interfacing with the VADS.

Many EDI software suppliers provide additional functions. These may include:

- A trading partner database integrated into the EDI Software. This can provide for code translation (e.g. internal customer codes to a trade sector standard code) and / or for the specification of the EDI requirements of each trading partner;
- Support of multiple EDI Standards. The selection of the appropriate standard may be determined by the trading partner database;
- Sophisticated facilities to ease the formatting of internal application data to and from the EDI Standard. 'Drag and drop' interfaces are available for this purpose. Various EDI Software suppliers have associations with the large suppliers of business applications (production planning, order processing, etc.) and provide standardised interfaces to those packages;
- Facilities for transactions to be sent by fax or e-Mail to customers that do not use EDI. The identification of such customers may be determined by the trading partner database;
- Interfacing with a variety of EDI VADS (including the Internet). The selection of the appropriate VADS may be determined by a trading partner database;

- The option to encrypt the EDI Message;
- Facilities for the automatic acknowledgement of the EDI message;
- Message tracking and an audit trail of messages sent and received;
- Direct input and printed output of EDI transactions – allowing free standing EDI Operation – in effect the EDI system provides the service of a fax machine.

EDI Software is available on a variety of platforms, from the basic PC up to a mainframe system. As with all classes of software the price varies: the basic PC packages starting at (say) 500 pounds sterling / 800 US dollars and the price then goes up from there for the larger machines, additional facilities and services such as consultancy. For some EDI software the support of each standard and / or VADS is an additional plug-in that is paid for separately. Yearly maintenance charges, that include updates as the new versions of the EDI Standards are released, tend to be quite hefty.

At the top of the range is the concept of an EDI Corporate Interface. This software, often mounted on its own, mid-range, machine acts as a central clearing house for all the e-Commerce transactions of a large organisation. The external interfaces can link to several EDI VADS's and translate to a variety of EDI Standards to meet the needs of a large number of trading partners. The internal interfaces can link to a number of business systems such as order processing and accounts payable, possibly systems that are replicated across the various divisions of the organisation. The system can also be used for intra-organisational transactions – if the interface for external customers and suppliers uses EDI, why not use the same interfaces for trades between divisions of the organisation.

9.4.2 EDI Integration

EDI software will do its job well at a relatively modest price. What pre-packaged EDI software cannot do is automatically integrate with the business application and a comprehensive solution to this requirement can take a lot of time and cost a lot of money.

The simple way to implement EDI is not to link the EDI software and the applications – a set-up sometimes referred to as EDI-Fax or EDInterruptus. This is, a course, followed by many organisations when they first start and persisted with by many small organisations who are only 'doing EDI' because a large trading partner has told them to. In this mode of operation:

- Incoming EDI messages are printed out from the EDI software and then manually keyed into the business application that they are intended for;
- Outgoing EDI messages are extracted from the business application and typed into the EDI software for formatting and onward transmission.

The use of EDI in this way ensures that the transactions get through quickly (hence the term EDI-Fax) but it rules out any of the other advantages of using EDI.

For full integration of the business application and the EDI Software there needs to be an interface to transfer data from the business application to the EDI software and visaversa. To ease this process, most EDI software provides for a 'flat file' interface. If the data to be sent is (say) an order then the business application can be modified so that:

- The supplier record in the order processing system has an indicator to say that its orders are to be sent via EDI;
- The order print run is modified so that orders for EDI capable suppliers are not printed;
- An additional run is included to take the orders from the EDI capable suppliers and format the data onto the flat file;
- The flat file is accessed by the EDI software and, using user supplied parameters, the order data is formatted into the required EDI standard and posted into the VADS.

The reverse process is used for incoming EDI messages. This will involve the creation of a batch input routine to run in parallel with the online facilities utilised by most business applications.

The additional worry with incoming EDI messages is validation. For orders, invoices and any other data manually input into a business application there will be (or should be) comprehensive primary and secondary validation built into the system and there is a human operator there to deal with any queries. For EDI messages there will not be any input errors at the receiving end but there is (normally) no guarantee that the data sent by the trading partner is correct or acceptable. Arguably the EDI routines taking input messages need all the same validation checks as the equivalent manual input routines and there needs to be procedures for correcting the problems or informing the trading partner and getting them to transmit a corrected message.

9.4.3 EDI Operation

Once the EDI system is set-up it, like any other data processing systems, needs careful and systematic operation.

A big difference between electronic transactions and their paper equivalents is that with electronic transactions there is no paperwork to fall back on should anything go wrong. In these circumstances, therefore, it is sensible to keep a security copy of all incoming transactions – preferably in their EDI format as soon as they enter the system. This then gives a fall-back position should any data be lost or corrupted and is an aid to the diagnosis of any problems.

The second aspect to EDI operation is how often should the system be run. EDI has been implemented, in part at least, to cut down transaction cycle time and there is no point in re-introducing unnecessary delays. For many organisations a daily download from the mailbox and processing run is sufficient – however, this is not entirely satisfactory if the daily run is timed for an hour before a major trading partner sends out their daily orders. In some circumstances, such as just-in-time manufacture in the vehicle assembly business, cycle times can be as short as one hour and obviously order processing needs to be very frequent / real-time.

9.4.4 EDI Alternatives

A large organisation that processes many electronic transactions is going to need its own EDI set-up. There are, however, many small companies that are dragged into EDI trade by a large trading partner but for who the set-up and running costs of an EDI facility would outweigh the benefits. For these organisations there are a number of alternatives:

- The low cost, PC based, free-standing EDI facility.
- Making use of an EDI clearing house. To do this the company contract for their EDI messages to be sent to a clearing house who decode them, print them out and then post or fax them on. The British Post Office is an example of an organisation that provides this service.
- Internet access via a clearing house. This is an update on the EDI-Post service outlined above where a clearing house is used but the inward and outward transactions are transmitted between the end user and the clearing house and accessed by the client using a standard web browser.

9.5   EDI Agreements

Setting up an EDI system requires a lot of discussion with trading partners. Manual systems rely a lot on the understanding of the people involved; when these interchanges are automated there is no understanding between the machines – they just do what they are told (well they do on a good day!).

The introduction of EDI may also be part of a wider process of business processing re-engineering that makes the effective operation of the supply chain much more crucial to successful business operation. Traditional logistics had buffer stocks in the factory's parts warehouse or the retailer's regional depot and stock room. In just-in-time manufacture and quick response supply these buffer stocks are eliminated – this reduces the capital employed and avoids the need to double handle goods. Without these buffer stocks the EDI systems become crucial – the orders need to be delivered on time or cars will be made with missing wheels and there will be no cornflakes on the shelves in the supermarket.

Hence to achieve a successful, electronically controlled supply chain, businesses have to talk. They need to agree the nature of the business that is to be done electronically, the technical details of how it is to be undertaken and the procedures for resolving any disputes that arise.

9.5.1 EDI Interchange Agreements

The appropriate way to document the details of a trading arrangement between electronic trading partners is an EDI Interchange Agreement. The agreement makes clear the trading intentions of both parties, the technical framework for the transactions and the procedures to be followed in the event of a dispute. The EDI Agreement is a document, normally on paper, and signed by both trading partners before electronic trading begins.

The first requirement of the agreement is to establish the legal framework. This has a special significance as most business law relates to paper based trading and how that law should apply to the less tangible form of an electronic message is not always clear (although a number of countries are updating their legal provisions to take account of electronic trade). This point is made in the commentary that is included in the European Model Electronic Data Interchange (EDI) Agreement (EU-IA):

> 'For EDI to be a successful alternative to paper trading, it is essential that messages are accorded a comparable legal value as their paper equivalent when the functions effected in an electronic environment are similar to those effected in a paper environment, and where all appropriate measures have been taken to secure and store the data.'

The EU-IA, in the text of the agreement, includes the clause:

> 'The parties, intending to be legally bound by the Agreement, expressly waive any right to contest the validity of a contract effected by the use of EDI in accordance with the terms and conditions of the Agreement on the sole grounds that it was effected by EDI.'

And the agreement also specifies:

- The point in its transmission and processing at which a message will be deemed to be legally binding – the usually accepted standard is that the 'document' achieves legal status when it arrives at the receiving party, the 'reception rule'.
- The timescale for processing EDI massages. One purpose of EDI is to speed up the trade cycle and this is not achieved if messages are not reliably processed within an agreed timescale.
- The time that copies of the message will be retained (a default of three years is provided for by the EU-IA but many member states require longer periods, e.g. seven or ten years).
- The procedure for settling any disputes. The EU-IA suggests a choice between arbitration by a named organisation, e.g. a chamber of commerce appointed arbitration chamber, or by recourse to the judicial process.
- The legal duristriction in which any disputes should be settled.

In addition to the legal (or legalistic) aspects of the agreement it is important to specify the technical requirements. These requirements include:

- The coding systems that will be used for identifying entities such as organisations and products and attributes such as quantities.
- The EDI standard that is to be employed and, within that, the messages and data segments that will be used. Updating of message standards as new versions are released is an issue that also needs to be covered.
- The network that is to be used – including details of scheduling and protocol where a post and forward network is not to be employed.

Model agreements are available from various parties, including trade organisations, and references to example agreements can be found on the web pages that accompany this book.

9.6 EDI Security

An important aspect of EDI is the privacy and security of the messages and their exchange. Points that are covered by the EDI Interchange agreement but may also be provided for in the technical implementation.

The first point is to ensure that interchange of messages is reliable. In the first instance this is a matter of procedures at both ends of the trading agreements. Procedures, rigid procedures, are required to ensure that all the processes are run and that they reach their successful conclusion – an old-fashioned requirement called 'data processing standards'. Procedures are particularly important where operations are manual (as opposed to being controlled by job control programs (JCP) run under the appropriate operating system). Particular attention is needed if the EDI software is run on a separate machine (say a PC) and the application software operates in a mainframe or similar environment; it is vital that all the data received on the EDI machine is passed to and processed (once only!) on the mainframe and that outgoing data is reliably processed in the reverse direction.

Further aspects of security are:

- Controls in the EDI Standards:
  EDI Standards include controls designed to protect against errors in, and corruption of, the message. The sort of thing that is provided is for segment counts in the message and message counts in the interchange (see 9.2.3).

- Controls in the Transmission Protocol:
  Transmission protocols include protection, such as longitudinal control totals, to detect any data corruption that occurs during transmission. Where corruption is detected the network system occasions a re-transmission without the need for outside intervention.

- Protection against Tampering:
  Where there is concern that the transmission might be intercepted and modified it can be protected by a digital signature. This is designed to ensure that the message received is exactly the same as the message sent and that the source of the message is an authorised trading partner.

- Privacy of Message:
  Where the contents of the message are considered sensitive the privacy of the message can be protected, during transmission, by encrypting the data.

- Non-repudiation:
  One potential problem is that the recipient of the message might deny having received it; the electronic equivalent of the idea that the unpaid invoice must have got 'lost in the post'. One way out of this is to use the receipt acknowledgement messages (see below) but the other alternative is a 'trusted third party'. The 'trusted third party' can be the VADS supplier or, if you don't trust them, some other organisation. The role of the third party is to audit trail all transactions (a role the VADS provider is ideally positioned to fulfil) and to settle any dispute about what messages were sent and what messages were received.

One aspect of security provided for by the EDI standard is the receipt acknowledgement message. This is a transaction specific message sent out by the receiving system to acknowledge each message, order or whatever. Trading partners that use receipt acknowledgement messages need to be clear about the level of security (guarantee) implied by the receipt of the acknowledgement. The EDI acknowledgement message can be:

- Automatically generated by the EDI Software (Physical Acknowledgement). It informs the sender that the message has arrived but there is no guarantee that it is passed to the application for processing or that it is a valid transaction within the application.
- Coded into the application to confirm that it is in the system for processing.
- Produced by the application once the message is processed to confirm that the message was valid and possibly to give additional information such as stock allocation and expected delivery date (Logical Acknowledgement).

The need for security in an EDI system needs to be kept in proportion; after all EDI is very probably replacing a paper based system where computer output orders, without signatures, were bunged in the post and eventually manually keyed in by an order entry clerk. Transmission and EDI message controls are automatic. Checks over and above that all come at a cost; encryption and digital signatures both require extra software and procedures; message acknowledgements require additional software to generate the message and to match it to the original transaction on the other side of the trading relationship. EDI orders and invoices for regular transactions of relatively low cost supplies do not justify too heavy an investment in privacy and security – if an extra load of cornflakes arrives at the supermarket distribution centre it can be sorted out on the phone and the error will probably be in the warehouse, not the EDI system (whatever the supplier tells the customer!). EDI payments require more care; normally the payment transaction is sent to a bank (with its own procedures) with the payment advice being sent to the trading partner.

The overall facilities for EDI privacy and security are summed up in Figure 9.9.

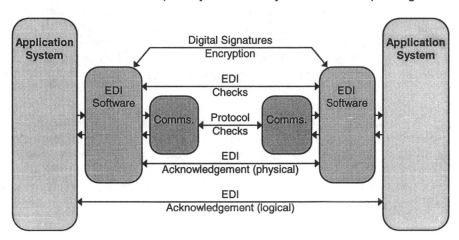

Fig. 9.9 EDI Privacy and Security.

9.7   Nuts, Bolts and the Tool Kit

The overall EDI 'technical' set-up is summed up in Figure 9.10. The business use and practices associated with EDI are examined in Chapter 10.

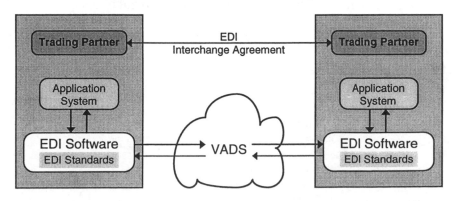

Fig. 9.10 EDI Summary.

Exercises

The following are suggested as individual exercises. They can be grouped together to make an assignment or a group exercise.

1. Using the EDIFACT standard information on the web page, format an invoice message for Packaging Solutions to invoice Pens and Things for the goods requested in the order shown at Figure 8.2.

2. Draw up an Interchange Agreement to cover the exchange of orders and invoices between Packaging Solutions and Pens and Things. You may use model agreements obtained from the web (or elsewhere) but the agreement must be fully tailored to the needs of these two organisations. Keep the agreement short, one page should suffice.

3. Draw up a plan for the implementation of EDI at Pens and Things. The plan is initially for the interchange of orders with Packaging Solutions but should take account of possible future developments. The plan should be no more than two pages long, state any assumptions you have made.

The web page includes an e-Commerce kit that can be used for further EDI exercises, see details on the web page.

Further Reading

A good introduction to EDI standards is given in Parfit (1992), see further reading in Chapter 8. More detail of the EDIFACT standard is given in:

Berge J. (1991) *The EDIFACT Standards*, NCC Blackwell.

Unfortunately, as is the case with Parfit, this book is now out of print.

Further reading on EDI is available on the Internet. This includes detail of EDI standards and model EDI Interchange Agreements. See the web page for a selection of appropriate url's.

10

EDI and Business

Summary

This chapter looks at the use of EDI in business and the implications of that usage for business.

The technical elements of EDI are relatively simple; of much more significance is the impact of EDI on the business. The use of electronic trading in an organisation can be part of a project to re-engineer the supply chain and can facilitate changes in the nature of the product that is offered to the consumer.

This chapter analyses patterns of EDI trading, examines a range of EDI transactions and introduces a model of EDI maturity. The chapter also uses a number of real life case studies to illustrate the effective strategic use of EDI.

10.1   Organisations that use EDI

EDI has potential applications in any organisation where the administration processes are computerised and that exchanges regular and standardised transactions with other organisations. Extensive users of EDI include:

* **Bhs**
  Bhs is a UK and European multiple retailer dealing mainly in apparel (fashion) goods. It operates some 120 large retail outlets and is represented in most major UK shopping centres.
  Bhs deals with about 400 suppliers on a regular basis and all orders for merchandise are sent by EDI. Using just-in-time supply it is important for Bhs to know what the suppliers have in stock and for the supplier to be able to anticipate demand by seeing Bhs sales data; this two way flow of information is also maintained using EDI. In addition to the orders, EDI is used to confirm supplier delivery and to communicate bar code information for use in delivery and packaging.

The use of EDI at Bhs is the back-end to an integrated merchandising, sales and replenishment system. Replenishment decisions are dependant on the sales plan and the stock available (updated from the EPOS systems). New EDI orders can be generated overnight and be with the supplier the next day. Bhs calculate that they can be making 4.5 million replenishment decisions each working week.

Derived from *The role of computers within Bhs (1994)*

- **Lucas Rist**
All volume car manufacturers make extensive use of EDI as a facilitator of just-in-time manufacturing systems. Typically parts supply is divided into categories, many smaller parts are stocked in warehouses at the assembly plant but a number of larger parts will be ordered for 'sequenced delivery' for the models that are to go down the line that day.

Lucas Rist manufacture the 'main harness' for Rover Cars. The main harness is a wiring loom that carries all the electrical cables for virtually every electrical part of a motor car. The loom can contain as many as a thousand individual wires and a thousand individual components; the configuration of the loom varies depending on the model, variant and component configuration of the specific car that is being built.

Rover send Lucas Rist a ten day build plan and later a provisional order, both by EDI. The actual, confirmed EDI orders are placed every two to four hours and are for delivery of the correct specification main harness, in sequence, to track side within 10 hours from the despatch of the order. Lucas Rist inform Rover, again using EDI, of when the part is to be dispatched; this gives Rover a chance to adjust the production schedule if there is a problem. Rover's requirement is that the part needs to be there, to be fitted to the body shell before it goes through the paint shop; without the part the production line stops.

Based of a case study supplied by *Perwill plc*

- **TeleOrdering**
The EDI system for the book trade is called TeleOrdering, a system that is linked to the Whitaker's catalogue *Books in Print*.

The book trade has a number of methods of supply. Some bookshops deal with the representatives of the major publishers and some with wholesale book suppliers but, for the academic bookshop, the Whitaker's catalogue is a standard tool.

Books in Print is a monthly catalogue issued on CD-ROM. It allows the bookshop to look up any book that is in print but not in stock. If the customer then wants the book ordering the system will format an EDI order that is sent via TeleOrdering to the appropriate publisher. The system is flexible and readily copes with the various types and sizes of organisations in the book trade. Smiths, for example, have incorporated Whitakers into their own Book Finder package that will also source from their own warehouse. At the other end of the scale, the small publisher that does not have an online connection to the system will receive a printed version of the EDI order, from TeleOrdering, in the post.

A good supply chain is important to both the virtual as well as the physical bookshop. Online bookshops must ensure that orders are satisfied as rapidly as possible and Blackwells, for example, have made a point of linking their online bookshop to TeleOrdering so that efficient supply can be assured.

10.2   EDI Trading Patterns

10.2.1 Hubs and Spokes

Many of the prime movers in the adoption of EDI have been large retail organisations, such as Bhs and component assembly manufacturers such as the Rover Group (both of these examples are used as case studies in Section 10.1).

These prime movers have set up extensive electronic trading networks with their suppliers. The EDI flows have been typified as a 'hub and spoke' pattern, the major organisation is the hub and the suppliers are the spokes. The orders are sent from the hub to the suppliers (spokes) and, after the goods have been delivered, the spoke will transmit the EDI invoice to the hub, see Figure 10.1.

Initially EDI is implemented with a small number of important suppliers and then, over time, the system is extended to encompass all suppliers to the core business activity. For many of these organisations EDI is made a condition of trade – if the supermarket is to sell your product then you will use EDI. Bray (1992) expresses it thus:

> 'Therefore, when it [the Hub] says, "thou shall trade electronically",
> the suppliers have little option but to reply "anything you say, Sir".'

Or, in a phrase attributed to the UK supermarket chain, Tesco:

EDI or DIE

The hub and spoke pattern of electronic trading leads to the formation of closed user communities. The supermarket or the car builder hub chooses the VADS and the EDI standard and the suppliers (spokes) are required to conform. The arrangements will in fact be more specific than that – the supplier will specify a number of very detailed requirements including a strict subset of the EDI standard that is specific to that closed user community (and is not always in strict compliance with the EDI standard).

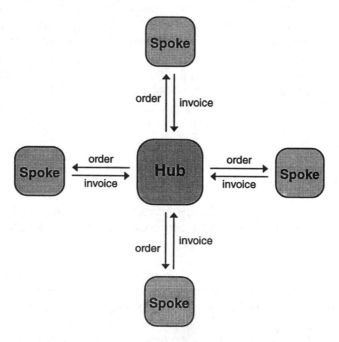

Fig. 10.1 Hub and Spoke Trading Patterns.

This arrangement can work reasonably well for a supplier that is a spoke serving just one hub. The EDI implementation decisions are already taken, they just need to be implemented. Some hub organisations will specify the system or even supply the software that is to be used. The position is less satisfactory when the supplier trades with more than one hub. The major food processors will typically supply most, if not all, of the major supermarket chains. In Britain, these suppliers will have to join at least two EDI VADS (most supermarkets trade using the GEIS/INS network but one of the majors uses IBM for its network) and then meet the different EDI standard and other conditions laid down by each of the hub organisations.

This situation is illustrated by Hood, *et al.* (1994). Their paper presents a study of one of the large supermarkets and four of its suppliers. One of the suppliers, a bakery, supplied several of the top ten food retailers and the following supply arrangements are recorded with different customers:

- EDI orders and invoices (with three customers);
- EDI orders only and manual invoices;
- Telephone orders and manual invoices;
- Manual orders but invoices on tape;
- Salesmen calling at the retail outlet.

The authors summarises the situation thus:

> 'Supermarkets see only their own systems whilst suppliers have to cope with multiple EDI systems, and the attendant coding problems, and combine this with a non-EDI system for other customers.'

The spread of EDI trading is increasing the number of electronic traders and the number of trading partners that any organisation might have. The hub and spoke pattern is becoming messy:

- The spokes are becoming intertwined and the hubs are spokes to other hubs.
- Different EDI standards, messages and message subsets are used by different organisations.
- The number of available EDI VADS is growing and interconnection with organisations connected to other VADS can be difficult.

These issues are further examined in the following sub-sections.

10.2.2 Overlapping User Communities

As illustrated above, electronically capable suppliers to organisations such as supermarkets and vehicle assemblers are becoming involved in EDI trading relationships with several customers. The user community looks like a hub and spoke network to the hub but more like a spider's web to the spoke organisation, entrapped by the conflicting requirements of a number of powerful and demanding customer organisations. An illustration of the nature of the overall trading network is given at Figure 10.2.

As EDI develops it is reasonable to suspect that networks will expand and grow more complex. Additional links are possible:

- Between the players in the network.
- To further tiers of suppliers or subcontractors.

Links to secondary suppliers are a logical development. If the supplier of cakes to the supermarket is receiving EDI orders then they might want to use the same system to purchase the flour and dried fruit they use in their baking. EDI links with secondary suppliers have not occurred at the same rate as with the major hub organisation. Many, but by no means all, supplier organisations are small or medium size firms which:

- Have enough on their plate coping with the EDI and JIT demands of their major customers.
- Are less computerised, automated and streamlined than their larger trading partners.

The extension of the trading network is further discussed in Section 10.2.3 below.

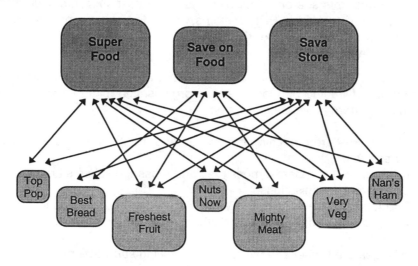

Fig. 10.2 Overlapping Supply Networks.

10.2.3 Differing Patterns of EDI Trade

The 'hub and spoke' is often presented as the general pattern of EDI trade. As EDI trade has developed differing patterns are beginning to develop for differing sectors. The patterns vary in the range of trading links established and the type of messaging that is used.

   Retailing is one of the sectors most advanced in electronic trading and a pattern has developed of:

- Major retail chains with EDI links to many (or most) suppliers;
- Suppliers with links to one or (typically) several of the major retail chains.

This pattern has already been illustrated in Figure 10.2 and has been discussed in Section 10.2.2. Automotive assembly is another sector that is making widespread use of EDI and the trading pattern is similar to that of the retail sector.

   The pattern of suppliers trading with a number of hubs gets further complicated when second tier suppliers start trading electronically.   As already discussed this has been happening but in general development has not been rapid.   There are, however, instances of large organisations introduced to electronic trading by their customers which have then gone on to make extensive use of EDI in their own supply networks:

> 'Spokes like Courtaulds Textiles (pushed into EDI by customer pressure), which are large companies and have their own suppliers, are busy becoming hubs of their own EDI networks, so that they can reap the same benefits as their own customers.'

(Bray, 1992)

The spread of EDI to second tier suppliers, when added to the picture at Figure 10.2, extends the network still further, see Figure 10.3. The addition of further layers of suppliers, and suppliers acting at more than one layer, has the potential for a significant increase in complexity (a complication if there are disparate EDI standards, messaging and networks in use).

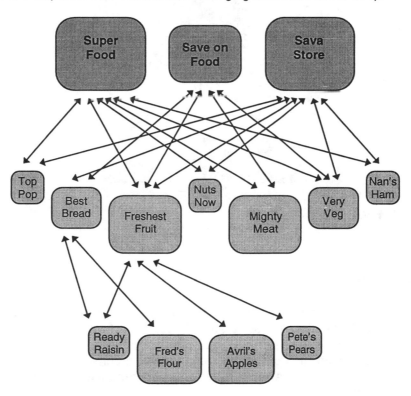

Fig. 10.3 Extended Supply Network.

The hub and spoke pattern, with the spokes networking to several hubs, seems to be the most common pattern but is not the only pattern of EDI trade. An alternative pattern is that exhibited by a wholesaling organisation. In a simple form the wholesaler has EDI links with a number of its (larger) customers and then is a traditional 'hub' of its own supplier network (maybe it could be called a 'corn sheaf structure', but then again perhaps not!). This structure is illustrated at Figure 10.4. It is, of course, very possible for wholesalers to be integrated into wider supply networks, the reader is left to construct a mental picture of this structure integrated with the links of the network shown at Figure 10.3.

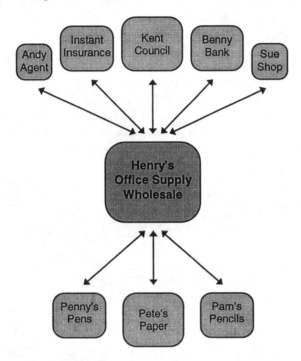

Fig. 10.4 Wholesaler Network.

10.2.4 Co-operative User Communities

The hub and spoke pattern of electronic trading is typically lead by the hub customer and, as already discussed, the suppliers who form the spokes are not necessarily willing participants. In many instances the customer organisation, in the hub and spoke, can also gain considerable competitive advantage from the arrangement at the expense of the supplier organisations.

EDI trading is not sold on this basis and there are EDI communities where the process of setting up the community is co-operative and where a win–win share of advantage appears to be achieved.

One such EDI network is TeleOrdering; the network used by bookshops for ordering books and featured as a case study at the start of this chapter; all publishers and book retailers, large and small can take part in this network, sending and receiving book orders on a broadly equal basis. Further such examples exist, particularly in Scandinavian countries where electronic trade systems are often set up by trade associations or organised as co-operative ventures.

10.2.5 Open User Communities

The opposite of a closed user community is an open user community. The hub and spoke pattern and the closed user community evolved to cater for the established trading relationships. The spread of electronic trading has produced unwelcome complexity within that model. That complexity has evolved while trade is still restricted to the core business of organisations. A new approach is required if electronic trading is to be extended to most, if not all, of the inter-organisational transactions that organisations make. EDI must be defined and implemented in a way that is appropriate to an open user community.

There are three principle barriers to the evolution of open EDI trade:

- Networks
- EDI Standards
- Product Coding

The norm for EDI trading is the use of a VADS – closed user communities will conduct all their business on a single VADS chosen by the hub. There are, however, some half dozen major VADS offering their services in the UK. There has been a tendency for any given trade sector to concentrate on one particular VADS and this has lessened the potential problem. However, by definition, miscellaneous trade will cross trade sector boundaries and the problem of the user community defined by the membership of a VADS will increase. The problem is both national and international. VADS have links to similar services in Europe, North America and across the world but again these partnerships only give access to the user community belonging to the connected VADS.

The EDI standards that have evolved are again associated with closed user communities. Standards have been evolved on a national basis (e.g. Tradacom or X12), on an industry basis (e.g. Odette) or even for one industry in one country (e.g. VGA). The requirement is for a common EDI standard and this is recognised by the European Community promotion of EDIFACT and the evolution of other standards towards the underlying structure of the EDIFACT standard. This move to a common standard starts to solve one of the problems but generates another. The EDIFACT standard, in trying to encompass the needs of all, is so vast that it cannot, readily, be fully implemented and dialects are being used – in effect reproducing the problem of separate standards that the use of EDIFACT was designed to overcome.

The final problem is that of product codes and the quantities they imply. Most manufactures code their products but it can be a problem unless the coding system is accepted on an industry basis. Many sectors use codes that conform with an industry standard, an ANA code for food or an ISBN code for a book are examples of this.

10.3 EDI Transactions

10.3.1 EDI Trade Exchanges

The main use of EDI is for the *execution* and *settlement* exchanges of the trade cycle. These exchanges take place within an agreed trade relationship and often in the context of a formal contract. The basic pattern of documentation for these trade exchange is:

- The Customer sends an Order to the Supplier.
- The Supplier sends the goods and a Delivery Note.
- The Supplier follows up the delivery note with an Invoice.
- The Customer makes payment against the Invoice and sends a Payment Advice.

This pattern is illustrated in Figure 10.5.

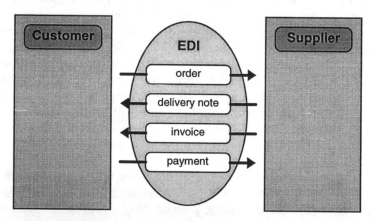

Fig. 10.5 EDI Trade Document Exchanges.

This is a simple, perhaps idealised, version of the trade documentation. The four exchanges shown are present in most trade exchanges even if not exactly in the form indicated above. Some of the important variations and complications that occur in each of the four phases are outlined below.

- **Order**

The order (often referred to as a purchase order) is a contract for one specific consignment of goods. It specifies what is wanted, in what quantity, where it is to be delivered, who will pay and often much more beside. The order may reference a contract or it may be against call-off order, see below.

Along with the order comes the need to amend orders. The customer may need to amend or cancel all or part of an order. The supplier might have a problem in fulfilling the order, for example errors in the order data or unavailability of stock.

The EDI order serves the same purpose as the paper order. Its merit is that it gets into the supplier's order processing system speedily, cheaply and with no transcription errors. EDI can also be used to amend orders or confirm receipt and availability; these later facilities will often not be implemented because of the system costs of setting them up.

Another form of order that is widely used in commercial transactions, is the 'call-off order'. This is an order for goods that will be needed but it does not specify when (and / or where) they will be delivered. It is arguably more of a contract than an order. It is perhaps most easily understood by considering a couple of examples:

- Call-off orders are extensively used by vehicle assemblers. The assemblers place large call-off orders with component suppliers. These specify product, price, etc., but not delivery. The assembler then places orders, weekly, daily or even hourly, for the delivery of the required quantity of components for the specific production plan.

- Call-off orders are also used in the retail trade. The call-off order can be placed for, say, a large quantity of a particular design of garment. The actual orders then specify the quantity, date and retail location for delivery. This then gives the retailer the flexibility to ensure that each outlet gets the stock it requires when it needs it (the advantage to the supplier is more debatable, the supplier could be left with stock that the retailer never asks for).

The call-off order will be for large quantities and / or for an extended period. It can be EDI but the real advantage is in using EDI for the many orders raised against the call-off order.

- **Delivery Note**

Goods arriving at a customer's door should have documentation to indicate who they are from and why they have been sent; there should be a notification of which order they fulfil. The document that does this is the delivery note. It may be that the invoice is sent with the dual purpose of notifying delivery and requesting payment but it is a common practice to keep the two functions separate: a delivery note for the lads (and lasses) in blue overalls and with dirty hands in 'goods-in' and an invoice for the nice clean people in the office.

The delivery note is used to check the goods in – the details from the delivery note then have to be input to the computer system and matched with the originating order (the system needs to know that the goods have been delivered before payment can be authorised).   There can be a discrepancy against the ordered quantity or there can be damaged or faulty goods.   This in turn sparks off a further exchange with a delivery variance or goods returned note.

The delivery note can be sent by EDI.   This saves the not inconsiderable effort involved in typing in the details from the delivery note and matching it to the corresponding order; the electronic delivery note will have all the correct codes and the matching should be automatic.   The problem with the EDI delivery note is that it does not prove that the package and the goods actually arrived.   There is still the need to confirm that delivery took place but this can be done with much less detail – many organisations use bar-code labels on the delivery to meet this need and to allow automated matching with the electronic delivery note.

- **Invoice**

When goods or services have been delivered, the supplier issues an invoice. This says what has been supplied, for which order(s) and the total cost (which we would now like paying).   Invoices can be issued for each order or at the end of the month for all orders sent out in that period (sometimes referred to as a statement).   The payment of invoices is often delayed to take advantage of credit, with or without the acquiesce of the supplier.

Most organisations check invoices against the original orders and deliveries to make sure that they are only paying for goods and services received.   The task is made more difficult by disparate invoice formats, incorrect / incomplete data and complications such as partial deliveries / multiple deliveries of an order.   The processing of paper invoices can be a costly and time consuming matter.

The use of EDI for invoicing means that the invoice gets through reliably and quickly and is accurately matched to the original order and subsequent delivery note.   The use of EDI should save time for the customer, cut out most invoice queries and improve cash flow with earlier payment for the supplier.   The excuse that the invoice was lost in the post loses its credibility.

- **Payment and Payment Advice**

The final step in the cycle is payment.   For paper systems this requires a cheque and a payment advice to indicate what the cheque is for.   The processing of the cheque is relatively easy, it goes to the bank.   The payment advice is another matching job, this time it is the supplier that needs to search the outstanding invoices and tick off those that are paid.

With EDI, both payment and payment advice can be electronic. Payment can be sent to the bank either using an EDI payment message or the BACS system. The payment advice can be sent to the supplier as an EDI message and is readily matched, within the computer system, to the invoice(s) for which it is the payment. Many banks offer an EDI payment service and will take instruction on payment from the supplier and forward the payment advice to the customer (arguably giving confidence that the payment advice actually represents a real payment).

10.3.2 Alternative EDI Trade Cycles

Not all organisations using EDI have kept to the traditional trade cycle. Variations to that trade cycle include:

- **Delegated Ordering**

A number of organisations have given up the order phase and have passed the responsibility of maintaining stocks over to the supplier. This practice is adopted by Willco in America where, for some departments, the system is to inform the supplier of what is sold and to only pay for those goods. The stock on the shelf remains the property of the supplier and it is their responsibility to make sure the right goods are displayed in sufficient quantities. A similar practice is adopted by some vehicle manufacturers. Rover have a supplier warehouse at their Longbridge plant – the suppliers have to make sure that the component supplies are at an agreed level but Rover only take ownership of the components when they are picked for use on the production line (this system is distinct from the JIT, sequenced delivery system used for many larger components and which has been discussed elsewhere).

- **Self Invoicing**

The trade cycle, as outlined in Figure 10.5, has four basic exchanges – each exchange after the initial order has to be matched to the preceding exchange – a process that can be time consuming and error prone (particularly with paper documents). The question to be asked, from a business process re-engineering standpoint, is 'are all these exchanges necessary'? It is a question that was asked at Ford UK with the conclusion that the invoice was a waste of time and a waste of space. Back in the late 1980's:

> '... Ford decided to take out the surgeons knife and reshape its accounts payable system. The aim was to ease the laborious task of handling invoices from the suppliers of its 1.2 million lines of production materials, from bolts to body panels, a task which

gobbled up people and time. Now 96% of our suppliers are paid by evaluated receipt. ... This means we pay the supplier for what we have received and produce a self-billing invoice which is used by the supplier for accounting and VAT purposes.

(Hamilton, 1991)

Self billing is now a practice that has since been adopted by a number of other large organisations.

- **Invoice Only**

For a number of trade sectors, ordering can be an informal, impromptu business. This is true of the catering and restaurant trade where the supplies that are needed depends on what is in season, what the customers are ordering and, possibly, the whims of the chef. The ordering is often in the hands of the chef but many large catering and restaurant chains process the invoices centrally.

The volume of invoices generated in this business can be very large. The processing requirement includes making payments but also needs to collect the detail necessary to calculate accounts for each cost centre (not a job that the chef does at the time of ordering). To handle this volume of invoices and to ensure that they get the information they need a number of catering organisations have turned to using EDI but only for the settlement phase.

10.4   EDI Adoption and EDI Maturity

10.4.1 Business System Evolution

The development of business computer systems has essentially taken place over the last 30 years. Initially, the commercial use of computers was limited to mainframe computers, the main administrative processes and to large organisations. The development of mini and micro computers allowed the adoption of information technology by medium and small size enterprises and, in many organisations, there is now a computer on every desktop.

The marriage of computers and telecommunications has enabled organisations to network their computers. Offices have local area networks linking one desktop to another, to a server and / or a central computer. Geographically dispersed organisations have wide area networks linking their locations and systems together, throughout the country and / or across the world. Many organisations have used these networks to interface or integrate their business processes with common customer files, interfaces to the accounting system and the like. At the simplest level this is achieved by numerous interface transactions but it can also involve the set-up of the corporate database or distributed databases on networked and client server systems.   The integration of systems has been a factor in improving customer service and customer care, it has also given birth to new products and services, particularly in the financial services industry.

However, this integration of computer systems stopped at the companies front (and back) doors. Inside the company, for example, the order processing system formulated the replenishment demand, updated the stock file and made a posting to the accounting system but then printed the order on paper. The paper order was then posted to the supplier where it would be typed into their order processing system with the inevitable quota of delays, transcription errors and coffee stained documents. It is calculated that, for a typical company, 70% of the documents they type into their system will have been printed out from another computer system and, of these documents, 50% will be input with mistakes in the transcription.

The answer to these difficulties and inefficiencies is the Inter-organisational System (IOS). The prime 'technology' of the IOS is EDI. The development of EDI and IOS systems is, arguably, a new generation of computer application that has changed inter-organisation business practices in much the same way as the evolution of IT and IS has radically changed intra-organisational procedures.

These developments of business information systems can be represented as three stages or three generations, see Figure 10.5.

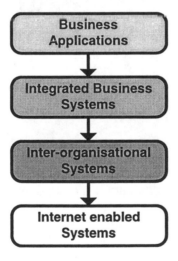

Fig. 10.6 Generations of Business Information Systems.

The development of Internet enabled systems is arguably the next stage in this evolution. The overall impact and implications of the development of the Internet on corporate systems is still to be evaluated. This is further examined in Part 4.

10.4.2 EDI Maturity

EDI development, it is suggested, follows a fairly standard pattern. This can be represented as a six stage maturity model, see Figure 10.7. The model had as its starting point a three stage model suggested in Saxena and Wagenaar, (1995) and has been developed using the author's own commercial and research experience. The model was first presented in a paper 'EDI: Re-Engineering the Competitive Edge', see Whiteley, (1995).

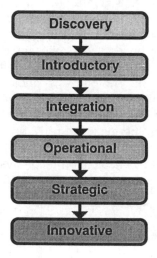

Fig. 10.7 EDI Maturity Model.

The stages of the model and some of the opportunities and implications of each stage are:

- **Discovery Stage**

The first stage in EDI development is the discovery stage. Discovery can be by an organisation choosing to adopt EDI to gain competitive advantage or to solve an administrative problem. Often it arises from the realisation that competitors are adopting EDI and that being left behind will result in competitive disadvantage. For most EDI users discovery has come in the form of a 'request' from a significant customer organisation that is converting its trade transactions to EDI – such 'requests' are not necessarily negotiable.

- **Introductory Stage**

Organisations setting out on the EDI path generally start with a pilot scheme. Initiators of EDI trading networks will choose one or two trading partners with which to pilot a single message (transaction) type. Organisations which are forced into EDI trading by an insistent partner start electronic trading in a similar way. This stage can be termed the introductory stage. This stage requires investment – there are direct costs in computer hardware and software but at least as significant will be the time commitment in establishing the parameters of the electronic trading relationship. This stage, on its own, does not result in any cost saving or efficiency gain.

- **Integration Stage**

Having found out about EDI and having gained some practical experience the system can be developed further. Very probably the introductory system was a free standing system with transactions being transcribed from the EDI system to the main business system (or visaversa depending on the selected message type). There is little benefit in an EDI system if, for example, orders have to be printed out and typed back into the order processing system. The next stage therefore is to interface the EDI software with the business application so that EDI messages can be transferred electronically and automatically between the two systems. This stage is referred to as the integration stage. The work involved in this stage is very variable but is often expensive. To establish the EDI service EDI software can be bought off-the-shelf. Integrating the EDI software and the business system will very often require writing an in-house interface system. The EDI software will provide interface file formatting facilities but is not likely to be able to match the validation and integrity checks that a business system would normally apply to data input. Integration is an essential stage for the large user of EDI. Many small organisations, often forced into EDI by a large trading partner, never achieve integration.

- **Operational Stage**

Integration realises the EDI benefits of saving time and avoiding transcription errors. Real business benefits only come when a significant number of trading partners and / or commonly used trade transactions are converted to EDI. Reaching a 'critical mass' in the volume of electronic trading gives cost savings – the staff dealing with manual transactions can be redeployed. The conversion of the major part of the trade cycle, both in volume of trading partners and in numbers of message types is the operational stage. Different organisations have placed differing emphasis on the completion of the operation stage. Large retailers have been keen to convert all their suppliers to EDI orders but there has been less emphasis on electronic invoicing and payment. The vehicle assemblers, however, tend to be more advanced in implementing other message types. Completing the electronic trade cycle speeds up business transactions and gives the opportunity to look at the organisation of the trade cycle and the supply chain.

- **Strategic Stage**

There are savings to be made by simply replacing paper documents by their electronic equivalent. The real opportunities come from making changes to established business practice.   These opportunities only arise when significant progress is made in the operational stage – the implementation of these changes is the strategic stage.   Possible areas of change and examples of where such changes have taken place are:

- The sequence of trade documents can be revised.   Document matching is a considerable problem in order processing: the customer have to match deliveries to the orders and invoices to the deliveries; the suppliers have to match payments to invoices – each process made more complex by disparate document types, part deliveries and incorrectly recorded codes.   EDI makes the process easier – at the very least codes should be correct and in the proper place.   The use of EDI has allowed companies to disband their order processing and invoice matching sections with large staff savings reported by the major EDI users.   EDI also gives the opportunity to re-engineer the trade document cycle; self invoicing, discussed earlier in this chapter, having been adopted by a number of major organisations..

- EDI can give dramatic time-saving. The time between formulating a replenishment demand to the order being processed by the supplier can be as short as Is required – for all orders, not just rushed orders. This has facilitated the reduction or elimination of stock holding (by the customer organisation at least) and is a part of the development of just-in-time (JIT) manufacture and quick response supply.

The establishment of electronic trading relations can involve considerable discussion and co-operation (although it can also be a case of 'EDI or die'- here is what we do – now you fit in). This is part of a pattern, in some trade sectors, of closer co-operation between customer and suppliers that involves co-operation in design, production and a long-term trading relationship. This can be reinforced by the electronic interchange of production plans or EPOS data – Bhs link POS data and EDI orders, they say of their suppliers 'by knowing the sales of his product, he can be more pro-active in his dealings with Bhs' (Bhs, 1994).

- **Innovative Stage**

The establishment of an operational EDI infrastructure and the change of operational procedures that it facilitates also gives the possibility of changing the nature of the product or the provision of new services.   These developments are termed the innovation stage in the model and it is contended that they open up new possibilities for competitive advantage. Examples of such developments are emerging as the early users of EDI achieve maturity in their systems. One example of such a development is:

- Rover Cars who, for the UK market at least, have stopped

producing cars for stock and only produce a car when they have the dealer's order. EDI and the associated changes in supply and production have reduced the time from production planning to delivery of a car from seven weeks to two. Rover dealers have been equipped with computer systems where the punters can specify their own car (well at least the options they want) and two weeks later there it is with sun roof, alloy wheels and gleaming pink paintwork. See *Computing, (1992)*, *Computing, (1995)* and Palframan, (1995).

A number of moves to product customisation rely on a mature EDI infrastructure. For example:

- Raleigh will build their top of the range mountain bicycles to a customer specification.

- Levi Jeans, if you are female and live in the US, will produce a factory made to measure pair of jeans. The measurements are taken in the store and submitted electronically to the centre.

Further moves to exploit a mature EDI infrastructure in an innovative way should be expected. A sector where the linking of EPOS and EDI is set to change the market is that of the 'best seller' book trade. Timely market intelligence can allow reprints of successful blockbusters to be rushed out before the stock disappears and the public interest is lost. This possibility was forecast in 1992 in a speech to the BIC Symposium by Eddi Bell, chairperson of Harper Collins:

> 'With EPOS and EDI working together on our behalf, we could have had the reprint out three weeks earlier; no bookshop need ever have been out of stock – and we could probably have doubled our sales during this early 'hot' period.'

The converse is that the same market information can dramatically reduce the half of all printed books that are remaindered or pulped.

10.4.3 IOS and Industry Sector Organisation

EDI has, for many sectors, becoming 'the normal way that business in done' (a phrase often quoted, and in this case adapted, from the report of the Massachusetts Institute of Technology – Management in the 1990s' programme). It also has the ability to be a factor in the restructuring of business sectors and the potential to be part of the new way of doing business.

The much quoted case of AHS was a factor in the restructuring of the US hospital supply sector. When the AHS's online ordering system was introduced there were 400 suppliers serving the 7,000 major customers, Earl

(1989). Following on from the success of the AHS system, and the resultant increase in market share for AHS, the sector underwent a period of rationalisation greatly reducing the number of suppliers. AHS itself became part of Baxter Healthcare.

Parallels to the case of AHS can be seen, or predicted, in two cases quoted in Jelassi's book of European Case Studies *'Competing through Information Technology'*:

- A case study by Jelassi and Loebbecke, (1994) outlines the recent introduction of EDI into Leroy Merlin, one of the larger DIY retailers in the French market. The French DIY sector is fragmented with a few medium size chains and many independent operators. This contrasts with the UK DIY sector which is dominated by a few large operators all of which have operational EDI systems. The use of EDI by Leroy Merlin will no doubt be emulated by the other players of comparable size but it seems likely to contribute to continuing the rationalisation that is taking place in this sector in France.

- Braun Passot, Jelassi, (1994a) is also one player in a fragmented market, in this case office supplies. By offering electronic ordering to their customers, using both the French Télétel teletext system and their EDI systems, they have been able to make rapid advances in market share. This market is restructuring – initiatives such as Braun Passot's are having an effect and the market is also being sized up by much larger organisations that operate in the German, UK and American markets.

The closer co-operation between customer and suppliers of which IOS is a part is also having a subtle effect on the market. It is argued that it is no longer the final component assembler, e.g. Fords and Rover, or the large retailer, e.g. Marks and Spencers and Bhs that is competing for the customer but it is these companies in conjunction with their supply chains. It is after all the suppliers of merchandise, to (say) the retailer, that give the distinctive product quality that, in conjunction with the ethos and ambience of the store, produces the overall marketing effect (although this is not to deny that an organisation, such as Marks and Spensers, exercise a very strong control over both suppliers and supplies).

The trend to outsourcing also emphasises the importance of the IOS. The ability to co-ordinate supplier and minimise transaction cost using EDI facilitate this trend. EDI is an important element in the operation, for example, of a number of franchised operations where both the retail and the supply side are run by third parties with the centre performing a limited range of functions which includes the co-ordination of supplies, to a standard pattern, using EDI.

10.5   IOS, EDI and Internet e-Commerce

The use of EDI is in no way rendered redundant by the introduction of Internet e-Commerce.   Internet e-Commerce provides for searching for products and for once-off purchases; it is, above all else, a person to application interface.   EDI is, in contrast, an application to application interface for repeated and standardised transactions.   As already discussed it is an essential part of the JIT or quick-response supply chain of many organisations.

   The user of Internet e-Commerce is looking for a quick response.   As discussed in Part 4, one of the problems of Internet e-Commerce is waiting for delivery and this problem is compounded if the online retailer does not have stock and there is a second delay while goods are ordered from the wholesaler or manufacturer.   The e-Commerce vendor needs their own quick-response supply chain to minimise 'stock-outs' and back-order delays. There is not much point in being able to order goods in a matter of minutes from home if delivery times are unpredictable and can stretch out to be several weeks.

   For many e-Commerce vendors EDI is, and will be, an essential element of their supply chain.   Existing retailers, supermarkets that start an e-Commerce / home delivery operation being an obvious example, have their supply chain and distribution operations already in place.   Other e-Commerce vendors are, as they grow, going to need to pay attention to their back-office systems.   The Blackwell's online bookshop is specifically designed to interface with the book trade TeleOrdering system and that is but one example.   The overall electronic supply chain is illustrated at Figure 10.8; this integration is a point that is further examined in Chapter 17.

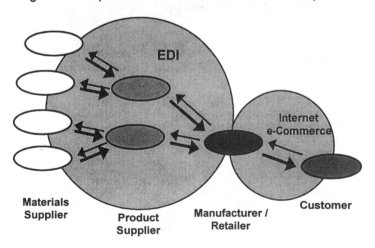

Fig. 10.8 EDI and Internet e-Commerce.

Exercises

Exercises for the chapter are as follows:

1. For each stage of the business trade cycle, see Figure 10.5, list the stage specific advantages (and any disadvantages) of using EDI.

2. What problems might be encountered by a small food processing company, which supplies several supermarkets, when required by its customers to implement EDI.

3. EDI is typically applied to trade exchanges, orders, invoices, etc. but it can also be used for non trade purposes. In the UK, students apply for university places through the UCAS clearing centre (and other countries may have similar schemes). The procedure is that students submit their applications to UCAS and the clearing centre passes the application onto the preferred universities. Each university then accept, reject or make an offer and the decision is passed back to the student via the UCAS clearing centre. Suggest how EDI (and other ICT technologies) might be used to update such a scheme.

4. Section 10.4.2 examples three instances where a mature EDI supply chain (JIT supply coupled with sharing of market information suppliers) can facilitate a change in the nature of the product of service – can you suggest any further real examples or possibilities that could be developed?

Further Reading

A number of EDI case studies are available in the book:

Krcmar, H., Bjorn-Anderson, N. and O'Callaghan, R. (eds.) (1995) *EDI in Europe: How it Works in Practice*, Wiley, Chichester, UK.

Further case studies are available online and references are given on the book's web page.

11

Inter-Organisational e-Commerce

Summary

The third e-Commerce 'technology', Internet e-Commerce, is most commonly seen as a business to consumer channel (the subject of Part 4). Internet e-Commerce, and related technologies are, however, of increasing importance for business to business transactions where the buying decisions are not readily automated.

This chapter introduces the business to business use in Internet e-Commerce and illustrates this use with case study examples. A full discussion of Internet e-Commerce is reserved for Part 4.

11.1 Inter-organisational Transactions

The Internet is (essentially) a network that provides an end-user interface, and gives those end users global access. The Internet with the WWW interface can be used to:

- Search:
  Organisations can use the Internet to search for goods and services that are not available from their established suppliers. The search process will not be as efficient as an electronic market but it is available where there is no electronic market alternative. The search may not be successful but 'there is no harm in trying'.

  The Internet can also be used to search for business opportunities. There are a number of sites where organisations advertise to find suppliers for the goods and services that they require.

- Purchase:
  Organisations can purchase goods and services over the Internet. This is not the way that a retail chain maintains stocks of hundreds of lines of merchandise or a car company is going to ensure the just-in-time supply of components, that is the province of EDI. There are, however, many purchases that are relatively low volume and outside the automated replenishment processes, and it is here the use of Internet e-Commerce can be appropriate.

- After Sales:
  Organisations may well need after-sales service and support for goods that they have bought. After-sales support can be an expensive commodity to provide and / or to purchase and a number of organisations have re-engineered their after-sales services to be effectively and economically delivered via the Internet.

These three uses of Internet e-Commerce for inter-organisational transactions can be disjoint – using the Internet to find a vendor does not necessarily lead to making online purchases and similarly online support may well be used for a product or service bought in a conventional manner. Many organisations, despite using Internet e-Commerce for these activities, will still make formal credit provisions with the supplier and this, if nothing else, implies a less impulsive relationship than might be the case for non-commercial user. These three areas of Internet, inter-organisational e-Commerce activity are shown on the credit trade cycle in Figure 11.1.

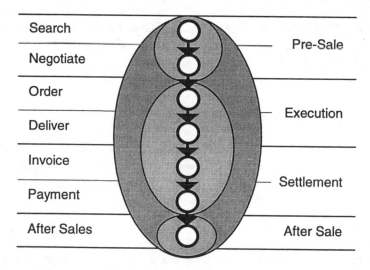

Fig. 11.1 Internet, Inter-organisational e-Commerce

The use of Internet e-Commerce for inter-organisational transactions is, in many respects, similar to business to consumer e-Commerce (the main difference is that credit may be offered, i.e. settlement is after execution as opposed to being co-incident). The detail of business to consumer e-Commerce is dealt with in Part 4 and this chapter is mainly devoted to examples of the application of these technologies to inter-organisational transactions.

11.2   Purchasing Online

The use of e-Commerce for inter-organisational transactions, as already explained, comes into its own for low frequency, non-strategic purchases. The use of online purchasing can be very convenient for the customer organisation and can provide competitive advantage for the vendor organisation. The cases of American Hospital Supply (AHS) and Brun Passot, both outlined in Chapter 3, are examples of such strategic advantage. In the case of AHS the company provided the hospitals with terminals that were online to its order processing system and in the case of Brun Passot the online ordering was provided using the French Minitel system (with EDI as an option used by some of the larger customers). The functionality and business purpose of these systems can now be replicated using web technologies and this is what a number of organisations are doing.

Examples of organisations that successfully provide Internet e-Commerce facilities for business are:

Del Computers, the direct sales specialists of the computing business who have made dramatic market gains against competitor companies – many of which are now emulating their online sales provision.

Dell takes its orders direct from customers; orders are placed by phone or online with online ordering increasingly being the preferred option. Dell builds its systems to order using a highly organised just-in-time approach. This system keeps inventory low and avoids the problems that other manufacturers have had with large stocks of obsolescent finished PCs.

The Dell web site can be accessed at www.dell.com.

CISCO Systems is one of the world's leading suppliers of networking equipment and the predominate supplier of routers used in Internet infrastructure. CISCO launched its web site in 1996 and it quickly became the preferred sales channel of the company and many of its customers.

At the time of writing, CISCO claim 83% of orders are transacted over the web and that online selling has resulted in a cost saving of $1.3 billion over a three-year period.

CISCO claim to take a commonsense approach to their web site design, they want it to work not to look fancy. Cunningham, CISCO's director of advanced customer services is quoted as saying:

> 'We roll something out, put it on the Web with a secret url, show a couple of dozen customers, listen to their comments, tune it, tweak it, let it out. Six months later we're going to have a change or two. We plan for it. Its not a surprise, not a shock, nobody's hurt. Our most successful tools (commerce agents), became that way because customers said, "Its what I want. I want the output on the screen, in e-mail, or a fax." Boom! We're not so smart, we just do what the customers tell us.'

The CISCO web site can be accessed at www.cisco.com.

Action Computer Supplies is a UK based supplier of computer equipment and computer consumables. It has a comprehensive catalogue of over 12,000 product lines; as of the end of 1998 Action carried out 12% of its business, worth some 30 million pounds, online – a proportion of the overall business that is conducted online continues to rise. Recently introduced features include:

- Tailor-made web sites for large corporate customers;
- The 'virtual warehouse' – a system that shows stock in the supplier's warehouse (for 3 day delivery) if the stock is not available from Action's own warehouse (one day delivery).

Action provide for group deals where orders can be placed by individual budget holders, throughout the organisation, but invoicing and an analysis of expenditure is available only to one central point.

The Action web site can be accessed at www.action.com.

Updated commentary on these sites is provided on the web page.

These online sites for sales to corporate customers provide for quick and efficient execution of once-off purchase decisions. Used appropriately they can cut out bureaucracy and let the staff get on with the real business of the organisation: providing banking services, educating students or whatever. The procedures they replace were often very time consuming and bureaucratic. It was not uncommon, in large organisations, for the procedures to purchase even the simplest item to take several weeks, require signatures of various managers and to cost considerably more to process than the value of the item being bought. Delegating authority to budget holders, within limits and with preferred suppliers, cuts out this wasted time and unnecessary cost. Vendor systems that require authorisation for exceptional expenditure and provide management with accounts of the expenditure complete the control loop.

A more detailed case study of the use of e-Commerce systems in outsourced, desk-top facilities management is given at Section 11.4.

11.3   After-Sales Online

Selling to corporate customers is one thing, providing ongoing support is another. For products of any complexity that are going to be used over a period of time, customers need product information, support and maintenance. For the supplier of such products there is the hope of further business if the customer receives a satisfactory service.

Providing ongoing support can be a complex and expensive business and in a competitive market it is a cost that can be difficult to front-load into the purchase price or to charge for at a viable price throughout the lifetime of the product. There are a number of ways that the Internet can be used to help provide this service at an affordable price. Two of these ways are:

- Online documentation:
  Providing printed instructions with a product is one thing, keeping them updated is another. Organisations that place documentation online can keep it updated without the need to send amendments to every customer.

- Online support:
  A fully staffed telephone help desk is an expensive facility. Online support via e-mail can at least cut the need to have operators immediately available when a call is made. Online facilities such as a good 'frequently asked questions' page can also help with sorting out customer queries.

PC and PC software suppliers are leading examples of the use of the Internet for after-sales support. Two notable examples are:

Microsoft

TM

Microsoft has an extensive site to publise its products and services and to support its software products. In terms of after-sales support the site provides an extensive rage of 'add-ons' and service packs. The add-ons are additional software that complements the mainstream Microsoft products, the Word 7 reader, for instance, is made available for users of old versions of Word whose software will not read the latest document formats. The service packs are bug fixes. Add-ons and service packs can be downloaded by any user without charge.

Also available is the 'knowledge base' which users can interrogate to assist them in diagnosing any fault they may think they are experiencing. e-Mail support is available to users taking part in beta-test trials.

The Microsoft web site can be accessed at www.microsoft.com.

TM

Sun is the market leader in UNIX workstations market with extensive installations at many universities. Technicians maintaining the systems and the students using them can use the Sun web site, the section on JAVA is very well known to many users of the language.

Software support, in terms of bug fixes, is available from local sites. For UK universities the site is hosted by Imperial College and sponsored by Sun. The Imperial site also contains a large library of software that can be downloaded and is available for free.

The SUN web site can be accessed at www.sun.com.

11.4   e-Commerce in Desk-top Facilities Management

Most businesses of any size have a large number of desktop computer systems. The purchase, installation and support of these systems and of the staff that use them is a costly and time consuming undertaking. In many cases organisations have outsourced end-user support and in an increasing number of cases the outsourcing company is providing an Internet (or similar) online support facility.

One such company ServePC (not its real name), is one of the largest corporate resellers of PC equipment in the UK. ServePC was bidding to take over the contract for supply and support of end-user systems for a large insurance company. The outsourcing company they were seeking to replace had an Intranet support system and it was a condition of the contract that a similar service was provided. To compete for the contract ServePC developed a support system and were successful in their bid for the contract. This section outlines the functionality of that system as an example of e-Commerce used to facilitate inter-organisational e-Commerce and to support after-sales service. The main facilities are:

- Equipment Register:
  The basic information requirement of a support system is a database with the details of the equipment that is installed and that requires supporting. The database also includes basic details of the staff to whom that equipment is assigned.

- Purchasing:
  The system included a comprehensive database of IT equipment available from the outsourcing company. The product list can be accessed using an index or searched using appropriate keywords. The database provides a brief specification of each product plus the price.
  Ordering can be done online through the system. Orders are initially routed to a member of the customer's staff authorised to approve procurement and from there, if approved, the request is forwarded, electronically, to the outsourcing company. Details of the progress of the order are then available from the tracking database for those with the authority to access it.

- Call Logging:
  Support calls are logged on the system. A logging system provides for the management of support requests and for any subsequent analysis of those requests.

- Technical Database:
  The outsourcing company is involved in a number of support contracts and maintains a technical database of problems it has encountered together with notes on the solution. The database enables knowledge gained at one site to be shared with support teams throughout the organisation.

- Asset Management:
  The system provides for an asset management database to be created for each customer. Using data collected in the overall system, problem areas can be quickly identified and facts and figures concerning cost per PC can be produced.

The system was developed using Lotus Notes. ServePC asserted that this software gives a superior service to the use of Internet technology and the customer was already a Notes user. This solution is good for a customer who is already a Notes user but the licence costs of installing the system with a customer that is not a Notes user could be prohibitive; Notes does, however, have an Internet interface and this can be used for access from customers or sites where Notes is not available.

The system seems to be a success. The customers found the system easy to use and were pleased that their orders were processed more quickly. ServePC gained from not having to key customer requirements into its main order processing system and from the reduced number of calls checking on their progress.

There is ,of course, an irony in co-ordinating desktop support using ICT, not a lot of help if the PC is defunct or you don't know how to operate it.

11.5   Pens and Things and the Web

Having put in an EDI system for some of its manufacturing supplies (see Chapter 8), Pens and Things (See Chapter 6 for the case study) is now facing pressure to provide electronic ordering systems for some of its trade customers.

The first step has been to install EDI for two of its largest UK accounts and the agent for the USA. These customers use EDI with other suppliers and wished to use the same system for transactions with Pens and Things.

This EDI Facility, now called Barker-EDI, is available to other corporate customers but it will not be of much help to the smaller customers who do not have their own integrated stock control systems and / or EDI facilities. To help these customers, Pens and Things is setting up an online ordering system based on the web. The system is to be called Barker-Web; it consists of:

- The Logon Page: Each business partner has to input their user-ID and password. Use is restricted to trade customers;
- Home Page: Space for the latest marketing update and a menu for the facilities of Barker-Web;
- Catalogue / Order Pages: The product catalogue with product summaries, delivery times and prices specific to the customer ID. Customers order by entering the quantity required next to the description of the product;

- Marketing Notices: Notification of new products, special promotions, etc.;
- Accounts Summary: A summary of orders, deliveries and invoices specific to the customer ID.

For each order placed online the system automatically generates an e-Mail to the customer confirming the details of the order. Orders entered online are passed electronically from the web server into the order processing system (to keep compatibility with Barker-EDI, Barker-Web orders are formatted as EDI orders on the web server and enter the order processing system through the same interface as Barker-EDI orders).

Exercises / Further Reading

There are no exercises or further reading for this chapter. Internet e-Commerce is further explored in Part 4, Chapters 12 to 16 and references and exercises are given at the end of each of those chapters.

Part 4

Business to Consumer Electronic Commerce

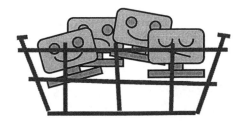

12

Consumer Trade Transactions

Summary

Business to consumer e-Commerce on the Internet is an area of rapid development. The chapter outlines the range of goods and services available, the nature of an online shop, and the phases of the trade cycle that the web can facilitate – these areas are dealt with in more detail in subsequent chapters.

Consumer e-Commerce has gained a new dynamic by the popularisation and commercialisation of the Internet but online business has been around for some time using technologies such as interactive videotext (notably the French Minitel) and TV shopping channels. These other consumer e-Commerce channels are briefly reviewed.

The application of Internet e-Commerce is illustrated using the case study of a stationery company: Pens and Things (first introduced in Chapter 6).

12.1 What you want, when you want it

At the heart of most that is good about the Internet lies the simple, seductive offering - what you want, when you want it. You want to buy an obscure book or track down a cheap holiday? Get online. Do it. Now!

(adapted from Waldman, 1999)

The Internet offers the opportunity to buy and sell almost anything. Books, CDs and IT supplies have been among the first products to make a splash online but buying tickets, contracting insurance, servicing a bank account or finding a house are just a few of the many products and services that are available.

Consumer trade transactions are open to anyone with an Internet connection. e-Shopping can take place using a computer at home, from work or at a cyber café. The e-shop can be anywhere in the world and it is open 24 hours a day.

All that said, shopping is still shopping and sometimes it is a pleasure and sometimes it is a curse. How it works out depends on who is buying, who is selling and what is being sold. This chapter looks at what constitutes an e-Shop and analyses e-Sales in terms of the stages of the trade cycle. Further details on the Internet, web sites, the components of e-Commerce and the nature of e-Business are provided in the next four chapters.

And just one more cautionary note. The shop might be available world-wide and open 24 hours a day but most goods still need delivery – that takes time and has to be paid for.

12.2   Internet e-Commerce

The basic elements of Internet use and of Internet e-Commerce are:

- The user of the system with a computer hooked-up to the Internet. The user accesses the Internet using software known as a browser, e.g. Netscape or Internet Explorer; the computer running the browser is the client.
- The content provider who has set up an Internet application and installed it on an Internet linked computer. The computer that holds the Internet content is known as a server.
- The Internet application may be linked to back office systems to process transactions and utilise information held on databases.

For Internet services provided through the World Wide Web (web) the data is formatted, for the basic web page, using the mark-up language HTML.

These elements are shown in Figure 12.1. Further details of the Internet are given in Chapter 13 and of web pages and HTML in Chapter 14.

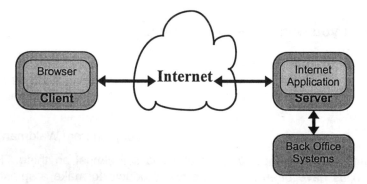

Fig. 12.1 A basic Internet Service.

12.3   The e-Shop

For e-Commerce applications that are selling goods or services the Internet application, held on the server, is an e-Shop. The infrastructure of the e-Shop can be very simple or it may be very complex. The basic element of an e-Shop is a web page that offers or advertises the goods for sale and provides a means for the shopper to make the purchase. A example of a simple e-Shop, set up by Charlie Bucket (and with apologies to Roald Dahl), are shown in Figure 12.2.

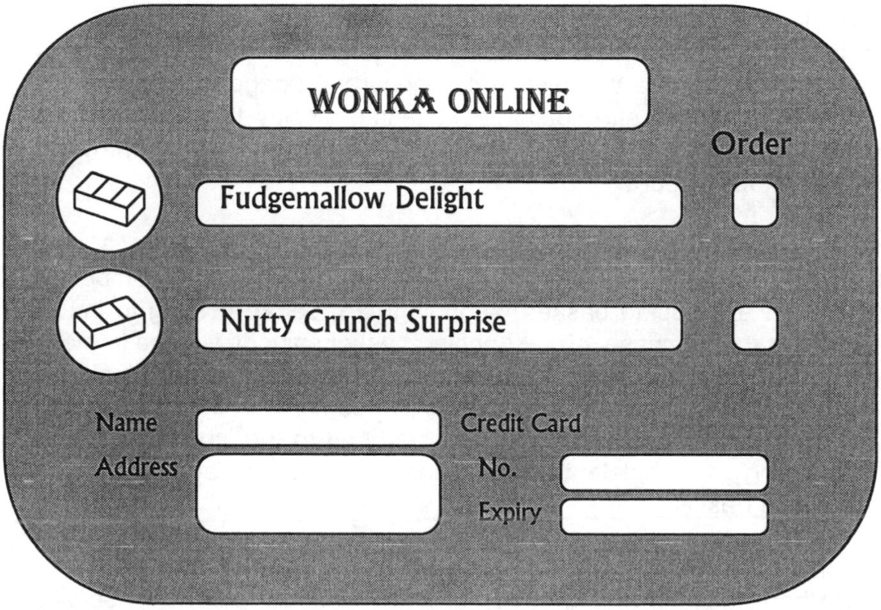

Fig. 12.2 A Simple e-Shop.

At its very simplest the e-Shop, or online advert, could simply list the products for sale or the services offered and invite the customer to phone, fax or e-mail their order.

The next step up, to make a 'real' e-Shop, is to add online purchasing. This adds a level of complexity, the site is no longer simply coded in HTML but needs some way of interacting with the server so that the customer and credit card details can be passed across.

Complex e-Shops have many more features, these can include:

* Customer Registration:
  Some e-Shops ask the customers to register and then store the customer details on a database. This then allows the vendor to tailor its information for the specific customer and saves the customer typing in details again on future visits. Registration can, it is thought, encourage a customer to return but it can also be off-putting for the first time customer – it is a hassle to input a lot of personal details and the customer may be concerned about how the information will be stored and used.

* Dynamic Web Pages:
  The basic web page is formatted in HTML and is then fixed; to change it

requires that the source is edited. A dynamic web page is built for each user when it is requested by the web browser. The dynamic web page may be built by reading a database in which case the page can include, for instance, the latest price and possibly whether the goods are in stock.

- Personalised Web Pages:
  This is another use of the dynamic web page. If the customer has registered with the site the system can generate a page for that specific customer. An airline site could, for instance, display the details of the customer's frequent flyer programme and feature flight deals from the customer's local airport.

- A Shopping Basket:
  Customers in a conventional shop are likely to collect a number of products, in a shopping basket / shopping cart, before coming to the till and making the purchase. The shopping basket analogy is used in many larger e-Shops. Goods can be selected and placed in the electronic basket. Facilities are made available for the contents of the basket to be reviewed and unwanted goods can be returned to the 'shelves'. When the shopping is complete the customer then makes payment for the goods in the basket.

- Additional Information:
  The e-Shop needs to let the customer know what the product or service is. The Internet has both advantages and disadvantages in this area. The customer cannot select their own bananas or try on the jumper but they can have additional information not normally available in a conventional shop. Examples of this are:
  - The wine shop that gives a detail assessment of each vintage;
  - Bookshops that provide customer reviews (both good and bad);
  - Music sites that can play a sample of the recording that is for sale.
  The provision of the additional information, if done well and kept up to date, can give the shop a buzz and keep the punters coming back.

- Community:
  Beyond the concept of additional information, is trying to create a sense of community around the store. Bulletin-boards are one such device in this area (but preferably not bulletin-boards where the shop and the products are criticised too much).

- Multiple Payment Options:
  The current norm for online payments is a credit card and most e-Shops will want to accept all major credit cards. Some e-vendors also have / accept:
  - Their own store credit card (often also available for use in conventional branches of the store);
  - Debit Cards;

- e-Cash, money represented electronically on the web and available for spending with sites that are participants in the scheme;
- Payment by phoning the credit card number or posting a cheque. A device that delays completing the transaction but that is made available for customers that are concerned about online payments.

- Encryption:
  e-Shops are very sensitive to the notion that e-Commerce is insecure, particularly when it comes to online payments. Most e-Shops use an encryption system to secure (or add security) to the transmission of personal and payment details. There are various security / encryption schemes in use or being developed and there are arguments as to which is best.

- Online Delivery:
  Electronic products such as software, information and music can be delivered online. Where it is appropriate, the use of online delivery cuts the costs of distribution and avoids the customer having to wait for the goods to arrive.

- Loyalty Schemes:
  Some e-Shops are introducing loyalty schemes. Each purchase made attracts a number of points and the points, accumulated electronically by the vendor, can eventually be used for discounts or free goods.

- Online Help:
  Having used the Internet for sales it can also be used for after sales. The web page can be used for product instructions and self diagnosis pages – all of which can be updated when the need arises. The customers can also use e-mail for online help (an expensive game for the vendor to play if the help service is free and it becomes popular).

- Shopping Mall:
  e-Shops may be setup as a part of an online mall. Like their conventional equivalent the online mall is designed to attract customers because there is a range of stores. e-Malls can help out the individual vendors with shared facilities, for instance a common customer file and a shared payment infrastructure.

Further details of these features and the technologies they use are given in subsequent chapters.

12.4 Internet Shopping and the Trade Cycle

As with any other trade exchange, a purchase on the Internet has a number of stages. Typically for a retail sale the trade cycle is simpler than for business to business transactions; there is no negotiation and settlement takes place at the same time as the order (there is no credit offered). The simplified trade cycle is shown in Figure 12.3.

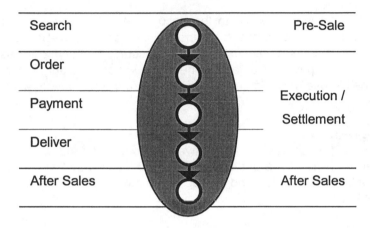

Search	Pre-Sale
Order	
Payment	Execution / Settlement
Deliver	
After Sales	After Sales

Fig. 12.3 The Retail Trade Cycle.

The stages in the retail trade cycle, and some of the differences when the selling is done online, are:

- **Search**

To make a purchase a shopper has to find an appropriate vendor. This is true for a business looking for supplies or a consumer going to conventional shops and is equally true of the online shopper. For the online shopper, the ways of finding goods are:

- Selecting a menu item or a button on the portal – the screen that is first shown when the user logs onto the Internet.
- Using a search engine to find an appropriate Internet e-Store site.
- Following a link to a store from another page that is advertising it.
- Selecting a page that has been featured on an advert or that is recommended by a friend.

And finding a shop that sells what is wanted in a way that the customer is comfortable with can be just as easy, or as hard, as it is on the high street. Once a useful store is found the customer is likely to want to return; Internet addresses are not necessarily memorable and bookmarking the site in the browser is the way this is done.

The issues surrounding Internet searching and how the vendor can make their e-Shops more visible are dealt with in more depth in Chapter 15.

- **Order**

Once on the site the consumer has to do their shopping. In the conventional shop the consumer can wander through isles or departments looking at the merchandise or ask an assistant for help. The online shop does the same, except electronically. The larger e-Store will have departments and there will be a search engine (or an index) that can assist in finding goods. There is less likely to be an assistant that comes to bother you (but the boffins are working on that one).

The goods, when found, are represented by a picture and a description rather than the real thing. This can be a disadvantage for goods such as clothes but it may be an opportunity to provide better information for items such as books and wine. Technical ways of overcoming the deficit are being developed; virtual reality to show off garments is one such approach.

Ordering of goods takes place by selecting the image, the name of the product or a selection box. The idea of an electronic shopping basket has been outlined in Section 12.3.

- **Payment**

Once the goods have been selected they have to be paid for. The normal way of paying for online purchases is by the input of credit card details; e-Cash is an alternative that is under development.

The options for payment and the issue of security have been outlined in Section 12.3; further detail on these topics is given in Chapter 15.

- **Delivery**

The smart way to do business is to get your customers to do the work for you. e-Commerce does this with the ordering process but not with delivery. In a conventional shop the customer usually transports the goods home, in an e-Shop the goods have to be delivered and that could be inconvenient and always adds to the cost.

The delivery issue associated with e-Commerce is an important one and it is one that is often ignored. An e-Commerce vendor needs a retail distribution network that matches the nature of the goods, the cost structures of the distribution industry and the expectation of the consumer. The delivery requirements differ for a book that can be posted from almost anywhere, fresh food that needs a local distribution depot and, for instance, software that can be delivered, at the time of purchase, online.

Delivery is further examined in Chapter 15 and is an issue that is looked at, in the context of various trade sectors, in Chapter 16.

- **After-Sales**

Goods that you don't like or that don't work can be taken back to the store (although how helpful the store is can be another issue). Sending back goods bought online can seem to be more of a problem.

The plus side for e-Commerce after sales is the opportunity to provide online support; the possibilities for online help have been outlined in Section 12.3 above.

12.5   Other e-Commerce Technologies

The Internet is not the first public access telematics system and neither will it be the last word in developments in this field.

The first attempt at providing public access to online facilities was with interactive videotext systems. These systems started in the 1970's and were developed by many national telecommunications authorities; examples were Prestel in the UK and Bildschirmtext in Germany. The French system was Télétel, more often known as Minitel which was the name of the terminal system that was distributed free to members of the public. The Minitel system was developed in the early 1980's, later than most of the other videotext offerings, but it was the only one of the many systems to gain general acceptance and to live on as a public access telematics system.

The French Minitel system, by 1993, had over six million subscribers and was used, at a conservative estimate, by 14 million people (nationally a higher access rate than has yet been achieved by the Internet in any country). The free distribution of terminals was an important factor in this success but, it is also to be noted that, one of the prime justifications for the system, and its most used service, was online access to the national telephone directory. Other uses of the Minitel were:

- Banking Services;
- Travel (Information and Reservations);
- Catalogue Sales.

Reports suggest that, after the initial excitement over applications such as the (sometimes) salacious messageries chat service, usage has settled down – users get online to access services that are useful to them and then get on with the rest of their lives – the Minitel has become a tool, not a toy.

Whilst Europe, and some other countries were using videotext; there was a development of a number of computer based telematics systems principally serving the US. CompuServe was founded in 1980 and is one of the worlds oldest online services. Initially it was a proprietary network with its own access software and, classically, all numeric account numbers; latterly it has also converted its service to be Internet compliant and given its users full access to the facilities of the web. A second such pioneering service was Prodigy. This service was launched in 1988 as a joint venture between IBM and the retail group Sears.

Prodigy started life using proprietary software but later on converted to the web and is now, effectively, just another ISP.

Another antecedent of e-Commerce, mainly in North America, was the television shopping channel. At one level the shopping channel is just a series of adverts but the difference is that it was designed for consumers to ring up and order the goods that were advertised rather than simply get the consumer into the advertised shop or buying a certain product when out shopping. The opportunity for a TV shopping channel occurred in the US because most homes were connected to cable TV that made available a multiplicity of TV channels; an opportunity that is being reproduced in other continents in the 1990's with the advent of a multiplicity of channels from satellite and / or cable TV systems.

It is to a combination of the TV shopping channel and the Internet that many pundits are looking to for further growth in Internet e-Commerce.   Many households own a personal computer and a sizeable proportion of them have an Internet connection.   Ownership of a home computer is largely limited to the developed countries and to the more educated and affluent in those countries. It may be that ownership of a home computer will become as commonplace as a TV and a video but a more certain way to spread access to e-Commerce services is to integrate the facility into the TV.   The proposition of interactive TV, used for e-Commerce, has interesting parallels with the videotext experience where most systems, excepting the Minitel, were designed to use the TV (connected to a phone line) as the home terminal. A more positive parallel with the Minitel is that competing satellite and cable TV service providers are taking to giving their 'set top boxes' away free; a trend that could continue when Internet access facilities are included (and where the cable operator has an obvious advantage over the broadcast only nature of a satellite operation).

A second combination that is being proposed is the combination of the Internet and the cell phone, a combination that is available at the time of writing.   In its favour the cell phone is achieving higher adoption rates than the home computer but a small screen on a portable telephone does rather limit the scope for the attractive display of merchandise.

The progress of Internet and e-Commerce use from its current limited consumer base depends, in part at least, on widening access to the majority of the population.   The e-Commerce market is important but is currently only a small percentage of the overall retail market. A report, dated 1999, from KPMG gives direct sales as 5% of retail sales in the UK and 4% in the US; 16% of US home sales and 1% of UK direct sales were electronic.

12.6   Advantages and Disadvantages of Consumer e-Commerce

The spread of Internet e-Commerce will depend on the perception of the consumer of its advantages and disadvantages. This perception depends, in part at least, on the individual, their circumstances and the goods or services that are to be traded. Among the advantages of Internet e-Commerce for both the consumer and the trader are:

- **Home Shopping**
  Shopping can be done from the home, hopefully quickly and conveniently. Internet e-Commerce avoids the hassles of travelling, parking, queuing and whatever else makes you mad in a shop.

- **World-wide, 24 Hours a Day Trading**
  The Internet home shopper can access an e-Shop anywhere in the world at any time day or night (although not all e-Shops will deal with a world-wide clientele).

- **The Latest Thing at Bargain Prices**
  Goods bought online may be cheaper or more up-to-date than goods available in a conventional retail shop.

- **Home Delivery**
  The goods are brought to your door – can be an advantage if you are there to take them in.

- **Online Sales Support**
  For some goods there can be information online on how to use them and how to fix them. e-Mail can also be an appropriate facility for after-sales services.

Disadvantages of Internet e-Commerce include:

- **Privacy and Security**
  The privacy of personal details and security of financial transactions are a concern to many users and potential users of e-Commerce.

- **Delivery**
  Where tangible goods are bought online they have to be delivered. Delivery can be an advantage but it causes delay, sometimes inconvenience and it adds another cost.

- **Inspecting Goods**
  The web can provide a good picture, an eloquent description and even customer reviews or virtual reality displays but you cannot actually see, feel or try on the goods you are buying.

- **Social Interaction**
  Shopping for some is a chore and for others is an excursion. A shopping trip on the Internet will not be the same experience as a shopping expedition with family or friends (for those who like such things!).

- **Return of Goods**
  Having to return faulty goods takes time and is an embarrassment. Returning goods to an online vendor can seem even more problematic.

The online trader has some of these advantages; access to world-wide markets may be one of these. Advantages specific to a trader are:

- **High-tech Image**
  Being known as an online trader gives an up-to-date image. Some customers will use the web site to look up products and then use the conventional store to make purchase.

- **Reduced Costs**
  The online trader does not have the expense of staffing and maintaining conventional retail outlets – premises for an online trader can be much more functional.

An additional issue for the consumer is whether they will always have the option to choose between e-Commerce and the conventional trade alternative. The possibility of submitting forms to public administration electronically or getting discounts / favourable terms for online services such as ticket sales and banking transactions may turn into compulsion. Service providers may be able to make significant cost savings using online transactions and the conventional alternative may, one day, be withdrawn.

12.7   Consumer e-Commerce at Pens and Things

Pens and Things now have their web site for use by their trade customers and would like to launch a similar service for direct sales to the public.
  Selling quality stationery items online seems like an ideal application. The goods are sufficiently expensive to make the individual transaction worthwhile but not so expensive that online customers would be unduly concerned about the security of their payments. Also the product is an appropriate size to be sent through the regular mail system and to be delivered through people's letter boxes.
  Pens and Things have set up their direct sales web site and are ready to launch – then the American agent hears of the plan!
  The American agent is not happy. She sees the plan for online selling as a threat to her market and that of her trade customers. She threatens to take the issue to court as it breaches her exclusive contract for the sale of Barker Pens in North America (or so she claims). It also appears that she was planning her own web site (although she is not admitting that).
  Pens and Things accept that the American agent has a point and realise that other agents might also raise similar objections. There is also a realisation that agents themselves could start selling online and this could raise further objections as the agents themselves poach sales from other people's territory. The whole issue of web selling needs talking about and the task is given to the marketing director to sort out.

The outcome of the negotiations is that there will be a web site, one web site for Barker Pens but that sales will be attributed to the agency for the area where the customer resides. Individual agreements are to be negotiated with each agency with two basic options being available:

- Option 1 is that the order is forwarded to the agent for packaging and despatch – Pens and Things take a fee for managing the web site.
- Option 2 is that Pens and Things handle the order and despatch the goods but make a payment to the agent in whose territory the customer lives.

Pens and Things is now ready to go online. Their home page is shown at Figure 12.4; like all web sites it will be improved as the company gains experience of online trading.

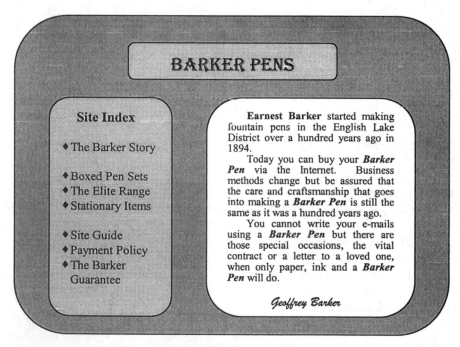

Fig. 12.4 Pens and Things – Front Page.

Exercises

If you are not already an experienced user of Internet e-Commerce, then look up a few sites to see what they look like. Use your favourite search engine to find two or three online bookshops. Use the search facility but also check out any adverts or menu items that click through to an online bookstore. Look up this book and any other course books and compare prices, delivery times and shipping charges. After you have looked up the book, jot down three reasons why you might buy the book online and three why it might not be advantageous.

If you did buy this book from an online bookshop then well done; you can still write down three reasons for and three against using an online bookstore.

Further Reading

Further detail on Internet e-Commerce is given in the next four chapters and that is the next place to read.

This book takes a critical look at Internet e-Commerce and concludes that it will not be the all embracing commercial channel that some commentators predict. For a less critical / more radical projection of the electronic future see:

Negroponte N. (1995) *being digital*, Coronet.

Cope N. (1996*) Retail in the Digital Age*, Bowerdean.

Also many magazines and newspapers have articles on e-Commerce, check some of them out.

Further detail on the Minitel is available in the case study book:

Jelassi T. (ed.) (1994) *European Casebook on Competing Through Information Technology: Strategy and Implementation*, Prentice Hall, Hemel Hempstead, UK.

The chapters on Managing Strategic IT Initiatives in the Public Sector and Developing and Diffusing Strategic IT are the most relevant although some of the other case studies detail Minitel applications. A paper that specifically attempts to draw lessons for the commercial use of the Internet, from the Minitel experience, is:

Hill R. (1997) 'Electronic Commerce, the World Wide Web, Minitel and EDI', in *The Information Society*, Vol. 13, No. 1, pp. 33–42.

13

The Internet

Summary

This chapter outlines the nature of the Internet, its history and the facilities that can be used for e-Commerce.

The Internet was born as a US military project and developed as an academic and research network. The use of the Internet by members of the general public and the commercial use of the Internet is a relatively recent phenomenon. The commercial use of the Internet involves service providers, content providers and software facilities; the chapter introduces the various categories of players and the range of services and facilities they offer.

13.1   The Internet

> The web is a big place, and tens of thousands of people have put hundreds of thousands of hours into making it enjoyable. The vast majority of them haven't made any money from their work yet, and many did it for the joy of starting something new.

> (Hoffman, 1995)

The Internet is a strange phenomenon. It had its origins as a military project back in 1969. It was adopted by the research and academic community; became the tool (or toy) of computer nerds around the world and then, in the space of a couple of years, it became the engine that, it is claimed, is to propel the world into the information age and the twenty-first century.

The Internet is also an interesting phenomenon because nobody owns it. It is unlike the railway, telegraph or telephone companies of the past that were owned by large private corporations or state monopolies. It is a pattern of usage of information and communications technologies that transcends any and all telecommunications infrastructure providers.

The Internet is, at a technical level, defined not by the equipment but by its communications protocol, Transmission Control Protocol / Internet Protocol (TCP/IP).

The Internet is, at another level, defined by the people who use it. The individuals, institutions and companies that make information available, send messages, access web sites and, in the case of e-Commerce, buy and sell.

The Internet is not the only, or the first, national and international data network. Other data networks have been put together by multinational organisations, EDI VADS providers and public access network companies such as CompuServe. The Internet has, however, despite its simple planning and lack of formal control, evolved into the global network; possibly its 'success' is because of that absence of formal controls.

13.2   The Development of the Internet

The origins of the Internet are commonly traced back to a US military project, the ARPAnet, commissioned by the US Department of Defence in 1969. The aim of the project was to explore packet switching technology in order to establish a network with distributed control that could still function if some of its nodes and links were knocked out in a nuclear war. The ARPAnet was demonstrated in late 1972 at an international conference in Washington DC: 'the first public demonstration of packet switching'.

In the late 1970's and early 1980's further experimental networks were created that were mainly used for e-Mail within and between university departments. CSNet (Computer Science Network) was established in 1981 and the military aspects were split from the ARPAnet in 1983. Further academic networks were put in place to provide access to supercomputer centres, notably JANET, Joint Academic Network in the UK (1984) and NSFNet, National Science Foundation in the US (1986).

The TCP/IP protocol was established in 1982 and introduced for use on the ARPAnet on the first of January 1983. Application protocols developed for and used in TCP/IP include the file transfer system (FTP), e-mail protocol (SMTP) and the remote login facility Telnet. The TCP/IP protocol also introduces the IP Address, a multipart numeric code used to identify all nodes in the network; TCP/IP addresses are also represented by an alphabetic equivalent in e-Mail and web site addresses.

In 1989 a group of scientists at the European Laboratory for Particle Physics (CERN) in Geneva, Switzerland developed an Internet Tool that would link information produced by various CERN researchers. The tool provided a way to link textual information on different computers and created by different scientists. The object was to overcome issues of computer incompatibility and utilise a new way of linking called 'hypertext'. Rather than presenting information in a linear or hierarchical fashion, hypertext permits information to be linked in a web-like structure. Nodes of information can be linked to other nodes of information in multiple ways. As a result, users can dynamically criss-cross the information web using pieces in the order most convenient to them.

In 1993 the National Centre for Supercomputing Applications (NCSA) at the University of Illinois pushed the CERN idea further by creating a software tool called Mosaic. Mosaic is an easy-to-use, graphical user interface that permits text, graphics, sound and video to be hyperlinked. Mosaic was the first of the Internet tools that are now referred to as 'web browsers'.

An alternative information access facility, developed at about the same time as the web, was Gopher. This provided for a series of menus that give access to character files. Gopher was, for a time widely used in the US but has largely succumbed to the now near universal application of the web.

The first commercial web browser was Netscape. The Netscape company was started in 1994 and included some of the programmers involved in the Mosaic Project. Some time after, some might argue rather late in the day, Bill Gates caught onto the Internet and Microsoft issued its Internet Explorer. With Netscape being the dominant web browser and Microsoft having a habit of wishing to dominate everything there ensued a period known as 'the browser wars'. Microsoft used their dominance of the PC operating system market to get Explorer pre-loaded onto most new PCs – Netscape protested that this was anticompetitive – Microsoft insisted that an Internet interface was central to the design of their operating systems and a court case ensued. Netscape and Internet Explorer vied with each other to add features to their browser. The added features were not always compatible with other browsers or HTML standards and in the process making the job of designing a web page more difficult (the provider of a web page cannot guarantee which browser the customer will be using). On the plus side, from the user point of view, the browser is now free. Netscape and Explorer are distributed to thousands of potential users, by Internet service providers, on CDs through the post and both packages are downloadable via the web.

On the other side from the browser and the client computer, there is the software on the server system. As with the client, the server can be any one of several boxes; UNIX and (large) PCs being the most common choices. Internet server software is available from a number of suppliers with Netscape and Microsoft both prominent and Apache, a public domain product is also widely used on UNIX boxes and with the Linux operating system.

Aside from browser wars is the need to add logic and system interfaces to web applications. The commonly used approach has been a Common Gateway Interface (CGI) program using Perl (or another programming language offering similar facilities). More recently JAVA from Sun Microsystems and ActiveX products from Microsoft have been issued with the capability to perform the same functions.

In 1994 there were approximately 500 web sites. One year later this had increased to nearly 10,000 and any further statistics that could be included in this book would be out of date by the time it is read.

13.3   TCP/IP

The network protocol used on the Internet is Transmission Control Protocol / Internet Protocol – TCP/IP. As has already been indicated this was introduced on the ARPAnet at the beginning of January 1983.

TCP/IP is a packet switching protocol. In packet switching, messages are split up into segments (packets) and despatched into the network with their source and destination addresses plus other header information including a package sequence number. The route a packet takes through the network is determined within the network and the lines used are shared with other packets that are travelling through the network (this contrasts with a circuit switched network where the line is used for just one transmission at any time). The packets are reassembled into the message in the destination system. TCP provides the transport protocol and ensures that the data that is sent is complete and error free when it is received at the destination. IP provides the routing mechanism. IP addresses consist of four sets of decimal numbers separated by full stops, e.g. 192.9.1.20. The IP address specifies both the sending network (netid) and the destination computer (hostid) – vital given the Internet's structure as a network of networks and the dynamic nature of the Internet. The IP address is used in conjunction with the port number, a logical number that specifies the application, e.g. 80 for the World Wide Web.

The TCP/IP protocol stack has five layers. The reference model for network protocols is the OSI seven layer model and the five layers of TCP/IP are commonly explained with reference to that OSI model. The five layers of TCP/IP are:

- **Application Layer**
  Equivalent to the OSI Model layers 7, 6 and (part of) 5.

  The application is the program that initiates the transfer. This may be the user's own program / application package or one of the TCP/IP defined applications:

  - FTP   File Transfer Protocol:
               Used to copy files across the network.
  - SMTP   Simple Mail Transfer Protocol:
               Used for all Internet e-Mail.
  - Telnet   Remote login facility.

  The message generated at the application layer, together with the IP address and port number, are passed to the transport layer for further processing. If the application does not have the full IP Address then the DNS (Domain Name System) / WINS (Windows Internet Name System) can be invoked to provide it.

- **Transport Layer**
  Equivalent to the OSI Model layer 4 (and part of 5).

  At this level, TCP establishes a logical connection with the receiving computer and determines the size of the segments to be sent.   TCP then divides up the message into segments and attaches a header to each; the header specifies the source and destination ports and the sequence number of the segment within the message.
  UDP is an alternative to TCP that is used for real-time audio or video.   UDP provides no error detection; there is little virtue in re-transmission of errored segments in such real-time applications.
  For both protocols the segments are passed to the network layer, together with the IP address.

- **Network Layer**
  Equivalent to the OSI Model layer 3.

  The Network Layer is responsible for routing the packet from source station to its final destination station, specified by the MAC address. If the MAC address is not already available then an ARP (Address Resolution Protocol) request is broadcast to the network and the machine with that IP address responds with its MAC address.
  The Network Layer may fragment the segments from the Transport Layer into smaller packets if this is necessary, to fit the frame size.
  The output packets from this layer (referred to as datagrams) are passed to the datalink layer.

- **Data Link Layer**
  Equivalent to the OSI Model layer 2.

  At the datalink layer, IP interfaces with the network to be used, e.g. Ethernet, or X25. The network protocol will typically add its own header (Nh) and trailer (Nt) that incorporate the MAC address.
  The packet is then passed onto the medium, the physical network layer.

- **Physical Layer**
  Equivalent to the OSI Model layer 1.

  The cables used for transmission.

See also Figure 13.1 (the diagram is based on Freedman, 1999).

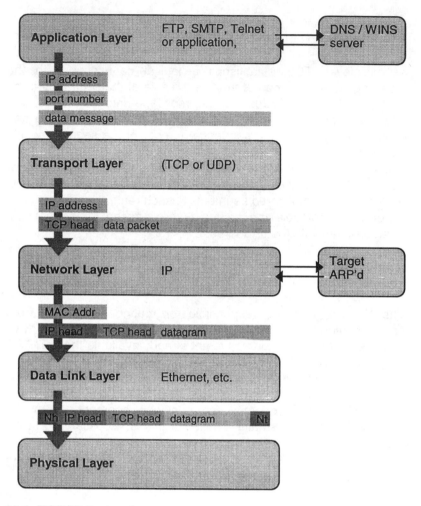

Fig. 13.1 TCP/IP Protocol.

At the time of its introduction, TCP/IP was seen as an interim measure with the OSI (Open System Interconnection) standard intended as an eventual replacement. In the event the use of TCP/IP has continued and interest in the OSI standard has waned. The OSI standards are still used in a number of commercial networks but the omnipresence of the Internet is tending to make TCP/IP the defacto standard for wide-area networking.

13.4   Internet Components

The TCP/IP is the unifying factor of the Internet – the software, hardware and connecting cables can be very diverse. Some of these components and the people who run them are:

- **Client:**

Users of the Internet access its facilities from a client machine; a PC, Apple Mac or Workstation that is joined to a network. The two most used facilities of the Internet are:

- **World Wide Web**
  The web is accessed from the client machine using a web browser; at the time of writing the two most popular browsers are Microsoft Internet Explorer and Netscape Navigator. The web page to be viewed is specified by its web address, the uniform resource locator (url), e.g. www.mcgraw-hill.co.uk; the url contains the addressing information needed to derive the IP address of the server that holds the web page.

- **e-Mail**
  Accessing e-Mail requires a mail client program; this may be a facility of the web browser or a separate software package. Incoming e-Mails are downloaded from a post-box (file) on the server and outgoing e-Mails are sent to the server for onwards transmission. Each e-Mail has to include the address of the recipient, e.g. susan.jones@mcgraw-hill.com (the name is fictitious); the second part of the e-Mail address (following the '@') is the domain name and is used on the mail server to derive the IP address.

- **Internet Service Provider**

Access to the Internet, for members of the public and small organisations, is via an Internet Service Provider (ISP). The user provides the client computer and uses a modem to connect to the ISP's server. Telecom providers and cable companies are increasingly providing digital services and open-all-the-time connections which give increased speed and convenience of access.

The ISP provides access to the web, an e-Mail address and very possibly user space for the client to set up their own home page. Some ISPs specialise in hosting business sites with services designed to meet the need of that market. The provision of Internet services has become very competitive and users have taken to shopping around for the best package. Users of the service get the ISP's home page displayed when they log on which gives the service provider the opportunity to create revenue from advertising and hosting links to commercial sites; many ISPs use the advertising revenue to support a free access service to the users.

For many large organisations the ISP is the company, the university or whatever. The organisation is wired with its own LAN and WAN and access to the Internet is via the company's own server.

- **Server**

The server is a computer system linked into the Internet and that can be accessed by the clients. The server may run a number of applications; Internet server applications include:

- **Web Server**
  Software that takes requests from client browsers, searches the web and passes back the resultant pages to the browser. The server software will support TCP/IP. The server will, very probably, store a number of home pages that are available to local users and other Internet users.

- **Mail Server**
  Software that acts as a 'post office' for the e-Mail system. Mail created on the client sites is passed to the appropriate post-box within the system or sent out over the Internet to its intended destination. Mail from outside is stored in post-box files and uploaded to the users machine when requested by the mail client. As with the web server, the mail server uses TCP/IP for its Internet transmissions.

- **Intranets**

A web site designed for use by the employees of an organisation – a private Internet. The Intranet can be used to replace documents such as staff manuals, internal telephone directories and office notices. Their advantage is that they are (hopefully) always readily available and that they can be easily updated. Intranet systems can include application systems where scripting languages give access to databases and the use of a browser gives easy access throughout the organisation.

- **Extranets**

Some organisations have web sites available on the Internet but with access limited to account holders by a password system; such a facility is called an Extranet. Extranets are used in business to business trading where customers are required to have an account, see Chapter 11. Another use of Extranets is by consultancies and business information services where business reports are made available online but only to clients and subscribers.

- **Webmaster**

The Webmaster is responsible for the provision of web services for the organisation. Responsibilities include setting up and maintaining the server software and the home page for the organisation. Where staff within the organisation can provide their own web content the webmaster will probably set the standards so that the organisation can ensure a professional appearance and consistent 'look and feel' for its users.

- **Governance of the Internet**

The Internet, as already described, is a network of networks – its co-ordination and development is provided by a number of voluntary committees. These include:

- Internet Society.
- Internet Engineering Task Force
- Internet Research Task Force.

The whole arrangement works well. It contrasts with the incompatibilities produced by competing commercial organisations such as the providers of web browsers. Whether co-operation or competition is a better model for innovation and societal progress is debatable.

13.5   Uses of the Internet

One use of the Internet is e-Commerce, an application that is more fully explained in Chapters 15 and 16. e-Commerce is, as indicated above, a relatively recent feature of the Internet. Other uses of the Internet are:

- Personal Messaging (e-Mail):
  e-Mail was one of the first applications on the Internet. The use of e-Mail is having a profound effect on the way people communicate and the way that organisations operate. An e-Mail message can be quickly typed and sent. Unlike the use of the telephone, it does not need the recipient to be available to take a call. The e-Mail can be sent to many recipients; it is a matter of record and its electronic content can be saved, edited and / or used in other documents. The e-Mail does not facilitate a conversation in the way that a telephone does but it can and is replacing most memos and many telephone calls within organisations and between individuals and organisations.
      e-Mail is not an invention of the Internet. e-Mail was a service available on the internal networks of many organisations and has been provided by other public access network services. The Internet, however, is an ideal tool for e-Mail as it is the one network that can connect all users – the Internet is the default option for an e-Mail service unless privacy requirements dictate a more secure provision.

- Data Interchange (EDI):
  EDI has been traditionally transmitted over proprietary VADS. EDI started before the Internet was widely or commercially available and made use of either VADS or point to point connections. Users of EDI have been reluctant to transfer their communication needs to the Internet because of concerns with security and reliability. Some EDI requirements are, however, being transferred to the Internet as its usage is generally cheaper than a VADS. There are also hybrid systems where EDI messages are taken in by a clearing house operation, decoded and forwarded, via the Internet, to small businesses users with limited EDI requirements and no EDI provision.

- Teleworking:
  Teleworking is another practice that predated the general availability of the Internet. Telework has a number of definitions but it generally involves doing work that has an IT component at home (or at least at a location that is away from the office) and using telecommunications to communicate with that office.

  Full-time teleworking has not materialised as the radical shift in working practices that was predicted by many pundits. Informal teleworking has, however, become a common practice with employees spending the odd day working from home (or spending time in the evening doing a bit extra); the general availability of Internet access has been an important facilitator of this change in working practices.

- Distance Education:
  The Internet is being utilised by colleges as a facility for the delivery of distance education. The traditional vehicle of distance education has been 'print through the post', supplemented in recent years by radio, television, video and computer aided learning packages. The Internet has the facility to replace all of this as a multimedia offering through a single delivery system. The Internet is been utilised by traditional distance learning institutions such as the UK Open University and is being leapt on by other institutions keen to get in on the act. The Internet can be a great facilitator of distance education; to be worthwhile it still requires quality material and thorough support of the students (and it seems likely that many of the newer providers will fall short of these standards).

- Entertainment:
  In addition to specific uses of the Internet there is a recreational use of the Internet, the surfer. On the Internet people can play games, find snippets of information, join a chatroom or just admire the intricacies of other web sites.

The Internet can even be place to find a partner – hopefully that does not classify as an e-Commerce transaction.

13.6   Internet Age Systems

Networks in general and the Internet in particular do not just exist in isolation; they affect and effect the businesses and individuals that use them. Networks are an essential technological component in many, or most, business information systems. Seddon (1997) suggested that the evolution of information systems can be divided into periods of 20 years as follows:

- 1955–1974 The Electronic Data Processing (EDP) era.
- 1975–1994 The Management Information Systems (MIS) era.
- 1995–   The Internet era.

A sequence that is represented diagramatically in Figure 13.2.

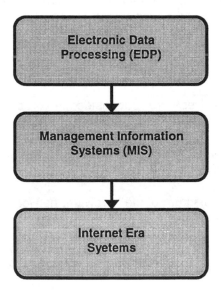

Fig. 13.2 From EDP to the Internet.

These systems types and their evolution have been enabled by a number of technological developments which have been required by various business imperatives. One of the facilitators has been the availability of networks. The essence of each era is:

- EDP was essentially batch. It was controlled by the DP professionals and used at the 'organisational level' within the company.

- MIS would normally utilise transaction processing (TP) and databases. The MIS system subsumed the dataprocessing functions of the EDP and enabled access to business data throughout the organisation and at all levels of the organisation. The internal network of the company was an essential enabling technology.
- The Internet era systems include the Inter-organisational System (IOS) enabled by EDI and the company to consumer, organisation to public systems enabled by the use of the web. The Internet epitomises these developments and is at the heart of many of these systems.

Seddon derives his definition of e-Commerce from this evolution:

'Electronic Commerce is commerce enabled by Internet-era technologies.'

Interestingly, Seddon puts a twenty year life span on each of these era. For Seddon the Internet era ends (or evolves into a new era) at 2014. It requires a brave person to predict the next stage!

Exercises

The following exercises are suggested in order to demonstrate an understanding of the chapter and the nature of the Internet:

1. Explain packet switching – how does packet switching differ from a switched network (i.e. a dialled call)?

2. Draw a simple diagram of the hardware, network and software facilities utilised when an e-Shop is accessed from a home PC.

3. Consider your college, university or place of work and suggest what uses / information would be appropriate to an intranet, extranet and the Internet.

4. The chapter lists some of the facilities available on the web (e-Commerce, e-Mail, etc). Add to the list and suggest business (as opposed to personal) uses for each of the facilities listed.

Further Reading

There is a dearth of books on the Internet. There are many books on how to author web pages and a number of very weighty volumes on TCP/IP but nothing, that the author has found, simply on the Internet. Details of the Internet, if additional details are required, are included as introductory material in many volumes on related topics.   One useful source of information is:

Freedman A. (1999) *The Computer Desktop Encyclopaedia* (2nd. ed.), Amacon, New York.

14

A Page on the Web

Summary

This chapter introduces HTML (the language of the Web) and indicates how it can be used to create an e-Commerce web site.

The chapter includes sufficient detail for the reader to construct his / her own web page.

14.1   HTML, the Basics

The basic building block of any web page is HTML – Hypertext Markup Language. HTML, as indicated by its name, it has two functions:

- Hypertext: a system of linking between documents (or to sections within a document) – click the link and the required document is selected and displayed. If this book was on the web in HTML there could be a link to Section 14.2 Introduction to HTML, and you could skip over this section and start learning simple HTML.

- Markup: a system for indicating the formatting of the page – headings, paragraphs, italics and the like – similar to the requirement to include formatting in a word processed document. The markups are sets of control characters inserted in the text, generally called 'tags'. Tags indicate the required format of the page but also other features such as the inclusion of pictures and the hypertext links.

The HTML page is stored on the web server system connected to the Internet. The user accesses the web page via a web browser on their own system, the client system. The web page, HTML tags and 'content', are downloaded from the server to the browser and displayed in the required format on the user's screen, see Figure 14.1.

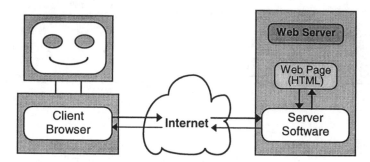

Fig. 14.1 Web Server and Client Browser System.

This is the basic system – it provides for the display of static information on the client's browser screen and nothing more.   The static information may be beautifully formatted, include pictures and sound, and provide links to other web pages but it is a static display – like a page in a book or a glossy magazine.   In order to include additional features, such as ordering goods or services from an e-Commerce site, the site provider has to go beyond the basics and outside the direct scope of HTML.   To go beyond the basics the site provider can:

- Include additional functionality in the web page that is to be executed on the server – using a CGI Script or Server Side Scripting.   This may, for instance, include in the web page data from a database, e.g. details of goods that are for sale, or process data from the client such as a completed order form for a product that the user wishes to buy.

- Include logic code in the web page to be sent to the client's browser and executed on the user's own machine – Client Side Scripting.   This is often used to provide eye catching moving images on the user's screen but can be used for more functional purposes such as validating user entered data before it is submitted.

This chapter outlines the basics of HTML, enough for the reader to set up his or her own web page; these details are supplemented on the book's web page. Further HTML features and facilities for client side and server side scripting are outlined but readers will have to access other, more specialised, sources for further details.   The basics of HTML are well established and do not change; the more advanced features can be much more complex and are being introduced and updated at a great pace.   There are a large number of books on these technical topics and a wealth of material available on the web – the web page for this book gives some pointers to relevant material that is available in this rapidly changing field.

14.2   Introduction to HTML

This sub-section is designed to show what HTML looks like and how it works. To achieve this an example of a simple web page to advertise this book: *Electronic-Commerce* by David Whiteley is used (and feel free to place it in the web – any free publicity is welcome!).

The formatting of the page in HTML involves inserting markup tags in the text to indicate the format that is intended. In HTML the tag starts with the < character and ends with the > character. Tags are often used in pairs with a start tag and an end tag, e.g. <H1> and </H1> at the start and end of the first level headings.

- **Headings**

The first item on the web page is likely to be a title, in this case the title of the book: *Electronic-Commerce* by *David Whiteley*. Formatted in HTML this can be as follows:

```
<H1>Electronic Commerce by David Whiteley</H1>
```

The HTML tags that specify the formatting are:
- <H1>   Start of major (level 1) heading.
- </H1>   End of major (level 1) heading.

HTML, unlike a word processor, does not specify the exact format, e.g. 20 point Times New Roman, but just the intention – a major heading. The result can be slightly different depending on the browser that is used but it is going to be something like this:

Electronic Commerce by David Whiteley

Not impressive! Using a bit more HTML the text can be centred, the authors name can be smaller, in italics and on a second line:

```
<CENTER><H1>Electronic-Commerce</H1></CENTER>
<CENTER><H3>by <I>David Whiteley</I></H3>
</CENTER>
```

The second line of headings is shown as a level 3 heading (levels 1 to 6 are available but levels 5 and 6 can be displayed in very small fonts and might not give the intended impression). Other HTML tags that have been introduced are:

- `<CENTER>`   Start centred text.
- `</CENTER>`   End centred text.
- `<I>`   Start italic text.
- `</I>`   End italic text.

The result is now something like this:

Electronic Commerce
by *David Whiteley*

- **Text**

After the headings comes some text to say what the book is about and what makes it a 'must buy'. The text needs to be put in paragraphs and, in this example, the title is shown in bold:

```
<P><B>Electronic Commerce</B> (e-Commerce) has
been brought to prominence over recent years by
the popularisation and commercialisation of the
Internet.  However, e-Commerce is not a new
phenomenon; it has been an important part of
trade for many years.  In addition to the
consumer oriented trade of the Internet, e-
Commerce is practised through Electronic Markets
and Electronic Data Interchange (EDI).  In broad
terms, these three areas cover the field of e-
Commerce.</P>
```

The new HTML tags that have been used are:
- `<P>`   Start paragraph
  (can also be used on its own to indicate a blank line).
- `</P>`   End paragraph.
- `<B>`   Start bold text.
- `</B>`   End bold text.

The result is that the text is displayed as a separate paragraph followed by a blank line:

> **Electronic Commerce** (e-Commerce) has been brought to prominence over recent years by the popularisation and commercialisation of the Internet. However, e-Commerce is not a new phenomenon; it has been an important part of trade for many years. In addition to the consumer oriented trade of the Internet, e-Commerce is practised through Electronic Markets and Electronic Data Interchange (EDI). In broad terms, these three areas cover the field of e-Commerce.

- **List**

The publicity for e-Commerce includes a bullet point list of key features. This can be replicated on a web page using the list facility:

```
<UL>
<LI>deals with the complete spectrum of
electronic commerce, markets and EDI;
<LI>treats the material using language which is
easy to follow and minimises jargon;
<LI>takes a practical approach with many
examples and exercises.
</UL>
```

The HTML tags for the unordered list are:
- `<UL>`   Start unordered list.
- `</UL>`   End unordered list.
- `<LI>`   List item (no end tag required).

(Ordered lists, i.e. with numbers in place of the bullets, have the same format but start with the `<OL>` tag and end with `</OL>` tag, the use of `<LI>` is unchanged).

The result is the following bullet point list:

> - deals with the complete spectrum of electronic commerce, markets and EDI;
> - treats the material using language which is easy to follow and minimises jargon;
> - takes a practical approach with many examples and exercises.

The web is multi-media so lets include a picture of the book's front cover:

```
<CENTER>
<IMG SRC="ec-cover.gif">
</CENTER>
```

The HTML tags for the picture is:

- `<IMG>` Image.
  The SRC attribute specifies the location (url) of the image file to be displayed.

And the picture, placed in the centre, would look like this:

(except at the time of writing the cover design was not available – a .gif file of the real cover is on the web page).

- **Links to Other Pages**

The last element of the example page is links to the web pages of the publisher and the author:

```
<P>Follow these links for further details about
the publisher
<A HREF="http://www.mcgraw-hill.co.uk">
McGraw-Hill</A> and the author <A HREF=
"http://www.doc.mmu.ac.uk/STAFF/D.Whiteley">
David Whiteley</A>.</P>
```

The HTML tags for the links are:

* `<A>`   Start hypertext link (A stands for anchor).
* `</A>`   End hypertext link.
                           The HREF attribute specifies the location (url) to which the
                           reader will be linked (if the link is selected).

The result is the following text with the links underlined and, normally, displayed in
a different colour from the surrounding text:

> Follow these links for further details about the publisher
> McGraw-Hill and the author David Whiteley.

* **Page Header and Footer**

The final element of the example web page is the HTML header and footer:

```
<HTML>
<HEAD>
<TITLE>e-Commerce by D Whiteley (McGraw-Hill)
</TITLE>
</HEAD>
<BODY>
The content of the web page.
</BODY>
</HTML>
```

The overall document starts and ends with an HTML tag (well it can be more
complex than that, but not in this book):

* `<HTML>`   Start HTML.
* `</HTML>`   End HTML.

The first part of the document is the header – it is not displayed but contains
information about the document as a whole. The header should include the title
and can include other elements that are not included in this simple guide:

* `<HEAD>`   Start header.
* `</HEAD>`   End header.
* `<TITLE>`   Start title.
* `</TITLE>`   End title.

The second part of the document is the body – the tags plus the content that are to
be displayed to the user – it is bracketed by the body tags:

* `<BODY>`   Start body.
* `</BODY>`   End body.

* **The Example Page**

Putting all the elements together the overall HTML for the web page (including text
that was not included in the example) is shown in Figure 14.2:

```
<HTML>
<HEAD>
<TITLE>e-Commerce by D Whiteley (McGraw Hill)</TITLE>
</HEAD>
<BODY>
<CENTER><H1>Electronic Commerce</H1></CENTER>
<CENTER><H3>by <I>David Whiteley</I></H3>
</CENTER>
<P><B>Electronic Commerce</B> (e-Commerce) has been
brought to prominence over recent years by the
popularisation and commercialisation of the Internet.
However, e-Commerce is not a new phenomenon; it has
been an important part of trade for many years.  In
addition to the consumer oriented trade of the
Internet, e-Commerce is practised through Electronic
Markets and Electronic Data Interchange (EDI).  In
broad terms, these three areas cover the field of e-
Commerce.</P>
<P>Written by an academic with many years experience
on the subject, this book covers all three areas.
The coverage ranges from the business use and
implications of e-Commerce to an outline of the
technical requirements.</P>
<P>Key features:</P>
<UL>
<LI>deals with the complete spectrum of electronic
commerce, markets and EDI;
<LI>treats the material using language which is easy
to follow and minimises jargon;
<LI>takes a practical approach with many examples and
exercises.
</UL>
<P>
<CENTER>
<IMG SRC="ec-cover.gif">
</CENTER>
<P>Follow these links for further details about the
publisher
<A HREF="http://www.mcgraw-hill.co.uk">
McGraw-Hill</A> and the author <A HREF=
"http://www.doc.mmu.ac.uk/STAFF/D.Whiteley">
David Whiteley</A>.</P>
</BODY>
</HTML>
```

Fig. 14.2 HTML for example Web Page.

And the page as it would be displayed is shown in Figure 14.3:

Electronic-Commerce
by *David Whiteley*

Electronic Commerce (e-Commerce) has been brought to prominence over recent years by the popularisation and commercialisation of the Internet. However, e-Commerce is not a new phenomenon; it has been an important part of trade for many years. In addition to the consumer oriented trade of the Internet, e-Commerce is practised through Electronic Markets and Electronic Data Interchange (EDI). In broad terms, these three areas cover the field of e-Commerce.

Written by an academic with many years experience on the subject, this book covers all three areas. The coverage ranges from the business use and implications of e-Commerce to an outline of the technical requirements.

Key Features:

- deals with the complete spectrum of electronic commerce, markets and EDI;
- treats the material using language which is easy to follow and minimises jargon;
- takes a practical approach with many examples and exercises.

-Commerce e-Commerc
e e-Commerce e-Comm
erce **e-Commerce** e-Co
mmerce e-Commerce e-
Commerce e-Commerce
e-Commerce e-Commer
ce e-Commerce e-Com
merce e-Commerce e-C
ommerce e-Comm Graw e
David Whiteley   M^c
Commerce e-Comr Hill e

Follow these links for further details about the publisher McGraw-Hill and the author David Whiteley.

Fig. 14.3 Example Web Page.

14.3   Further HTML

The example already given covers a number of HTML constructs (and it is not the function of this book to be an HTML or a web authoring manual) but there are three more constructs that can be usefully mentioned:

- **Tables**

```
<TABLE Border=1>
<TR><TD></TD><TD>CW</TD><TD>Exam</TD></TR>
<TR><TD>Susan</TD><TD>56%</TD><TD>40%</TD></TR>
<TR><TD>Yousif</TD><TD>79%</TD><TD>67%</TD></TR>
<TR><TD>John</TD><TD>28%</TD><TD>34%</TD></TR>
</TABLE>
```

The HTML tags for the table are:
- `<TABLE>`   Start table.
- `</TABLE>`   End table.
                     (Border=1 sets the width of the lines around the cells of the table).
- `<TR>`   Start table row.
- `</TR>`   End table row.
- `<TD>`   Start table data cell.
- `</TD>`   End table data cell.

The result is the following grid:

	CW	Exam
Susan	56%	40%
Yousif	79%	67%
John	28%	34%

- **Frames**

Frames are a way of dividing up the browser window into a number of sub-windows. Using frames a separate HTML file can be displayed in each window. A common configuration is to have a site index in a narrow page down the left hand side and the current page in its own window on the right of the screen.

Frames, to be effective, get quite involved and the user is asked to reference specialist HTML material for the details.

- **Forms**

Forms are a way of asking the user to input information. The information can consist of selecting a menu item, clicking a button or the input of text. The following HTML is an example of an online order form, an abbreviated version of a simple form that could be used for the e-Shop shown below:

```
<H1>WONKA ONLINE</H1>
<FORM ACTION="url of CGI script" METHOD=GET>
<PRE>
Fudgemallow Delight
<INPUT TYPE="checkbox" NAME="fudgemd"
VALUE="yes">
Nutty Crunch Surprise
<INPUT TYPE="checkbox" NAME="nutcrun"
VALUE="yes">
Name: <INPUT TYPE="text" NAME="customer">
<INPUT TYPE="submit">
</PRE>
</FORM>
```

The resulting form would look like this:

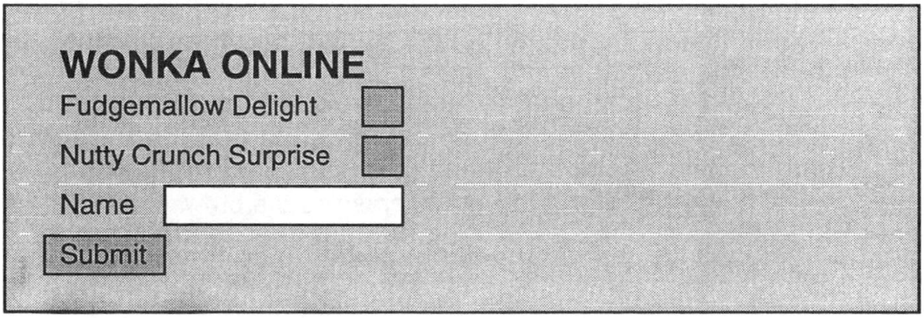

WONKA ONLINE
Fudgemallow Delight ☐

Nutty Crunch Surprise ☐

Name [   ]

[Submit]

With additional formatting it would look more presentable but this has been omitted to make the HTML easier to follow.

Processing of the data from the form requires the use of a CGI script or some form of Server Side Scripting. General purpose CGI scripts to process forms are available; they can be downloaded from the web but ask your web-master for a recommendation before finding your own.

- **General Notes**

And a few general notes on HTML syntax:

- Tags can be in upper or lower case: `<H1>` is the same as `<h1>` and `<CENTER>` is the same as `<center>`.
- All tags start with the `<` character and end with the `>` character – and if you want to use a greater than sign, less than sign or the & sign (which is also used in HTML) on your web page, the simple answer is don't.
- Many, but not all, tags come in pairs. The closing tag matches the opening tag but is preceded by a / (within the `<>`).

14.4   Client Side Scripting

The standard 'technology' for Client Side Scripting is the JavaScript. Essentially a JavaScript is a program, usually a small program, that is embedded in the HTML source, downloaded with the HTML source and executed on the client (the user's machine).

The JavaScript is normally used to change the screen in some way. Examples are to open an additional window, adding a message in the status bar, or a mouse rollover effect (where a button is changed when the mouse is pointing at it).

The JavaScript is included in the HTML using the `<SCRIPT>` tag within the `<HEAD>` section of the page. The JavaScript is then invoked using HTML at an appropriate point in the `<BODY>` section of the page.

More complex functions can be achieved by downloading Java Applets. These are mini-executable programs that are downloaded and then run on the client machine. There is a range of tasks or effects that can (or could) be performed by Applets – slowing down the client system and crashing the browser are two of the unintended effects.

Client side scripting is outside the scope of this book and this introductory chapter.   Readers wishing to use this facility should refer to a source that specifically deals with the subject. For Java Applets the Sun Microsystems Java web site is a good starting point.

14.5   Server Side Scripting

A Server Side Script is a small program that is run on the server. The traditional form of Server Side Scripting is a Common Gateway Interface (CGI) script. In an e-Commerce application CGI scripts could be used to:

- Access the product database for the catalogue information to be included on the pages of the e-Shop.
- Accept the user data input on forms and pass it to the order processing system for processing.

CGI scripts have typically been written in Perl but other languages such as C++ and Visual Basic can also be used. There are a number of CGI scripts available for commonly required functions and it is usual to use one of these scripts, possibly with modification, as opposed to taking on the task of writing a new script that is specific to the application.

More recent developments in this area have been the introduction of Active Server Pages by Microsoft and JavaServer Pages by Sun. These serve the same purpose as the use of CGI Scripts but offer a more integrated solution when used on the server software from the same supplier.

Server side scripting is also outside the scope of this book and web sources or more specialist references should be consulted if further information is needed.

14.6   HTML Editors and Editing

A HTML file can be created using any text editor; for PC users the most readily available is Notepad that is supplied as part of the MS Windows operating system. An HTML file can also be created using a word processor file but it must be saved as a text only file (a normal word processor file includes markup details inserted by the word processor software).

In order to avoid having to remember the different tags and having to type them in an HTML Editor can be used. These are like a word processor or desk top publishing packages; the user provides the content and selects the required formats, the editor inserts the HTML tags. Typically the user can view the HTML source or switch to a display format to see what the page will look like when it is viewed by the browser. Some web browsers include an HTML editor and there are a number of free-standing packages on the market; many of them can be downloaded from the Internet and used free for a trial period.

The third approach is to use the HTML formatting facilities included in some standard desk-top packages, for example, some word processors that include the option to output documents in HTML format.

Once written, an HTML file can be viewed by simply opening it as a local file in the browser – a good way of checking what the page will look like. To let the whole world see your web page the HTML file has to be placed on the server. This placement can be done using file transfer (FTP) to logon to the server and transfer the file. It may be that the ISP that is being used has its own way of doing this and, if this is the case, the appropriate instructions should be followed.

You could even use the web to send a birthday card next time you don't get to the shop in time. The card in Figure 14.4 was produced using the draw facility of MS Word, saved as a .gif file in Paint Shop Pro and then called in HTML. Having loaded the card on your home page, just send an e-Mail giving the url and the job is done (and it is cheaper than e-Flowers).

Fig. 14.4 Happy Birthday Dear Lena.

The full card, all four pages of it, is on the book home page in full, garish, technicolour.

Exercises

This chapter has just one exercise:

> Create your own home page

A home page can say what you like and look as you want it to. You can:

- Scan in a picture of yourself or take one with a digital camera – if you don't want your face on the page then put in a picture of your hamster or the ring in your navel;
- Say what you like and what you do;
- Tell a joke or write a poem (if you must);
- Put in links to your favourite web sites.

It is probably not a good idea to include home addresses and telephone numbers – there are plenty of nuts out there on the net. Preferably don't be too tasteless – the ISP might object and certainly the university will if the page is to be on their server.

A home page can be developed over the years and might help you get a job – include the url on your CV.

Further Reading

There are a number of good HTML guides on the web (see the book's web page) and lots and lots of books on how to write HTML. They range from the 'noddy guides' aimed at the raw beginner to cryptic reference works aimed at serious web designers. Two books that reflect these two categories and that were used by the author are:

Hoffman P. (1995) *Netscape and the World Wide Web for Dummies*, IDG Books.

Niederst J. (1999) *Web Design in a Nutshell*, O'Reilly, Sebastopol, CA.

These books were useful but it is not intended to recommend them in preference to the many other similar volumes that are available. A point to bear in mind when selecting a text is that while the basics of HTML stay the same there are new features coming out all the time; look at the publication date when selecting a book.

15

The elements of e-Commerce

Summary

This chapter looks at how the facilities of the Internet can be used for e-Commerce transactions.

EDI and Electronic Markets are appropriate to specific trade sectors, trade cycles and parts of the trade cycle. Internet commerce has, however, the potential for a wider applicability. It can be used for marketing in the pre-sale phase of the trade cycle; for sales the execution and settlement phases and / or in the after-sales phase. Each of these uses has potential advantages, requires differing techniques and can have its risks (the security of on-line transaction settlement being just one example).

15.1 Elements

The basic elements of Internet e-Commerce are an e-Shop on a server, a user with a web browser and an Internet connection between the two; these elements were outlined in Chapter 12 and further details on the Internet and web pages have been given in Chapter 13 and Chapter 14 respectively.

The basic e-Shop could be analogous to a market stall or a pitch at a car boot sale. For an enterprise wishing to establish a substantial online business the set-up needs to be much more sophisticated. The large e-Commerce sites cost millions (in any currency) to set-up and similar sums to maintain and update. The additional issues to be tackled in such a site include:

- Visibility: Getting the site noticed and the online customers visiting the store;
- Ease of Use: Once the customer arrives at the site they have to be able to find what they want with the minimum of hassle;
- Order Processing: Online orders have to be processed. Logically electronic orders are linked into computerised back-office systems;
- Online Payments: Goods bought online normally have to be paid for electronically;

- Security: Online payments need to be secure and the customers have to be confident they are secure;
- Delivery Systems: With Internet e-Commerce there has to be a system of home delivery; the customer cannot take the goods home with them (although there are some products and services that can be delivered electronically);
- After-Sales: Queries and faults need to be processed online; the customer can no longer simply pop back to the shop.

These aspects of e-Commerce are reflected in the trade cycle given in Chapter 12; they are represented in Figure 15.1 and are examined in detail in the remaining sections of this chapter.

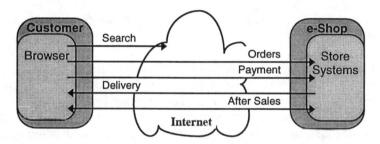

Fig. 15.1 e-Commerce Facilities.

15.2   e-Visibility

Having an e-Shop is not much use unless customers are 'coming in through the door'. A small retailer, with a low investment in their web site, might be content with the level of business that is obtained by chance hits and return visits. A large retailer, that has invested a lot in a web site and where e-Commerce features prominently in the business plan, needs to do rather more. Ways of advertising a web presence and getting customers in through the door include:

- Site Name
- Conventional Advertising
- Portals
- Malls
- Search Engines
- Links
- Personal Recommendations

- **Site Name**

The surest way of finding an e-Commerce site is the url. If the url is simple (and they often are not) and the punters can remember it, then the site is made. At the time of writing there is one such site:

```
amazon.com
```

A sensible simple site name can be guessed by users and might be easily remembered one such example is britishairways.com; it contrasts with flycontinental.com and cdnair.ca where, whatever the motive for the name, it is unlikely to be guessed.

- **Conventional Advertising**

An irony of e-Commerce is the apparent urge to advertise them through conventional media: in the newspaper, on the television and even on the carrier bags used in real shops.
   Conventional advertising of Internet addresses has a threefold effect:

- It boosts the image of the organisation and any conventional facilities it might have – it gives an air of modernity and 'high-tech';
- It lets the customer know that the organisation has Internet facilities;
- It can give users access via the url. A little difficult if it is a complex url that is flashed on a TV screen or is printed on a bag that has been thrown away.

- **Portals**

On loading the browser and connecting to the web the user is presented with a first page. This page is the portal, the place from which to access the facilities of the Internet.
   The portal is a valuable piece of property. It is the one place through which all users are likely to pass. An advert on a popular portal is the web equivalent of a TV advert at half time in the cup final or in a break during the Superbowl – it is seen by millions. An advert on a popular web search engine is a similar piece of property.
   Adverts on the portal can be banners, little boxes or background. Portals also provide a menu of services and inclusion in that list is another way of picking up business. Similar adverts appear on search engines; Figure 15.2 shows a couple of adverts from search engines for amazon.com. In the second instance, amazon have configured their advert to pick up the search requirements and advertise books on that topic; the result is not always appropriate.

Fig. 15.2 Example Adverts from Amazon.

- **Malls**

An Internet shopping mall models itself on the American shopping mall, a lot of shops, under one roof with a pleasant shopping atmosphere. To own a shop in a conventional mall is usually a good way of getting noticed by customers; hopefully there are a lot of people using the mall. The intention of an Internet mall is much the same, hopefully the customers who have been there before come back again, look around, see new shops and the interest in the location increases to the benefit of all the shops in the mall.

An Internet mall can, like its conventional counterpart, provide common services. Possibilities include:

- Shared advertising – publicising the mall and hence attracting customers to all the shops;
- Common facilities – the mall will very probably provide the software to link the shop to the back office and facilities like security and credit card processing can be common;
- e-Cash – the mall can provide or join an e-Cash service that is useable in all the stores;
- Common customer files so that publicity can be sent out to a wide range of users.

The drawback of joining a mall is that, as for any good retail location, the rents can be high.

- **Search Engines**

A search engine is a standard way to find any Internet site and that includes e-Shops.

Finding a specific e-Commerce site, or a site for a particular service, may or may not be easy.   Type in bookshop or airline into a search engine and you get thousands of entries. Figure 15.3 gives summary search results for bookshops on three popular search engines (results of searches can change on a daily basis).

Bookshop:	Excite rank	Excite advert	Lycos rank	Lycos advert	Infoseek rank	Infoseek advert
• amazon	-	Yes	-	-	1	-
• boarders	-	-	-	-	-	Yes
• barns and noble	-	-	-	-	-	-
• blackwell	7	-	-	-	4	-
• dillons	-	-	-	-	7	-
Total Hits	n/a		42,724		43,831	

rank is the position within the top 10 hits.

Fig. 15.3 Searching for a Bookshop.

A successful e-Shop could do with appearing in that top ten list of hits whichever search engine the user uses and whatever relevant term the user might choose to search on. As can be seen, not many of the main online bookshops achieved this with the search terms used (although some of the bookshops did appear as links). Many of the entries that did appear were of more specialist bookshops; these included:

- The Economist Bookshop
- The Haunted Bookshop
- Virtual Bookshop (rare books)
- Dog Lovers Bookshop

The search engines, and there are many of them, index the web. The index is constructed by a combination of:

- Manual indexing: The search engines employ people who search the Internet for relevant sites to include in the indexes of the search engine;
- Automatic Indexing: The search engine provider uses software robots, called *spiders*, that crawl the web to find pages to index.

The coding of the site can help the search engine to index the page. The prime target for the search engine is the `<TITLE>` and an appropriate choice of information will help (but remember that the title is also the default for use in the bookmarks so it needs to be appropriate for that use as well). In addition to the title, many search engines inspect the contents of the (optional) `<METTA>` tag and additional information or keywords can be included using that tag.

A site owner, who knows the tricks of the trade, can submit information to a search engine that ensures they get listed – some sites submit a multitude of entries to ensure their prominence and to ensure that they would be found using a variety of keys (and the search engines attempt to detect such ploys).

The search engines list only a small number of the sites that are out there on the Internet. About 15% of the web sites is all that the best of the search engines manage and, as the Internet expands, the task does not get any easier.

- **Links**

Online adverts on the web are also links to the site – hypertext links. The issue of advertising web sites on portals and search engines has been discussed above (and two adverts / links for amazon.com are shown in Figure 15.2).

Links are included on a variety of other sites with a variety of deals being done. Links to online bookshops occur on, for instance, sites of professional organisations and the pages of academics. Some links are paid for, some are a mutual arrangements and there are those odd individuals who just have to share their shopping experiences with us all.

Links can be a good way of getting customers (particularly given the rather hit and miss nature of searching). A broken link that simply gives an error is not very helpful, and there are a lot of them out there on the web.

- **Personal Recommendations**

The final way of getting customers onto the site is the personal recommendation. The satisfied customer will bookmark the site, come back to the site again and recommend it to their friends (be those friends real or virtual), the Internet is like that.

15.3   The e-Shop

e-Shops come in all shapes and sizes. They range from, at the simplest end of the spectrum, a few simple web pages to highly complex sites offering a range of products and services including online ordering and payment

The simple online presence is appropriate to advertise a facility such as a bed and breakfast establishment or the services of a local tradesman or craftsman. The issue of helping people find the site is much more important than the facilities on the site; links from the local tourist information site or some sort of professional register of tradesmen can be important.

The full service e-Store needs an extensive range of facilities; these include:

- Company information, frequently asked questions and customer support facilities;
- Customer registration and online mailing of customers with information / special offers tailored to be relevant to customer interests;

- Dynamic web sites integrated with product databases and possibly providing individual customisation;
- Site indexes, search facilities, etc.;
- Online order entry and payment systems;
- Sophisticated security protection systems;
- After sales service and support;
- Feedback systems to improve the service and promote a community of users.

- **Online Information**

Trust is an issue on the Internet and it is not an issue that is likely to go away. One element of this issue is knowing that an e-Commerce site is a bona-fide trader and not just a scam. Part of the reassurance is having a known brand name and trading record. Further elements are:

- A site that gives a professional image.
- The inclusion of company information on the web site.

Company information lets the potential online shopper know what sort of outfit the e-Shop is (or represents). The information can include a company profile, summaries of annual reports, messages from a director, etc. All of this does not prove that a site is genuine but it has been shown that it reassures potential customers.

- **Customer Registration**

e-Commerce customers have to give their suppliers details about themselves; a name and address are a minimum requirement if goods are to be delivered. This, and more, information would be required if the customer were to open a bank account or purchase an insurance policy but it is not information that we normally provide when we buy cornflakes at a conventional grocer or some light reading at a station bookshop. The provision of information to the online vendor raises a number of privacy issues, these include:

- Will the information be put to further uses after this sale? Will the customer be e-Mailed with further offers and updates; will the details be sold onto other organisations and is it possible to stop the further use of this information?
- Will the e-Vendor compile a profile of the customer's purchases and what use would be made of such a profile?
- Is the information secure? Can unauthorised users hack into the vendor's system and modify or steal the information?

The context in which the e-Commerce vendor asks for this information is also important. The e-Commerce site can require:

- Customer registration prior to using the site;
- Customer details only when an order is placed and the information is needed.

Prior registration of customers can allow the site to be customised to that user's needs and it facilitates the building of a marketing database by the e-Vendor. Prior registration does, however, annoy or scare away many potential users; they don't want to go through the hassle and invasion of privacy involved in registration before they make a purchase.

- **Site Navigation**

Large complex web sites (and some smaller ones) can be slow to download, difficult to navigate and, horror of horrors, contain erroneous hypertext links. Good site design and intuitive site navigation are vital:

> 'if a site is not designed with usability in mind, people will be frustrated with the site. People that are frustrated with the site don't bookmark, don't buy, don't revisit, and won't tell other people about the site."

> (Rhodoes, 1999)

Site navigation is aided by:

- A site index, preferably accessible from every page;
- A site search engine;
- Logical sequencing of facilities with clear links to the next stage in any process.

Great care needs to be take in site design. An e-Commerce site must aim to appeal to the experienced user and to be readily accessible to the novice.

- **Product Database**

e-Commerce sites sell a variety of products and the layout and technical design can be similarly varied.

At its simplest an e-Commerce catalogue can be hard coded in HTML. The web site contains a series of product descriptions, prices and possibly a picture of each product. Such a hard coded HTML page is simple and can be effective. The drawback to such a page is its inflexibility; any change to the product catalogue requires a change to the HTML and a re-release of the page.

Many e-Commerce applications require a more sophisticated provision than the fixed format HTML page. The need for something different arises where there is a rapid change to the product details, there is perceived to be a need to use a common data source for the e-Store and the back office function and for services that are specified in response to customer demands. These type of requirements need the integration of database systems into the e-Shop and the construction of the web page 'on the fly'. Two examples of where this integration is required are:

- The Online Bookshop requires a catalogue of books that it is prepared to supply; for the larger bookstores this is not just the books that are in stock but also those it can order as and when a customer requires them. This database of books needs regular updating as new books are published, old books withdrawn, prices change, etc. In addition to these changes in data the bookshop will have a number of different formats for displaying the information on a book. The book search requires a summary of the book, mapped onto a page with details of the other books that met those search criteria. From the book search the user can select full details of the book and for that a second format is required. Overall it is not a job for hard coded HTML; the catalogue will be held and updated on a database and that data will be mapped to the appropriate screen format at run-time.

- The Airline Website needs to integrate its site with its airline seat booking system. For a scheduled airline the product is specified by a combination of departure point, destination, date, time and ticket type; there is no simple list of discrete products – the number of possible combinations is vast. To sell an airline seat, to make a booking, the site needs to collect this information from the customer, look it up in the booking system and construct a web page setting out relevant options and availability. Again this is not a job to be hard coded in HTML. Airline booking systems are large complex systems serving a host of online users and an airline will need a sophisticated web site if it is to successfully integrate the front end and back end of the system.

Bookshops and airlines are just two examples of systems where the web system and backroom business systems / database systems have to be integrated. e-Shops which want to emulate the facilities of the leading online bookshops will need to match them for technical sophistication. The provision of online services such as e-Banking, e-Insurance and e-Sharedealing need to integrate web systems and business systems in much the same way as the airlines do if they are to provide a meaningful service.

- **Online Orders**

The most common analogy on a web site is a shopping basket in the UK and a shopping cart in the US (will the UK move to a shopping trolley as e-Commerce volumes grow?).

Fig. 15.4 Baskets and Carts at Amazon.

In e-Shops selling tangible goods, the customer is invited to browse round the shop, select goods and put them in their basket. On a good site the contents of the basket can be inspected at any time, the total value of the goods is shown and any of the goods can be 'returned to the shelves' if the customer decides against the purchase.   Once satisfied the customer proceeds (electronically) to the checkout.

In a service site such as an airline, the search process, indicated above, is also the shopping process. The site displays available flights and prices and the customer will choose, change the search or go elsewhere.

The checkout involves filling in a form. The form filling is reduced for customers who have pre-registered and have not subsequently lost their passwords. To pay the customer has to provide a credit card number and for delivery the name and address. Often the e-Vendor will want to get more details for marketing purposes. Further issues concerning payment are discussed at Section 15.4.

- **Payment, Delivery and After Sales**

These three functions are discussed separately below (see Sections 15.4, 15.5 and 15.6 respectively).

15.4   Online Payments

Goods and services bought using the web have to be paid for and, given the transaction is online, cash will not do.

For a retail transaction, the norm is that the payment is made at the time of purchase coincident with the exchange of goods. The retailer takes cash, cheque or a credit / debit card as payment and the customer takes the goods. This simultaneous exchange of value gives both parties reasonable confidence in, what is normally, a 'casual' trade exchange. It contrasts with many business to business transactions which are part of an ongoing trade relationship and where credit is given; the despatch of the goods takes place first and payment is made later after an invoice is received.

To replicate retail trade exchanges online there needs to be a way of transferring value electronically. The ways of paying for e-Commerce transactions can be classified as:

- Credit Cards
- Debit Cards
- Stored Value Cards
- e-Cash
- Delayed Payments

And it is noted that while online payments give reasonable assurance to the vendor that payment is being made there is no equivalent assurance to the customer that the goods or service will be delivered and will be of acceptable quality.

- **Credit Cards**

The most common way of paying for an e-Commerce transaction is with a credit card. The customer types the card number, expiry date and billing address on the order form and the vendor can verify the details and be confident of payment.

Credit Cards used in a conventional retail application are recorded on a transaction slip and verified by the use of a signature. In addition to this, credit card companies allow for 'customer not present' (CNP) transactions. CNP transactions were initially used for telephone ordering and the same facility has been adopted for e-Commerce payments.

There is a general concern that CNP transactions are less secure than the conventional use of credit cards; there is no signature that can be checked and no possibility of assessing if the customer gives the impression of being genuine. Concerns for the security of online credit card payments include:

- Fraudulent Use of Credit Cards:
  Fraudulent use of a credit card in a shop requires the possession of the card, fraudulent use online only needs the card and account holder details. The credit card company can carry out checks that the transaction 'seems reasonable' and there is an audit trail of the use of the card in the vendor's records but the system can be and is abused.

- Interception of Credit Card Details:
  Credit card details sent over the Internet could be intercepted. The card details travel over a public access network, very possibly the transmission travels via a number of nodes and there is the possibility of abuse by hackers. Credit card details obtained by hackers could then be used fraudulently, as outlined above.

  The possibility of interception has been an area of considerable concern and can be addressed by making the transmission secure, normally by encryption, see Section 15.7.

- Remote Storage of Credit Card Details:
  Many e-Commerce sites that require registration also retain credit card details on their system. Doubtless it is convenient for customers to make further purchases using a PIN and without having to send the credit card

details again but there is the risk that someone else might use that account or hack into the system and get the card details. Many sites that retain credit card details enhance the security of their customer details by firewall systems and encryption of the data.

Processing a credit card transaction involves some expense and there are also charges levied on the vendor by the credit card companies – credit card transactions, as in conventional shops, do not make sense for small transactions. The credit card payment is also traceable and is therefore not suitable for a transaction where the customer may wish to remain anonymous.

- **Debit Cards**

Debit cards / cash cards can be used for e-Commerce transactions in much the same way as a credit card. Fewer sites offer the facility to use debit cards and arguably the debit card offers less security than the more commonly used credit card. Debit cards are also not appropriate for very small transactions and do not afford anonymity.

- **Stored Value Cards**

One of the most common forms of electronic payments is the stored value card; the most widespread use of this technology is the telephone card that is available for use in public call boxes. Further uses of this technology are in some public transport operations and, for instance, for prepayment of usage on laser printers at universities or on portable telephones.

On a more general scale, there have been a number of schemes to promote stored value cards as a replacement for cash – the electronic purse. Mondex is one such scheme that has been trialed in a number of countries including the UK. These schemes for general purpose stored value cards have not proved to be popular; whatever the other advantages and disadvantages it would seem that the general public is reasonably happy with good, old-fashioned cash.

Stored value cards could be used for e-Commerce, it would be (or could be) anonymous and would be suitable for fairly small payments. Any such use in e-Commerce would probably be dependant upon the general acceptance of stored value cards and there is no evidence that this is about to happen. It would also require that the customer's terminal was fitted with the appropriate card reader and the French experience with Minitel's suggests that the customer would not wish to pay for such a device.

- **e-Cash**

The online equivalent of a stored value card is e-Cash or network money. The system operates by the user transferring money from a credit card or bank account into an e-Cash account. The e-Cash can then be used to make payment for e-Commerce transactions.

The advantage of the system is that it can be operated cheaply as the whole operation of the system is on the net. The system can, or could, be used for very small payments (micro-payments). The system can also be anonymous if that is of relevance. There is an obvious security risk but the intention would be that e-Cash accounts would store limited sums and any loss would be an annoyance rather than a disaster (like loosing the change from your pocket as opposed to loosing your credit card).

The problem with e-Cash systems is that there is no one system that is generally accepted. There is little point in having an e-Cash account if that currency is not accepted in the shops that you visit. It is not clear that if there were a generally accepted e-Cash scheme the public would use it; they might but the acceptance of e-Cash has much in common with stored value cards and that has not yet caught on except for very specific purposes.

- **Delayed Payments**

The final option is to pay off-line. A number of sites, seeking to reassure customers who are uncertain about the security of online payments, will accept credit card details by telephone or fax or cheques through the post. It is obviously not a preferred option as the transaction has to be stored and released for delivery once the payment is received. It causes extra work for the e-Vendor and delay for the customer.

Overall it seems that credit cards are likely to continue as the preferred means of payment for medium to large amounts. Processing costs and service charges are between (say) 3% to 5% of any transaction but that is an overhead that retailers, conventional and electronic have had to accept. It is noted that credit card companies have attempted to increase charges for retailers that only trade online and that can be a problem for new enterprises seeking to start an online business.

15.5   Delivering the Goods

Internet e-Commerce allows the user to order what they want, when they want but then they have to wait until the postman arrives. That can be OK but it is not so helpful if the requirement is for a cinnamon, blueberry bagel for breakfast or a book for an essay due of Friday.

The delivery system for e-Commerce purchases has to depend on the size of the product, its nature, urgency and the distance that packet will have to travel. Examples of delivery systems are:

- Post: The post is relatively cheap, reasonably rapid and is useful for small packets of non-perishable products; books and CDs are ideal products for posting. For the customer, there is no requirement to wait in for the delivery – the packet can, in most instances, be simply posted through the letter box. It has been said that you can sell anything online provided it will fit through a letter box.

- Packet: Call them parcels or call them packets, there are a variety of organisations that provide a home delivery parcel service. Packed delivery services are not that cheap and if next day delivery is required then there is a premium rate to pay. Like post they are essentially for reasonably robust types of merchandise, computer equipment could be one example Delivery can be problematic; if the customer is not at home then the delivery service (should) take the packet back to the depot, an extra hassle for those who are rarely at home.

- Local Delivery: The idea that all e-Commerce can be conducted from a central warehouse with minimum overheads starts to break down when it comes to perishable (and possibly very bulky) goods.

    Food sales are a case in point.   To provide an online grocery service there will have to be a local depot and a local delivery; currently where such a service is provided that local depot is a conventional supermarket and the e-Commerce service rides on the back of the infrastructure and logistics (including EDI) that are in place to run that store. Also, as the quote says, the groceries cannot just be dumped on the doorstep and the online customers are normally asked to agree a time slot when they will be at home to take delivery; not an arrangement that would suit everyone (particularly if the slot convenient to the customer is already fully booked. An interesting alternative, apparently already in use in the Boston area is for the customers to have a safebox with a refrigerator compartment and for the supplier to hold the combination or key so that the goods can be safely delivered when the householder is out (Cope 1996).

    A second issue with local delivery is cost. There is no real savings to an e-Commerce retailer of groceries that can be offset against the costs of picking, packing and delivery.   The consensus among UK food retailers is that delivery charges will need to be at least £5 (US$8) for a home delivery service to break even. Groceries are a cost sensitive item in many budgets and many shoppers are looking for special offers, not extra charges – time will tell how many customers want to take on this delivery package.

- Collect your Own: An alternative to local delivery, that is suggested, is for the customer to collect their own goods. The produce is ordered electronically, paid for online, picked and packed by the vendor but then the customer picks it up at the local depot or supermarket – cuts out the queues at the checkout and the customer only has the local traffic jam to cope with.

One application suggested for the collect your own is with the online bookshop. The books could be ordered online but collected from the local branch of the book retailer without the imposition of delivery charges. A possible competitive advantage for those online retailers that also run conventional bookstores as opposed to Amazon.com which does not.

- Electronic Delivery: The one way to not only order what you want, when you want but also get it when you want is electronic delivery. A lot of software is sold online and downloaded with savings in packaging, distribution costs and time for both the supplier and the customer. It is suggested that music and books have the same potential but it does increase the risk to the copyright and the result is a product that is not quite the same.

- No delivery: The final category is for those intangibles where there is no need for delivery. An insurance policy bought online can be confirmed there and then; airline tickets can be substituted by an e-Ticket, etc. There are security implications that were perhaps not present with the traditional ways of contracting for services but these electronic replacements are achieving an increased acceptance.

Overall the issue of delivery of electronically purchased goods is somewhat problematic – there are issues of cost and issues of trust. A tendency of strategic information systems has been to transfer tasks to the customers of the system. Inter-organisational systems achieve this trick and many Internet e-Commerce systems can achieve similar savings for the order and payment stages of the trade cycle. However, for the delivery stage of the trade cycle the task of delivery is transferred from the retail customer to the vendor and the vendor generally finds it necessary to recoup those costs as delivery charges. These charges can wipe out any discounts that the e-Vendor is offering; this is often the case, for example, with online bookshops.

15.6   After-Sales Service

The Internet can have considerable advantages in the area of after sales. A good web site can provide excellent product information and diagnostic support; both Microsoft and SUN are renowned for this aspect of their websites (arguably these are more aimed at the corporate customers than the retail customers who are the focus of this chapter).

The advantages of the Internet over conventional manuals and postal updates are:

- No printing costs;
- Material is readily corrected and updated;
- Hyperlink indexes and search facilities can be provided;
- No mailing costs;
- For software, bug fixes and updates can be downloaded.

These advantages are particularly applicable in the computing and software field where access to the internet is fairly readily available (it is noted that online instructions on how to switch on the computer or what to do if the computer breaks down are somewhat problematic). These advantages could apply in other sectors, electrical goods could be an example, but the manufacturers are not sensibly able to expect their customers for these categories of goods to be online.

The other aspect of after sales is when things go wrong; the new shirt that falls apart at the seams or the electric heater that expires with a puff of blue smoke the first time it is used. When these problems occur with goods bought in a conventional shop you take them back; it is not necessarily pleasant or convenient but it can be done and there is a person there to whom the problem can be explained. For goods bought online (as is the case with any direct sales channel) the goods have to be wrapped up and posted off to the supplier. Doubtless many online suppliers are very good in dealing with such problems but it seems more problematic, and there is nobody available to shout at!

15.7   Internet e-Commerce Security

There are numerous threats to the security of Internet e-Commerce, some of them already alluded to in this chapter. Security breaches are most frequently discussed in terms of the Internet and the danger that hackers will intercept messages, misuse the information or modify the content of the message. The internet is only one potential source of insecurity; further elements of the problem are:

- The customer side where a customer can be impersonated, with or without the use of the customer's equipment. The use of stolen credit card details is the simplest example.
- The vendor side where the vendor can trade inappropriately or dishonestly. Problems can range from customer details being stolen from the vendors files to bogus traders who set-up online and take money with no intention of supplying the advertised goods or services.

The security issues, across the network and at both ends, fall into a number of categories. Henning (1997, quoted in Rebel and Koenig, 1999) identified four pillars of secure e-Commerce:

- Authentication: The sender of a document must be identified precisely and without any possibility of fraud;

- Confidentiality: The contents of a message may not be scanned by unauthorised parties;
- Integrity: Changes made in messages without according remarks must be impossible;
- Non-Repudiation: The sender of a message is directly connected to the contents of the message (and the recipient cannot deny that the message was received).

These four pillars tend to emphasise network security but with appropriate interpretation can cover all of the issues involved. Some of the solutions to these issues are:

- **Encryption**

Encryption is the conversion of data into a code so that it cannot be read by unauthorised users. The data is converted into the code by the sender and then decoded by the receiver. Hopefully only the sender and the receiver know the rules for encoding and decoding and thus nobody else can read the message.

Modern encryption methods use an encryption algorithm and a binary number that is the key. Using a secret key system, only the sender and the receiver of the message know the key; the problem is, of course, keeping that key secret, particularly for an application such as e-Commerce with thousands of users involved. The alternative approach is the public key / private key system. The public key is used to encrypt the message and can be made available to anyone. The private key is used to decode the message and is only known to the recipient of the message. Secret key systems have the advantage that encoding and decoding is much quicker than the public key systems.

For Internet e-Commerce the leading encryption method is *Secure Sockets Layer* (SSL), developed by Netscape, using a combination of both public and private key encryption. The stages are:

- The vendor transmits the public key (ka) to the intending customer's web browser – if the key is intercepted it does not matter.
- The customer's browser generates a secret key (kc) for the session.
- The customer's browser encrypts the secret key (kc), using the public key (ka) that it has just received, and transmits it to the vendor.
- The vendor decodes the message using a private key (kb) and now has the secret key (kc).
- Further interchanges between the customer's browser and the vendor's server can now be encoded and decoded using the secret key (kc).

The use of encryption should meet the requirement for confidentiality and goes a long way to ensure integrity; a hacker cannot make meaningful (fraudulent) changes to a message if the message cannot be deciphered.

Security is not only important on the network but it is also important to preserve the integrity of customer details, including credit card details, held by the e-Vendor. Encryption of the details on the vendor's server is an important way of ensuring this security.

- **Digital Signatures**

A digital signature is used to authenticate the sender of the message and to check that the integrity of the message, i.e. that it has not been altered in transit.

The authentication element requires a digital ID, also known as a digital certificate, that is issued by a third party certification authority. The digital ID is sent with the message and is designed to verify the identity of the sender. Digital signatures plainly need to be encrypted when they are delivered from the certification authority and when they are used in a message.

The integrity of the message is ensured by a hash function of the contents of the message. The hashing algorithm is applied in the sender's system and included as part of the digital signature of the message. On receipt of the message the hash algorithm is applied again and a match of the two hash totals shows that the message has not been tampered with. Again, as with the digital ID element the signature, the hash total would normally be encrypted.

Digital signatures are, in terms of transmission authentication and integrity very secure. Some countries have put in place legislation that accepts that a digital signature is valid as authentication of a contract. The problem arises in cross border transactions where legal and technical provisions for digital signatures may not be compatible. The digital signature is also insecure as, in reality, it identifies the sending system and not the person it purports to authenticate; an unauthorised use of the system can potentially misuse another person's digital signature.

- **Trusted Third Parties**

If authentication, confidentiality and integrity have been dealt with, that leaves non-repudiation. The way to deal with this issue is to also transmit a copy of the transaction to a third party, trusted by both sides, and where the record of the transaction could be used to settle any disputes; obviously for this purpose the message would require a digital signature to verify its source.

Trusted third parties have been much talked about and are used to record some commercial transactions. Arguably the use of a provision such as this is a bit excessive for a transaction such as buying a book or a football jersey.

- **Good old fashioned Fraud**

All the provision for encryption, digital signatures and trusted third parties does nothing to prevent:

- The use of a stolen credit card or credit card details;
- The setting up of a fraudulent web site by a bogus trader.

There is no technical quick fix to the fraudulent use of credit cards in e-Commerce and there is a suggestion of an added problem of some e-Customers using their own cards online and then denying that they made the transaction.

Similarly there is no technical quick fix to the problem of bogus web sites. There is advice that customers should stick to well known brands (and that would suit those brands). There are proposals for schemes to issue certificates to reputable online traders. Such schemes may well help but the fraudsters will quickly find the obvious ways round.

- **Example**

Amazon.com has been put forward as a model for the way to deal with security and for the reassurance they give their customers. They start from the good position of being both a well known brand and the best known e-Commerce brand. Their web page has a section on e-Commerce security which, at the time of writing, included:

- Reassurance that all personal data, including credit card numbers, is encrypted for transmission over the Internet.
- The option to enter only part of the credit card number online and then ring in to give the rest of the number.
- A guarantee that if ever there was fraud arising from a transaction with Amazon that they would refund the part of the loss that is not covered by the credit card provider.
- A statement on their policy on the privacy and use of customer data.

It can be, and is, argued that online trade is no less secure than conventional trade. This is particularly true in the case of credit card fraud where any retailers can keep and misuse the customers credit card details when a credit sale is processed. Whatever the truth of the argument, people feel particularly vulnerable in e-Commerce transactions. In e-Commerce there is not a salesperson there with whom one might think one has a bond of trust, there are no bricks and mortar to which one can return to complain and there is no simultaneous exchange of value; you pay now and hopefully get the goods later. The Internet / e-Commerce community would like to persuade the customers that there is a technical fix for this (and any other) problem but there is not; technologies, such as those outlined in this section do help, but they can never cover all aspects of the Internet e-Commerce security problem. Security is a vital issue for e-Commerce as is shown by all the attitude surveys on the issue. e-Commerce users have decided to trust the system for at least some purchases with some vendors but there are a lot of potential users that are not prepared to give that trust. There is a steady drip, drip of horror stories in the media and from friends and acquaintances that reinforce the opinion of the wary and, almost whatever the industry does, those stories and that mistrust is not going to go away.

15.8   A Web Site Evaluation Model

Figure 15.5 shows an e-Commerce evaluation model developed by Ian Hersey in a project supervised by the author.   The model was subsequently tested by evaluating a number of airline web sites (Hersey, 1999; Whiteley, *et al.*, 1999a).

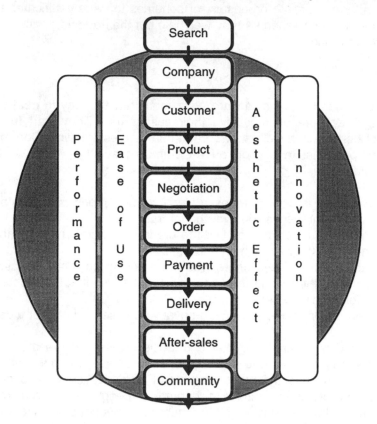

Fig. 15.5 Web Site Evaluation Model.

The model is designed to evaluate e-Commerce web sites but it also serves as a checklist of the issues to be dealt with when an e-Commerce site is designed and implemented.   To evaluate a web site using the model the following statements should be assessed.

- Company Information: The web site gives me all the information a person could reasonably require on the company before undertaking an e-Commerce transaction.
- Customer Information: The requirements to provide customer information are appropriate and there is good reassurance about the security and use of the information.

- Product Information: The web site contains all the product information which a person could reasonably require before undertaking an e-Commerce transaction.
- Negotiation: The web site allows all the customisation of the product / price that the user could reasonably expect.
- Order: The web site provides as comprehensive a range of options for ordering the product or service as could reasonably be expected by the user.
- Payment: The web site provides as good a range of payment options as could reasonably be expected.
- Delivery: The web site provides as wide a selection of delivery options as could reasonably be expected which are generally satisfactory, convenient and reassuring.
- After-sales Service: Overall the after-sales customer support service on offer is excellent.
- Aesthetic Effect: Overall the web site is aesthetically pleasing.
- Performance: Overall the site loaded quickly and operated without error.
- Ease of Use: Overall the site was extremely easy to navigate and to use.
- Innovation: The web site is extremely innovative.
- Community: The web site is excellent at fostering community among its customers.

A simple approach to evaluation is to assess the statements on a five point Likert scale:

1	2	3	4	5
Strongly Disagree	Disagree	Neutral	Agree	Strongly Agree

If it is felt appropriate, the scores for each aspect can be added up to compute overall usability rating for the site. Note that there is no statement for assessing the Search factor. Search is outside the site and dependent upon the search engine and the search term that is used, too many variables for the assessment approach outlined above.

Exercises

An underlying theme of this chapter is that while Internet e-Commerce might be a very attractive facility to many customers it does not solve all shopping problems for everyone that might use it. There are two exercises given and both reflect this theme.

1. Select two categories of goods, for example groceries and books and list the advantage and disadvantages to you of ordering these products online. The lists can be compared across a group of students and the differences analysed.

2. Use the Web Site Evaluation Model and the associated questions from Section 15.7 to evaluate a couple of web sites. For this evaluation use two web sites from the same sector, possibly one of the sectors used in Exercise 1. Compare the results of the two evaluations and compute an overall score for each of the sites.

Further Reading

A useful overview of payments for e-Commerce Services is provided in the following chapter in an edited book:

> Lee B. (1998) 'Payment for Goods and Services in an Information Age', in Romm C. and Sudweeks F. (eds), *Doing Business Electronically: A Global Perspective of Electronic Commerce*, Springer, London, pp. 163–73.

And the follow-up book from the same editors tackles e-Commerce security (although much of the chapter concentrates on the electronic signature aspect of the topic):

> Rebel T. and Koenig W. (1999) 'Ensuring Security and Trust in Electronic Commerce', in Romm C. and Sudweeks F. (eds), *Doing Business on the Internet: Opportunities and Pitfalls*, Springer, London, pp. 101–12.

Also look at the security section of one or two well known online brands, the web page for the book includes suggested sites.

16

e-Business

Summary

This chapter looks at the use of Internet e-Commerce and evaluates its application and potential across a number of trade sectors.

Despite the development of Internet e-Commerce and the hype that surrounds it, the amount of business done online as a proportion of all retail sales remains stubbornly small. This chapter looks at e-business applications and, through the use of mini case studies, examines the scope of e-Business on the Internet and the factors that lead to a successful retail web operation.

16.1. Introduction

Consumer Internet e-Commerce uses a single set of technologies.   The infrastructure for an e-Shop selling books is essentially the same as is used for the online sale of airline tickets.   The important differences between e-Commerce applications are how they fit into the consumer market, how they are supported by the supply chain and their potential to alter the role of players in that supply chain. These essential components of the business structure are shown in Figure 16.1.

Fig. 16.1 e-Vendor Business Links.

Consumer Internet e-Commerce facilities, an e-Shop, may be set up by:

- A new entrant to an existing market;
- An existing player in the market using the Internet to develop a new sales channel.

New entrants to the market have the potential to threaten the market position of existing players but they have to build up expertise to support their operations. Existing players in a market may respond to the new entrant by sharpening up their conventional retail act or by setting up a competing online channel; the latter course of action adds to the threat to their investment in the conventional distribution channel.

The e-Commerce applications also need an effective supply infrastructure; the online purchaser is not going to be impressed by lines that are out-of-stock or goods that take forever to arrive. An existing retailer has supply chain arrangements that have been built up and tuned over time. The new entrant to the market has to match this efficiency by quickly setting up similar arrangements or developing an alternative infrastructure that better meets the needs of its way of conducting business.

A number of contrasting sectors are examined in this chapter. These sectors exemplify the range of consumer e-Commerce services that are available. The chosen sectors are:

- Bookshops;
- Grocery Supplies;
- Software Supplies and Support;
- Electronic Newspapers;
- Banking;
- Auctions;
- Share Dealing;
- Gambling.

16.2   Internet Bookshops

- **General Description**

One of the first applications of e-Commerce on the net was the Internet Bookshop. The story is that Jeff Bezos, when he decided to set up an online business, sat down to work out what he could sell online and decided it was books – the result was amazon.com.   Books, as an item of merchandise, have four significant advantages for the online retailer:

- They can, in most cases, be adequately described online. They are not like clothes that the customer might wish to try on or bananas where the customer could want to check the size and ripeness.
- They are moderately priced – expensive enough to make the transaction worthwhile but not so expensive that the transaction exacerbates customer fears about online payments.
- Many customers are prepared to wait for the goods to arrive (and there is often a similar wait for books ordered through a conventional bookshop).

- Delivery is manageable. Postal / small packet services can be used at reasonable prices and the customer does not have to be at home to receive the goods; they can be posted through the customer's letter box.

The start-up and subsequent success (in terms of growth and sales volume) of Amazon came as something of a shock to conventional booksellers. The shock was in terms of loss of sales but also the discount pricing of Amazon that threatened existing pricing structures within the book trade. The reaction of other players in the book trade has been threefold:

- Defensive reaction by large traditional players that set up their own e-Bookstores; Barns and Noble in the US is one such example (and in setting up an online alternative, the existing player adds to the threat to their investment in conventional trade outlets).
- Competitive reaction by new operators in the field who have copied Amazon's initiative; bol.com is one such example in Europe and the UK. Some new entrants have been aggressive in their advertising and pricing, displacing Amazon adverts on some portals and pushing them to increasing their discounts.
- Enhancements of conventional bookshop offerings; many multiple book retailers have made considerable investments in their conventional bookshops converting them into, what could be termed, book emporiums. Apparently the conventional book retailers don't intend to let the online vendors have it all their own way.

The advent of retail e-Commerce customer interfaces has not altered the supply chain arrangements of the book trade. Bookshops have two main sources of supply:

- Book wholesalers (and it is Amazon's relationship with a large wholesaler in Seattle that, arguably, made their operation possible). Wholesalers tend to deal more with 'popular' books than with specialist or academic requirements.
- Direct supply from the publisher, either from a sales representative or using direct ordering (direct ordering is typically via EDI, e.g. TeleOrdering in the UK).

The book trade supply chain is summarised in Figure 16.2.

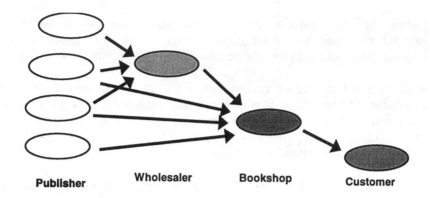

Publisher   **Wholesaler**   **Bookshop**   **Customer**

Fig. 16.2 The Book Trade Supply Chain.

In competitive terms the Internet bookshop has the advantage that it does not have to maintain expensive retail premises and the staff that go with such an operation. A warehouse operation where the customer does the data entry is cheaper to operate although the IT infrastructure is an additional expense.   The major disadvantage for the online bookshop is that the customer does not collect the product and delivery has to be paid for. The exact balance of the equation is not clear.   The online retailers do discount but the high headline discounts are concentrated on a few best-sellers and many books are sold at the publisher's recommended price. Also the online retailer, seemingly, need to pay for promotion to a greater degree than their conventional competitors. The online only retailers, at the time of writing, are all making substantial losses.

The large online bookstores need a sophisticated web site, both to attract and retain the attention of their customers and to ensure the efficiency of their backroom operations. The facilities of the online bookshop may include:

- A large database of books. The details available for display include a picture of the cover, description of the book, price and possibly customer reviews;
- A search engine for author, title, subject, etc.;
- Details of stock and hence an accurate picture of delivery times (this is, for example, provided by Blackwells which also has a wholesale function and thus has access to this data);
- Software to record the readers interest and to suggest other titles that might also appeal;
- Integration into the supply chain, e.g. facilities to send EDI orders to the publisher (again this is a feature of the design on the Blackwell's online bookstore).

The system has to be up-to-date, robust and comprehensive.

- **Noteworthy Sites**

Large online bookshops include:

- Amazon   www.amazon.com, www.amazon.co.uk
- Barnes and Noble www.barnsandnoble.com
- Bertetsmann AG   www.bol.com
- Blackwell   www.bookshop.blackwell.co.uk
- Chapters   www.chapters.ca

There are also a large number of sites for bookshops dealing with specialist interests; these sites are much smaller and tend to have fewer features than the major online bookstores.

   Some online bookshops have been merged, re-named or gone out of business. Some of the sites listed may not be available at the time of reading; see also the book web site.

- **Case Study**

amazon.com

TM

Amazon opened for business in July '95. Amazon was a new start-up business and its founder Jeffrey Bezos had no previous experience of the book trade. As indicated above, the basic decision was to start an online retailing company; the decision to retail books was based on an assessment of which types of merchandise were suited to online selling.

   Amazon started in Seattle and the company worked in close association with a large book wholesaler that was also located in the city. Expansion has been rapid and by 1999 Amazon had four despatch bases in the US and further operations in Germany and the UK; each European operation has its own web site.

   As of 1998, Amazon's turnover was US$610 million, a growth of 313% over the previous year. In its four year of existence Amazon has never made a profit; the loss for the third quarter of 1999 was US$79 million on sales of US$356 million. The trend in growth and the inability to make a profit both seem set to continue for a number of years.

   In 1997, Amazon sold shares in the company. The shares quickly rose to dizzying heights (as did shares in a number of other Internet based companies). The market valuation of these and other Internet shares is not a reflection of the turnover or profit record of the company; there is an expectation of the rapid development of online markets and a feeling that 'first movers' will be uniquely positioned to exploit this potential.

   Amazon is certainly intending to exploit its position as an Internet trader. Amazon has diversified into selling recorded music, videos and, more recently, electronic equipment. Amazon are also buying into, or linking up with, other online traders, such as pet supplies, groceries, pharmaceuticals, and the auction house Sotheby's.

- **Comment**

Online bookshops have garnered a substantial part of the bookmarket in the US and other developed countries look set to follow suit. The extent of the market penetration that this electronic sales channel will eventually achieve is difficult to predict, a ball-park figure of 20% has been suggested in some reports and this is possibly a realistic figure.

As has already been discussed, the online book trade is fiercely competitive. At the time of writing the game plan is to achieve market share as opposed to profitability; a strategy that is encouraged by stock valuations of Internet traders that measure such companies on the number of customers rather than the more conventional measures.

Online traders such as Amazon that do not have conventional sales operations are looking to diversify into other online markets. The other online traders that do have their own bookshop chain are looking to make their online facility complement their bookshops; ordering online and then picking up the books from the store is one approach to keeping costs down.

16.3   Grocery Supplies

- **General Description**

Going to the supermarket for many people is just a chore, often the time they can go is the time everyone else can go. The car park is crowded, the aisles are jammed, the queues at the checkout stretch out for miles and then the goods have to be unloaded onto the checkout, reloaded into bags, loaded into the car, taken into the house and loaded yet again into the refrigerator and the cupboards. How much easier if one could call up the home page of the friendly local supermarket, a few clicks of the mouse and the weekly shop is done.

The online supermarket is set up to meet the needs of those who cannot get to the supermarket or those who do not want to go. It is an updated version of the many home delivery services that existed 40 years ago and have been in gradual decline ever since.

The online supermarket works much like any other shop. The customer logs in and selects the groceries that are required. The staff pick the goods, pack and despatch them. That said, the logistics are a bit different from other online stores:

- Selecting Goods: The typical food supermarket carries a product range of several thousand items and a customer may well select (say) 60 of them on a weekly shopping trip. This is a task that can take some time and the online supermarket tries to help with facilities such as an online

shopping list.
- Delivering Goods: Groceries are both bulky and perishable and leaving them outside the back door is not necessarily appropriate. Common practice for home delivery is to arrange a delivery slot with the customer, delivery within a specified two hour period and to make a small charge for delivery.

In the UK most of the large supermarkets have started online shopping services. There is strong competition between UK supermarkets and possibly the rollout of online shopping is more to do with a need not to be seen to be falling behind than a great enthusiasm for the new channel. In the UK, the first food retailer with a (modern) home delivery service was Iceland, a frozen food chain that also does general groceries. The Iceland home delivery service does have a web connection but the main method of access is telephone ordering and a sizeable number of the customers are senior citizens who have a problem getting to the shop but are readily available at home to receive deliveries.

In the US, one of the pioneers of online groceries has been Peapod, a software company; they have set-up the online facility and have found other organisations to stock and deliver the groceries. Amazon have also recently joined in with their Homestore brand offering its services in selected locations.

The logistics of the online grocery business are very different from the e-Bookstore. A warehouse in Seattle can do nation-wide (or even world-wide) delivery of books but would not be appropriate for general grocery supplies. The home delivery grocery business requires local depots and it needs the same supply chain infrastructure, co-ordinated by EDI, that the supermarkets have in place. The organisations that have the infrastructure to enter this business are the existing food supermarkets; the only part of their facility that is not entirely appropriate is the retail store which is a much more lavish facility than would be required in a purpose built, home delivery depot.

The supply chain of the home delivery grocery operation is diagrammatically very similar to the bookshop; a vital difference is that supply has to be from a local depot rather than a central warehouse. The supply chain is shown at Figure 16.3.

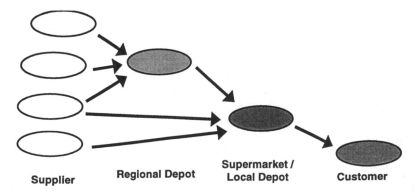

Supplier   Regional Depot   Supermarket / Local Depot   Customer

Fig. 16.3 The Supermarket / Grocery Trade Supply Chain.

It is noted that there are a number of online suppliers of specialist food products. These operators work with a limited product range of specialist products at premium prices. These operators can work from a central warehouse and use the postal / packet delivery system. Selling chocolates or wine online is a very different operation from general groceries.

- **Noteworthy Sites**

  - Peapod   www.peapod.com
  - Homestore   www.homestore.com
  - Sainsbury   www.sainsbury.co.uk
  - Tesco   www.tesco.net

- **Case Study**

Peapod started selling groceries in 1989. Peapod claim to stock a full range of groceries 'from fresh items like meat, seafood, produce and baked goods to non-perishable grocery staples' at prices comparable with those in the local store. Orders are completed by clicking the items that are required, each item has a simple entry giving its name, price and pack size.

Items can be found through the classification / menu system or using a search. Shopping lists can be stored, modified and reused which saves time for the regular shopper. Orders have to be put in at least a day in advance and with more notice if the customer needs to be sure that their required delivery time will be available; the customer has to be at home at the appointed time to receive the order. Payment can be made by most methods, excluding cash, but the customer must have a credit card to open an account. A refreshing change is that a first time user can use the store, fill the virtual shopping cart and only needs to register if they decide to take the plunge and proceed to checkout.

Peapod currently operate in six metropolitan areas in the US. Their web site quotes a prediction that 20% of US grocery shopping, by volume, will be online by 2003, possibly a little optimistic given the current stage of development.

- **Comment**

Grocery shopping has not taken off in the same way as the online bookstore and perhaps it never will; the nature of the product and the needs of the customer are intrinsically different. There are problems at every stage of the trade cycle. The issues are as follows:

- Selecting Goods: Navigating an online grocery shop takes time. Some products are difficult to locate (asking the search engine for toilet tissue will not help if the store lists the product as lavatory paper) and when selecting fresh products the customer cannot pick the reddest apples or the leanest meat. This point is reinforced by a quote from Michell of Sainsburys (one of the UK's largest supermarkets):

  'It took the customer ages to order, and they got fed up. They ended up ordering less than usual. It was too much like hard work finding things.'

  (Cowe, 1998)

- Delivering Goods: The groceries ordered online have to be picked and packed by an employee and delivered to the customer. The process takes time, costs money and mistakes can and do occur. Reid of Tesco (the UK's largest supermarket chain) is quoted as saying that groceries are:

  '... the most difficult product to deliver. Food is perishable and vulnerable as well as bulky. It cannot just be dumped on the doorstep and it cannot be returned if it does not suit.'

  (Cowe, 1998)

- After Sales: If something is wrong, an incorrect product, something is missing or there is fresh produce that is not of acceptable quality, what then? Rectifying these mistakes is not convenient for the customer and, as indicated by Reid, not very easy for the store.

The extent that Internet e-Commerce can make inroads into the grocery market will be an important indicator of the extent of the e-Commerce revolution. If Marie-Antoinette were to be around in 2010, would she order cake online or send out a servant to collect her gateaux?

16.4   Software Supplies and Support

- **General Description**

Software supplies is both a business to business market and a business to consumer market. The topic of software supplies (for the business to business market) has already been discussed in Chapter 11; it is included in this chapter as it is also a consumer market and as it contrasts with the other trade sectors discussed in this chapter.

The Internet as a channel for software sales, including computer games, has two distinct advantages:

- The customers are presumably computer literate and will be able to operate the medium.
- The product is electronic and can be delivered via the net.

The supply chain for software delivered over the net is therefore very simple. It is a straight transaction between the customer and the supplier without the need for any agent or retailer. The supply chain is shown at Figure 16.4.

Supplier

Customer

Fig. 16.4 Online Software Supply Chain.

Problem areas are the transmission times for the larger software packages (and most software seems to take up more space every time it is released) and the problems of software piracy (although, arguably, software bought online is no more likely to be pirated than software supplied on a small CD in a large box).

Another phenomenon, facilitated by the Internet, is the free software movement. Linux is the most notable product of this sector. Linux is a PC operating system that is more efficient than the equivalent product from Microsoft. Linux has a kernel developed by a young Finn when he was a student; the rest of the software in the operating system has been developed and de-bugged by an ad-hoc grouping of enthusiasts brought together via the Internet. Linux is available free to anyone who wants to use it.

- **Noteworthy Sites**

- Qualcomm / Eudora   www.eudora.com
- FAICO / DiDa   www.faico.net

- **Case Study**

TM

One example of a small software company distributing its software over the web is DiDa; its product is an HTML editor and viewer.

DiDa was one of a number of early HTML editors. Since they started some of the big software companies have got into the act with products, such as Microsoft FrontPage, that offer greater functionality than the likes of DiDa. DiDa however is still available; it advertises itself as both fast (as fast as NotePad) and small (can be run off a floppy) – it will happily run on a 286 laptop.

The system is available as a trial version for free (without time limits) and the full specification version is available as shareware. Both versions can be downloaded over the Internet.

DiDa has had a number of customers; the author is one of its users. A search of the Internet reveals a number of the sites created using DiDa; the <TITLE> tag defaults to 'Created with DiDa' and some users have not updated it with a real title for their web page and hence their pages are found using DiDa as a search key.

- **Comment**

For the larger software companies, online sales (if used) are just one sales channel and it is additional to software supplied through agents / dealers and the local computer store. For these larger companies, the real advantage in the use of the Internet is for after-sales with information, support and bug fixes being available online. Online support is used by organisations such as Microsoft, Sun and also by software suppliers for mainframe systems (see Chapter 11).

For the small software outfit, the Internet provides the only readily available marketing channel. Using the Internet, the small software company does not have to cut a CD, write a manual and get a box printed. More importantly the small software company does not have to fight to get its product stocked by retailers, it can do its own retailing on the net and it can release its product for a free trial for any customer who is not sure that the product is one that will suit them.

Small software companies using the net sometimes have a limited lifespan. Good ideas that are piloted by small software companies can be taken over by the bigboys and the originators are left out in the cold – that is unfair but then that is business (and it is good to see the likes of Linux causing some concern to Microsoft).

16.5   Electronic Newspapers

- **General Description**

The web, it is suggested, provides a new channel for news distribution that overcomes the shortcomings of both the printed newspaper and of broadcast news on radio and television. The web can give news coverage that is as up-to-date as broadcast news but has the in-depth coverage available from a serious newspaper. Further than that, the browser could be set to select the news of interest to the reader and to leave out the rest.

That is the potential but it has not yet happened, possibly it never will. The simplistic assessment given above perhaps misses out on a more complex way that news is 'consumed'. Radio and television news is often consumed while people are doing other things, eating their breakfast or driving a car; they happen in the background. Newspapers are read on the train or in the park and then may be shared with someone else. The newspaper gives the reader the chance to be selective (and that selection process is to do with moods and time in a way it would be difficult for any software to emulate).

There are a number of online newspapers available and most of them are web versions of existing newspapers. The Washington Post is the one that has, to date, received the most favourable coverage. Currently access, with a couple of exceptions, is free.

The online newspapers, it seems, are often used to look up something that has been missed in a previous issue or to look at the job advertisements, rather than being read as a newspaper. Online magazines attract some readership but they have had a hard time attracting subscriptions – there is the ethos that the net should be free and there is also a concern that the magazine might not be as good as it pretends to be or that it may not last the period of the subscription.

There is, however, a threat to conventional newspapers from the web. A large part of the revenue that pays for newspapers comes not from the cover price that the reader pays but from the money received from advertisers. The web has the potential to advertise jobs, houses and used cars at a fraction of the price of a newspaper – should the advertising of these items shift to the web then it might not be possible to buy our daily or local newspaper, at least not at a price that the public is prepared to pay.

The supply chain of the online newspaper is also much simpler than that of the paper version. No need for a midnight deadline before the papers are loaded onto lorries, delivered to wholesalers in each major town, re-packaged for delivery to newsagents and then possibly to the door by a paper boy or girl. The supply chain of the online newspaper is direct from the company to the reader's screen; see Figure 16.5.

Supplier

Customer

Fig. 16.5 Online Newspaper Supply Chain.

- **Noteworthy Sites**

  - Guardian   www.guardian.co.uk
  - New York Times   www.nytimes.com
  - Washington Post   www.washingtonpost.com

- **Case Study**

The Guardian Unlimited is an online version of the conventional print on paper version of the newspaper. The site is attractive and easy to use. Major news stories appear on the home page as a title and a single paragraph and there are similar summary pages for each of the major sections. The sections are accessed using an index on the home page. The full text of the article is accessed by clicking the relevant title; the text is the same as in the paper version. For stories that have continued over several days or weeks the summaries from previous stories are also available.

The online edition is not festooned with adverts. The news pages do have the odd banner advert and the classified job adverts can be accessed. Given access is free and there is not much advertising, it is unclear how the online edition can cover its costs. The online edition may even detract from sales, particularly in the case of the customers who buy the paper just once a week for job adverts in their professional area and who can now access these adverts online.

Statistics show that the online edition of the Guardian is being used. Katz (1999) reports a hit count of 50 to 80 thousand a day in comparison to the paper's circulation of 400 thousand a day. How much of the paper is read by its online users is not made clear.

Currently there seems to be no real indication as to why the Guardian, and other newspapers, are producing an online version. Is it to support current sales, part of a long-term strategy to move entirely online or just a marker to deter other, non-newspaper organisations, moving into its market segment? Probably it is a marker whilst everyone waits to see what will develop.

• Comment

Newspapers are both a cultural and a political institution. For many people they are part of their way of life, a relaxation on the train or bus on the way to work, a break on a Sunday morning when there is time to savour a cup of real coffee. They are also part of the political process, a forum where current affairs are considered and views are modified and moulded. They are imperfect vehicles but the zeal with which some regimes seek to repress them is an ample justification for keeping the newspaper, or something like it.

The traditional newspaper is convenient, it can be transported and read anywhere that there is light to see it. The newspaper is a superior technology, for the purpose, to any current computer technology, however portable.   The development of future technologies such as electronic paper may change that, we will have to see.

Newspapers offer diversity of political view. Most people are able to pick up a paper that suits their way of seeing the world but they are also influenced by other papers as they themselves make news. This diversity is the best system that we have but it is by no means perfect. The main newspapers are owned by press barons that can and do influence and control what is said. The progression from Hurst and Beaverbrook to Rupert Murdock is perhaps no more than a change in personnel and a move onto Bill Gates will not be an improvement but it is arguably no worse. The move to an electronic newspaper has the potential to increase diversity but there is little likelihood that it will. It will, however, be important that, if I buy my role of electronic paper and an interface device, I can use it to download whatever flavour of news I want and not just the thoughts of chairman Gates.

Overall the development of electronic newspapers is fine but not if it removes choice, and having news on paper is one of those choices. It is possible that the economics of the newspaper industry and the shift of advertising to the Internet may in a real sense deny us all that choice.

And finally a comment from Piers Morgan, editor of the Mirror (a UK national tabloid paper):

> 'The century is littered with experts claiming the death of the newspaper. Radio was to kill it, they wailed. Television will kill it, was the next cry. Now it's computers. But history will record that each new medium did not replace the existing one, it complemented it.'

> (Morgan, 1999)

However, newspaper editors don't have the greatest record on predicting the future.

16.6   Internet Banking

- **General Description**

There are times when the bank customers want to know their bank balance or make an urgent payment and a visit to a branch is not convenient; Internet banking (and telephone banking) can solve these problems. The use of the telephone or the Internet also has advantages for the bank; it reduces the cost of processing each transaction (by a factor of between 10 and 100 depending on which report you read) and has the potential to enable the bank to reduce the overhead of the branch network.

Online banking allows the customer to check their balance or pay a bill at any time of the day or night. The services offered by online banks typically include:

- Online balances and statements giving up-to-the-minute information. The statement can be used to check that any specific debit or credit has gone through;
- Credit transfers so that bills can be paid online. Included, is the facility to set up a transaction now for the bill to be paid at a later date;
- Maintenance of standing orders and direct debits.

The major service that is not provided is cash in and cash out; for this service the account holder has to leave home and visit an automatic teller machine (ATM) or a bank branch (assuming it has not been closed down).

A problem is that doing your own banking allows you to make your own mistakes and there are reports of customers sending money to the wrong account or just out into cyberspace. Banks also make mistakes but when they do it is comforting to have someone other than oneself to blame.

For online banking, security is obviously an issue. At the Bank of Scotland logging on reportedly involves a customer number, three passwords and eight different pages before the balance could be accessed; and the service needs special software downloaded onto the ᴼC. It is, of course, right that security is taken seriously but it does not necessarily make for an easy to use, or a fun, service.

The supply chain of the bank, using e-banking, reduces usage of the branch network (although a branch or ATM machine will still be required). The supply chain of the online bank is shown at Figure 16.6.

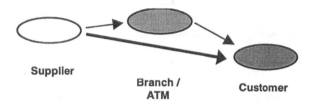

Supplier   **Branch /**   **Customer**
                       ATM

Fig. 16.6 Internet Bank Supply Chain.

- **Noteworthy Sites**

  - Bank of Scotland   www.rbs.co.uk
  - The Co-operative Bank   www.smile.co.uk
  - First National Bank of the Internet   www.fnbinternet.com

  (Obviously you will not be able to use these sites if you are customer.)

- **Case Study**

The Co-operative Bank grew out of the Co-operative movement, had strong trade union and labour movement links; it carries forward this heritage in terms of its ethical banking policies.
The Co-operative Bank is a relatively small UK bank with about two million customers and about a 5% market share. The bank has a very small branch network. Typically its customers had banking facilities at their local Co-op store and as that link weakened the development of ATM facilities obviated the need to grow the branch network. In an era of branch closures the bank is now well positioned; it does not have the expense and adverse publicity that other banks are suffering as they try to cut back their branch networks.

The bank has over recent years developed new banking facilities, including an Internet front end written in Java. The system, it is claimed, is in advance of that used by any other bank. Java is designed to be portable and hence the system should cope with changes in Internet e-Commerce technology; for instance the use of a portable digital assistant PDA or set-top box.

Using this system the bank has launched (re-launched) its Internet banking service under the name 'smile'. The launch has been accompanied by eye-catching adverts and an equally eye-catching interest rate of 4.5% on the current account (impressive when most customers of the large UK clearing banks get no interest on current accounts – whether the rate lasts is, of course, another matter). The Co-operative Bank is clearly out to capture new business.

Smile's banking service includes:

- A full range of accounts: current, savings, loans and credit cards;
- Online money transfer to and from any account that provide for electronic funds transfer;
- Flexible paying in arrangements, for example cash can be paid in at Post Office branches;
- Online payment of bills with the system maintaining a list of accounts to which bills are paid;
- Online maintenance of standing orders and direct debits;
- Use of ATM machines in the Link network for cash withdrawals;
- Conventional cheques;
- A guarantee of reimbursement should there be a failure in the system or a breach of security (although errors and omissions on the part of the customer are excluded).

The bank also seems to be happy to let the users mix Internet banking with more tradition *f*!al forms. Contact can be via the web page (secure messaging system), e-Mail, post or telephone.

The head of Channel Development at the Co-operative Bank recognises that change in attitudes takes time. He is reported, in a case study issued by Sun Microsystems, as saying:

'Within 15 to 20 years, using the Internet will be normal business. It takes that amount of time for there to be a massive shift in customer behaviour. It has taken over 25 years to reach the point where 70 percent of customers take all their cash out from 23,000 ATM's around the country.'

The Co-operative bank is, it seems, ready to move with their customers as their banking habits evolve into the electronic age.

- **Comment**

Banking is a complex product with important security, tax and legal implications – an online bank has to be a bit more serious than an online bookshop.

Banking has over the years been at the forefront of the use of computer technology. All banks are heavily computerised with a terminal at every counter in the branch, each linked to extensive, centralised computer resources. The large banks typically head the league tables of IT investment with sums of up to and over £200 million in the annual IT budget. The use of IT in the banks facilitate the wide range of financial products currently on offer and an extensive use of EDI in, for example, the CHAPS and SWIFT network provides for the rapid transfer of monetary value between accounts across the globe. For the customer, the use of IT has enabled:

- The automated teller / cash point machine (ATM);
- Telephone banking;
- Online banking via the Internet (and prior to the Internet on Minitel or with other online banking software).

The use of ICTs has also cut the need for the link between the customer and the branch; the customer's account details are available at any branch or ATM. The introduction of, firstly, the ATM and more recently telephone and Internet banking have reduced the need to visit the branch and the banks are competing to reduce costs by closing branches and reducing their staff levels.

The large banks have a range of complex financial products and a diverse customer base. Arguably there is no one technology that will adequately service all these products for each and every consumer. The banks are trying to move the simple transactions out of the branches and would probably like the customers to move away from cheques to electronic means of payment. The ATM can deal with cash withdrawals and deposits. Telephone banking or online banking is appropriate for most simple enquiries and money transfers. The branch, those that are left, are increasingly concentrating on the sale of financial products, a 'financial car showroom'. Arguably the city centre branch is also part of the bank's image, an imposing building is what many customer expect of their bank even if they never visit it (and a truly virtual bank will not necessarily receive the same trust as one that has at least some physical presence).

The use of ATMs and the Internet is something the young prosperous customers may require and can certainly cope with. For the old and the poor these developments are less likely to be welcome. There is a problem of exclusion from financial services and the retrenchment of the branch network will do nothing to help the situation. Social exclusion is a growing problem both in and for society – the banks do protest that they also care but there is scant evidence to back up those claims.

16.7   Virtual Auctions

• **General Description**

Second hand goods, collectables and antiques are sold in shops, auctions, car boot sales and now on the Internet. For online sales the Internet is used to put the seller in touch with the buyer, a bit like small adverts in the local newspaper or a collector's magazine but, using the interactive capabilities of the net, the method of sale is the online auction.

The way the virtual auction works is that:

• The person with something to sell puts a description up online, sets a minimum price and a deadline for the auction to end.
• Other people looking for collectables (or whatever) browse the auction catalogue and can bid for any item they require; their bid will be listed online.
• If there is considerable interest in the item the prices will go up. As the deadline approaches bidders may return to place a second and a third bid.
• At the time set the auction ends and the item is sold to the highest bidder (provided of course any reserve price is met). The buyer then pays and the seller despatches the item.

The online auction differs from most other e-Commerce implementations. The operator does not have any merchandise to sell; unlike a conventional auction the items are not even at the auction site. The online auction site is providing a virtual meeting place where people with things to sell can tie up with people who may want to buy – it is like a marriage bureaux but there are safeguards built in to try and avoid any breach of promise between the two people that the auction eventually beings together.

The supply chain of the online market is something new. It matches that of the advert in the local newspaper but misses out a stage if compared to selling and buying via some variety of second hand shop. The supply chain is shown at Figure 16.7.

Seller   **Online Auction**   **Buyer**

Fig. 16.7 Virtual Auction Supply Chain.

• **Noteworthy Sites**

• eBay	www.ebay.com, www.ebay.co.uk
• Yhahoo	auctions.yahoo.com
• Sothebys at Amazon	www.sothebys.amazon.com

- **Case Study**

 eBay was started in 1995 by Pierre Omidyar and is a rare phenomenon among Internet e-Commerce sites, it operates at a profit.

The story is that Pierre's fiancée, a keen collector of Pez character-based sweet dispensers, complained to him about the difficulty of making contact with other collectors. This tied in with thoughts that Pierre was having about efficient markets and enabling ordinary people to use the net for business and the result was eBay (McCellan, 1999).

As of November 1999, eBay was listing over 3 million items for sale under 2,500 categories. Just one example, listed under 'Photo and Electrics' on the front page and 'Vintage and Collectible' on the second level menu was:

Item #201176461 – Zeiss BLACK Contarex body, rare rare rare

The item had attracted 18 bids. Bidding had started at $100 and had risen to $2,370, the reserve price had not been met but there was still 4 hours and 59 minutes to get an offer in before the auction closed. The camera was being offered by a guy in Milano, can he be trusted? Click on his profile – there are 63 responses from previous buyers, 62 of them positive, for example:

'A true gentleman, very pleasant to deal with, highly recommended!! Thanks.'

Sounds good and there are not many of this model around that are black and in good condition – put in a bid!

Once the bidding is complete, the seller contacts the buyer. The buyer makes a payment according to the seller's instructions and the seller despatches the item. Most eBay users, it appears, deal honestly (and if they don't their record is there online to warn other users). If there are any problems there is insurance, an eBay dispute solving service and for high price items there is an escrow service (a third party who holds the payment until the item is delivered and accepted and then passes the payment onto the seller). Oh, and finally, eBay charges a commission – a Pez collection is an expensive hobby to maintain.

Overall eBay seems to be a great success. It helps collectors buy and it helps people find new homes for items they no longer need. Over and above just buying and selling it has created a buzz, a community for whom eBay is a fun part of their lives.

- **Comment**

e-Bay claims to be an 'online trading community' and community seems to be what it is. It is people all over the world buying, selling and having fun without the need for or involvement of big business (except eBay is now a big business).

The interesting part of eBay is the way that the dealing seems to be fair and honest. The fairness is reinforced by a system of user profiles built up from the comments of other people with whom they do business. It seems to work and long may it continue to do so.

eBay is not without its competitors and there has to be the suspicion that those competitors are more about money than community. A successful online auction needs a critical mass of people taking part. Not all the online auctions that have sprung up seem likely to last; hopefully those which offer a real service will be the ones that stay the course.

16.8   Online Share Dealing

- **General Description**

The use of the Internet is taking off among private investors in stocks and shares. The Internet can make available to the private investor the up-to-the-minute information that, until recently, had only been available to those working in financial institutions. The use of online brokerage services automates the process of buying and selling and hence allows a reduction of commission charges. Also the commodity being traded is intangible; the ownership of stocks and shares can be recorded electronically so there is no requirement for physical delivery.

Internet share trading sites are been set up by stock broking organisations and by new entrants to the market (the latter need clearance from the regulatory authorities before they can operate). The Internet is also being used for information sites and chatlines, some provide information free and some require a subscription.

Current developments are, essentially, converting off-line practices to an online equivalent. The private investor who may have received a stockbroker's report through the post and looked up share prices in the morning paper can access the information online (with the current market price being available). The investor who might have made calculations about trends and valuations by hand can download the information from the web into a spreadsheet or a personal finance program that runs on their PC. That same private investor who used to ring up a stockbroker to buy or sell (a process that might take some time when the market was busy) can issue that same instruction online for immediate execution.

> 'The investor is able to deal at a price viewed immediately, whereas using more traditional dealing services an investor will often have to wait in a telephone queuing system to get through to the dealing desk and when trading may have to wait for the price of the trade to be confirmed.'

(Allgood, 1999)

The number of sites and the usage of them is mushrooming. Figures for 1999 show 7 million online traders in the US and a rapid growth in the UK since the first site opened at the start of 1998. In the UK the sites are offered by some of the traditional British stock broking firms, a number of the banks and a few large US companies that have set up in the UK.

In the US the availability of online share dealing services has created the phenomena of daytrading. The daytrader's aim is to make a profit from volatile shares that are bought in the morning and sold in the afternoon. Daytraders are often just ordinary members of the public who have given up their jobs to spend the day glued to a screen watching the price movements of a few selected stocks. Some daytraders make money but many do not; the unsuccessful daytrader looses all their savings and often a great deal more as many take out loans or trade on credit.

The supply chain for share dealing is unchanged, the use of the net just speeds up the whole process (and that can be vital in some share dealing). The supply chain (from broker to investor) is shown in Figure 16.8.

Broker

Investor

Fig. 16.8   Online Share Dealing Supply Chain.

- **Noteworthy Sites**

  - E*Trade   www.etrade.com, www.etrade.co.uk
  - Market Eye   www.market-eye.co.uk
  - Charles Schwab   www.schwab.co.uk

- **Case Study**

E✳TRADE E*Trade traces its origins back to 1982 with the first online trade taking place in 1983. In 1992 E*Trade
TM opened for business on CompuServe and AOL with the net version coming online in 1996. The services they list are:

  - Free real-time quotes;
  - Market news and research that can be customised to the user's investment interests;
  - Choice of order types;
  - Low commission rates with substantial discounts for heavy users of the system;.
  - Portfolio tracking (a system that tracks the value of the

account holder's shares);

- Customer accounts (with a facility to borrow further funds using stocks and shares already held as security);
- Discussion groups so that investors can share news and views.

The main indexes (US in this instance) are on the home page and the details of any share is available to the investor who is interested in it.

NASDAQ	3329.96	▼	-62.60
DJIA	11013.07	▼	-76.45
S&P 500	1406.88	▼	-14.06
30-YR BOND	6.187 %		0.00

- **Comment**

Internet share dealing seems like a sector set to grow and grow. Why trade through a broker when you can get a better information and a better service by trading online. For many years the people in the trade have had up-to-the-minute information on share prices that has not been available to the general public. Now members of the general public can compete on equal terms.

The problem with online trading is that it increases the temptation to indulge in short-term speculation rather than long-term investment. It is a risky business for the individual and of doubtful benefit to the overall economy that the financial markets are supposedly designed to service. That said, if the financial institutions can and do speculate, often in a thoroughly irresponsible manner, why should the ordinary punter not have a chance to join in if they wish to?

16.9   Gambling on the Net

- **General Description**

Gambling takes many forms, from the simple scratch card, through betting on various sports events to casino type games (often played for high stakes). All these forms of gambling can be replicated on the web.

Internet gambling can be dated back to 1995 with the establishment of the first online casino. From that start the industry has mushroomed with, four years later, over a thousand casino sites online. The way Internet gambling works is much like any other e-Commerce site; the punter chooses the service and pays with a credit card. Gambling sites can be sophisticated with the facilities of the web used to display the odds, report on the result of the event or simulate the playing of the game.

The gambling supply chain is very simple, the transaction is between the bookmaker or casino and the punter, that applies both online and offline. The supply chain is represented in Figure 16.9.

**Bookmaker /
Casino**

Punter

Fig. 16.9 Online Gambling Supply Chain.

- **Example Sites**

  - Blue Sq / City Index   www.bluesq.com

- **Case Study**

Blue Square is the interactive division of City Index, a UK sports and financial bookmaker. Blue Square are concerned about their credentials; they emphasise that they are based in the City of London and not in some offshore island.

The site covers a wide range of betting; topics include UK and international football (soccer to US readers), snooker, NFL, cricket, horse racing, dog racing and even who might be elected to be Mayor of London. Click on UK football and odds are given for the current weeks matches, which team might win the league and which player will be the season's top goal scorer. The site matches the sort of bet that could be placed with any licensed high street bookmaker. There are no card games or gaming machines; it is all strictly within the parameters set out in UK law.

The site requires registration before it is used and emphasises that customers must be at least 18 years old.

- **Comment**

For some, all gambling is immoral but most would agree that a little 'flutter' does no harm – and possibly a little good if the profits go to a good cause.

Gambling has, however, a darker side. Gambling addicts ruin their own lives and, not infrequently, the lives of many other. On the other side of the business there is an issue of criminal involvement. For these reasons there has been considerable effort by governments to use the law to regulate gambling (with some of the most restrictive legislation being in North America). A further area of involvement of the state, in gambling, are the levying of gaming taxes and the support of casino development as a tool of economic development (an involvement that runs somewhat contrary to the social case for the restriction of gambling).

The use of Internet gambling blows apart the regulatory framework and social controls that consist in conventional gambling. Problems include:

- Social controls that might be exerted over a gambler in a betting shop or a casino do not apply online; at the simplest level there is no closing time;
- The gambling facilities can be based in a country with minimal legislative restrictions and from there it is open for business on a world-wide basis (thus circumventing national legal restrictions);
- Offshore gambling circumvents national taxation requirements;
- Any attempt by a state to monitor online gambling activities would raise civil liberty concerns – the use of encryption for transmission makes any monitoring that is undertaken more difficult;
- The difficulty in regulating online gambling makes it prone to illegal activity, possibly more vulnerable than its conventional counterpart.

Overall it is difficult to see what can be done about these issues. The problems are compounded by the very different legislative frameworks that operate in different countries. Any attempts that are made to tighten up legal controls in one country may well be evaded by the operator simply moving their activities to another location with a less restrictive reglme.

16.10 e-Diversity

This chapter has examined the use of Internet e-Commerce in eight different market areas. The technology for online operation and the issue of payment security is much the same whatever the area of operation. Differences include how adequately the product can be described online, the ease with which the product can be delivered to the customer, the extent to which the price to the consumer can be cut by operating online and the possibility of offering an enhanced service by operating electronically. Thus, the appeal to the customer differs across market sectors and from individual to individual. Examples could be:

An academic might order a book from the online bookstore that is not held in stock in the local bookshop but she will use the airport bookstand for something light to read on the plane. In contrast her brother who reads a couple of thrillers a week on the daily commute to work might plan his reading in advance around the special offers available at the online bookstore.

The same academic might have toyed with ordering groceries online but can never be sure when she will be in to take the delivery. Her father, retired and living alone, has no problem being at home to take the delivery and has got his daughter to help him understand the online grocery store.

In the sale of physical goods, Internet e-Commerce is particularly suitable for products such as books and CDs. These products are adequately described and easily delivered and e-Commerce outlets already have a worthwhile market share. The use of Internet e-Commerce for other merchandise: groceries, clothing and furniture, for example, is more problematic; for these items an online description is likely to be less satisfactory and the delivery problems are greater. There is and will be an online market in all classes of goods but the market share will vary across the different trade sectors. In no market for physical goods is online trading likely to become the dominant channel.

For the provision of many services the story may well be different. For banking, insurance, share trading and gambling there is no physical product to deliver. For these services, the customer who wishes to transact online, can gain considerable benefit (if only the ability to deal with their 'paperwork' when and where they like. The other beneficiary of putting these services online is the supplier who can make considerable cost savings by dispensing with traditional outlets and the staff that used to serve in them. There seems to be a distinct possibility that some of this provision will become online only (or the conventional service will only be available for those prepared to pay a premium price); not a healthy development for those too old, poor or disabled to make use of online facilities.

Finally, Internet e-Commerce has a darker side. It can allow legitimate regulation to be bypassed or tax to be avoided. Online gambling has obvious dangers and the proliferation of pornography online is another problem area.

Exercises

This chapter is intended to show the diversity of e-Commerce and how the infrastructure and business model differs across trade sectors. The exercise is to follow up on this analysis by:

- Further investigating one of the sectors outlined in the report. Take for instance electronic newspapers and checkout a range of papers. Look at the newspaper, the use of adverts and any background information that the sites might give. Identify how the different newspapers use the web and try to establish how this might complement (or compete with) their conventional paper publication.
- Identify a sector not covered in the chapter and carry out a similar investigation. Sectors that might be chosen are insurance, fashion, cosmetics, etc. Choose a sector that sells tangible goods and one that offers a service and contrast the two.

This exercise can be done individually or it could for the basis of a tutorial with each participant ivestigating a named site and the findings then being discussed in class.

Further Reading

The main recommendation for this chapter is that the reader investigates the diversity of web sites and business models that are evolving by looking at the e-Commerce sites online, see exercise above. For a radically different view of how e-Commerce might (should?) evolve the following book is recommended:

Rowan W. (1999) *Net Benefit, Guaranteed Electronic Markets: The Ultimate Potential of Online Trade*, Macmillan, Basingstoke, UK.

See also the book's web site for updates on the business use of e-Commerce.

Part 5

Conclusions

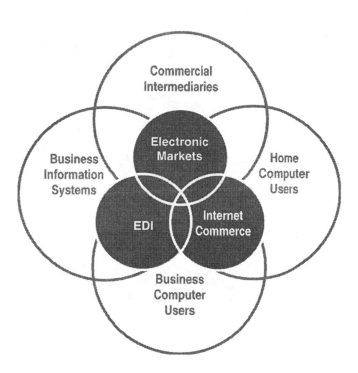

17

Electronic Commerce: Let a thousand Flowers Bloom

Summary

EDI and Electronic Markets have established their place and their utility in the way business is done. Their effect has been considerable but not as all embracing as some early theorists predicted.

Internet based commerce, just one of the many applications on the Internet, is still at an early stage of development. It is set to become an important commercial channel and its wide availability and diversity will ensure it a developing role. However, as with other new forms of commerce, it too will settle down as just one of a range of ways of doing business.

This chapter looks at all forms of e-Commerce in their wider commercial context. It concludes that each way of doing business has a role to play and that the road to competitive advantage, for many organisations, is in the integration of appropriate e-Commerce technologies throughout the supply chain.

17.1   The Full Set

The study of e-Commerce is much broader than the current enthusiasm for home shopping on the web. As this book has explained, e-Commerce includes:

- Formal business-to-business transactions using EDI;
- Electronic markets used by commercial intermediaries;
- Informal business-to-business transactions using Internet e-Commerce;
- Consumer transactions with business, or other members of the public, using Internet e-Commerce.

This range of e-Commerce is illustrated in Figure 17.1.

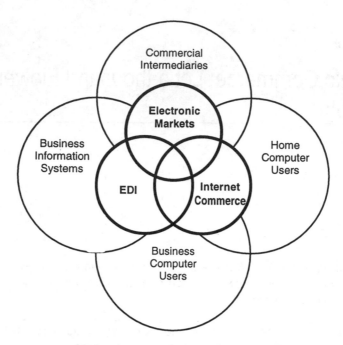

Fig. 17.1 e-Commerce Technologies.

These developments in e-Commerce have been intimately linked with the development of networks. Initially networks were confined within the organisation. These networks were then expanded to form inter-organisational links and subsequently reached out to members of the public (with the Internet as the most obvious manifestation of this later phase). Each development in e-Commerce has taken place in parallel with other business and technical changes. The development of EDI was accompanied by, for example, EPOS systems and resulted in the development of the inter-organisational information systems that control the supply chain in many retail and component assembly trade sectors. The emergence of Internet e-Commerce arose from the availability of affordable home computers, the popularisation and commercialisation of the Internet and the development of multi-media and graphical user interfaces. Each development has added to the range of e-Commerce facilities but the previous technologies have not been superseded. Each e-Commerce technology has its own appropriate area of application; it can now be argued that there is a 'full set'. The technologies of e-Commerce and the equipment used with e-Commerce will be further developed and popularised but there is now an e-Commerce technology applicable to each category of trade exchange.

17.2   Technology Adoption

The history of technological adoption, both with e-Commerce and in the wider sphere of ICTs, is a chequered one. There seems to be a pattern of each new technology being welcomed with great fanfairs and exaggerated claims. Examples of this include:

- Interactive videotext for information services and e-Commerce application; a part of Harold Wilson's (the British Prime Minister at the time) 'white heat of the technological revolution'.
- Telework which was to close offices and factories, cut traffic and pollution and create flexible and fulfilling lives '... the most anti-productive thing we can do is to ship millions of workers back and forth across the landscape every morning and evening.' (Toffler, 1981).
- EDI where Sokol (1989) said 'unless a company is doing EDI in a few years, it will be at a marked competitive disadvantage' and MIT in their report of the Management in the 1990s, programme which famously said 'EDI is not a choice ... it is the inevitable way that business will be done'.

These enthusiasms were soon to evaporate and, in some ways, turned into a pessimism or rejection that was equally unjustified. Interactive videotext systems only took off as a consumer telematics channel in one country but elsewhere the system was extensively used, by business, for applications such as financial market information and the booking of package holidays. Telework is significant in a number of organisations, has helped many people who had a particular need for flexibility but it has not changed the general pattern of peoples' working lives; its main contribution is perhaps in informal teleworking where employees will work at home on the odd day to finish a report or to combine a working day with some other domestic commitment.   EDI has similarly failed to meet the original expectations of near universal business adoption but it has become 'the inevitable way that business is done' in important trade sectors where the trade cycle most closely matches the specific advantages of the technology.

Internet e-Commerce has been greeted in much the same way as these earlier technologies. Bill Clinton, President of the United States was impressed:

> 'Anyone who wants to form a business to deliver information will have the means of reaching customers. And any person who wants information will be able to choose among competing information providers, at reasonable prices. That's what the future will look like – say, in ten to fifteen years.'

Bill Gates of Microsoft (a somewhat late convert to Internet enthusiasm!) is quoted as saying:

> 'The rise of the Internet and the increase in subscribers to online services is a fantastic thing ... virtually all agree that by the end of the decade the Internet will be a significant business channel.'

And Tony Blair, the British Prime Minister, adds his predictions (in somewhat similar terms to Sokol on EDI ten years earlier):

> 'To British business I deliver a pretty blunt massage: if you don't see the Internet as an opportunity, it will be a threat. ... If you're not exploiting the opportunities of e-Commerce you could go bankrupt.'
>
> (Teather, 1999)

The Internet serves a great number of functions and not all of them should be classified as e-Commerce. The e-Business applications of the Internet are developing but they are a long way from fulfilling the predictions of the pundits. Internet e-Commerce has changed the life of a few web entrepreneurs but its effect on the lives of most other people has been very slight (unless you are a Pez collector). The e-Commerce guru of ICL put it thus:

> 'Everyone agrees that electronic commerce is going to be big, very big or enormous. But nobody knows when. There is considerable disagreement about the historic impact of electronic commerce, let alone the future one. Although all commentators present forecasts for the short-term which contain truly eye-catching growth, their figures fail to achieve anything remotely approaching the size of existing modes of trade. And yet no commentator doubts the power of electronic commerce to challenge those existing modes.
>
> In order to explain this paradox, many observers allude to technical, cost and infrastructure impediments. While playing their part in impeding adoption, these alleged impediments have arguably limited validity. For electronic commerce to deliver its full promise, there will have to be business, social and cultural changes and these will take more than two or three years to complete.'
>
> (Emery, 1999)

And that change to a wired society will not render redundant previous technologies. The use of e-Mail has not eliminated the use of telephone, fax and good old-fashioned post (and the post has an important new role to play in the delivery phase of the e-Commerce trade cycle). The development of the supermarket and the shopping mall did not eliminate the specialist shop and the corner store (though they have had a hard time). The widespread adoption of e-Commerce will take many years; it will not be 'the' shopping and communication channel but just another channel that is additional to the several that already exist. Its adoption and use will become part of everyday life and, like England losing at sport, it will hardly be noticed.

17.3   Integrating the Supply Chain

e-Commerce is sold as an instant technology and a one or two day wait for delivery does not quite fit the image. The image of e-Commerce, or at least the e-Store, will be further tarnished if the product that is being ordered is out of stock and the delivery time extends out from a day or two to a week or more.

The need is for an efficient supply chain that matches or exceeds the capability of supermarkets and other multiple retailers to maintain high levels of stock availability whilst holding minimum levels of stock. The multiples use e-Commerce, typically EDI, to manage their supply chains and the efficient e-Vendor is going to need the same or similar systems. The requirement is summarised in Figure 17.2.

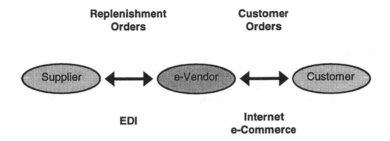

Fig. 17.2 e-Commerce enabled Supply Chain.

This is a requirement that was, for example, specifically included in the design of the Blackwell's online bookshop where EDI links to book trade systems are specifically built in. There is also an interesting variation on the web pages of Action Computer Supplies who include the stock figures of key suppliers in their product database; goods supplied from Action's stock are next day delivery and goods brought in from suppliers require a three day turn round.

17.4   e-Choice

And finally, how will the future look? Will the local supermarket be boarded up and has Mr Ali in the corner store switched to a job with a parcel delivery company – probably not.

I, for one, will still be going to the supermarket to select my own extra ripe bananas and those stuffed olives that take my fancy and look good in the jar; both of which the supermarket has ordered using sophisticated EDI systems.

Later that evening, marking essays and out of cola (my fuel to keep me going), it is off to Mr Ali's late night corner store, a store that is still replenished by the owner doing a trip to the cash and carry.

A recommended book that I know the local bookshop will not have in stock, the online bookshop should do nicely. But to get a book for my mother-in-law's Christmas present I would rather browse round the shelves in a friendly real bookshop – might even have a cappuccino as well.

Finally, off to Canada with a pile of unmarked essays in my bag. As I rush for my plane, brandishing (virtually) my e-Ticket I stop at the real newsstand for some light reading (student essays are rarely light reading). On the shelves is a book on China and I remember the words of Chairman Mao:

'Let a thousand flowers bloom.'

... but he probably did not have e-Commerce in mind.

Further Reading

Nigel Cope in his book *Retail in a Digital Age* sets out a vision of a time where e-Commerce has in fact replaced most other shopping channels. It is 2006 and:

'Jim drives back, passing on the way two boarded-up supermarkets and the old shopping mall on the edge of town that was converted to a virtual reality fun park three years ago. There were still a lot of derelict superstores and shopping centres. They had become real eye-sores with their crumbling brickwork and car parks sprouting weeds. So many of them had failed to recognise the full impact of the digital revolution or seen it too late. The new 'virtual' grocery chains like InterGrocer and SmartShop had stolen a large share of the market.'

It is reassuring to see that at least urban decay will still be with us! (and to be fair, Jim does occasionally still visit a real store called Safebury, the name is reassuringly familiar). The full reference of the book is:

Cope N. (1996) *Retail in a Digital Age*, Bowerdean.

A book that sets out a vision somewhat similar to eBay but where almost every aspect of life can be conducted as an online transaction is:

Rowan W. (1999) *Net Benefit, Guaranteed Electronic Markets: the ultimate potential of online trade*, Macmillian Business.

Bibliography

Allgood B. (1999) 'Internet Based Share Dealing in the New Global Market Place', *Bit World '99*, Cape Town, South Africa.

Andre A. and Wickens D (1995) 'When users want what's not best for them', *Ergonomics Digest*, Vol. 4, No. 4, pp. 10–4.

Andrews K. (1971) *The Concept of Corporate Strategy*, Irwin, Homewood, Ill.

Been J., Christiaanse E., O'Callaghan R. and Van Diepen T. (1995) 'Electronic Markets in the Air Cargo Community', *Third European Conference on Information Systems*, Athens.

Benjamin R., de Long D., Morton M. S. (1990) 'Electronic Data Interchange: How much Competitive Advantage', *Long Range Planning*, Vol. 23, No. 1, pp. 29–40.

Berge J. (1991) *The EDIFACT Standards*, NCC Blackwell.

Bhs (1994) *The Role of Computers within Bhs*, Bhs plc. Information Technology Department, London.

Bloch M., Pigneur Y. and Segev A. (1996) 'Leveraging Electronic Commerce for Competitive Advantage: a Business Value Framework', *The Ninth International Conference on EDI – IOS*, Bled, Slovenia.

Bloch M. and Segev A. (1997) 'The Impact of Electronic Commerce on the Travel Industry: An Analysis and Case Study', *Thirtieth Hawaii International e-Commerce Conference*, Hawaii.

Bray P. (1992) 'Electronic Trading: Web of Wheel', *Which Computer*, January, pp. 50–8.

Camphuisen A (1998) 'Corporates now Boarding!', *Internet World*, September/October.

Cats-Baril W. and Jelassi T. (1994) 'Managing Strategic IT Initiatives in the Public Sector: Establishing a National Information Technology Infrastructure: The Case of the French Videotext System', *European Case Book on Competing through Information technology: Strategy and Implementation*, Prentice Hall, pp. 166–98.

Computing (1992) 'Eyes for the Road', *Computing*, 20 February, p. 32.

Computing (1995) 'The Focus: Electronic Data Interchange', *Computing*, 26 January, pp. 37–47.

Cope N. (1996) *Retail in the Digital Age*, Bowerdean, London.

Cowe R. (1998) 'Bringing Home the Bacon', *The Guardian*, 10 October, p. 26.

DeCollect (1999) 'Way, Way too Cool', *Canadian Business*, 27 August, pp. 30–5.

Doward J. (1999) Observer Business, p3, Doward J., 31 Oct, BA sells 2% of tickets online and intends to increase that to 50% over the next 5 years.

Earl M. (1989) *Management Strategies for Information Technology*, Prentice Hall, Hemel Hempstead, UK.

Earnest and Young (1994) *Report to Whitaker Telerdering: O&M Study: Book Ordering Process within Book Retailers*, Earnest and Young.

Electronic Commerce (1996) 'Saving Energy', *Electronic Commerce and Communications*, Issue 4, March, p. 30.

Electronic Trader (1994a) 'Rover rolls out with EDI', *Electronic Trader*, Vol IV, Issue III, February, p. 14.

Electronic Trader (1994b) 'An Interview with Alan Sheppard, General Manager ODETTE Europe', *Electronic Trader*, Vol. IV, Issue III, February, pp. 16–8.

Electronic Trader (1995) 'Health: A suitable case for treatment by EDI' *Electronic Trader*, Vol. V, Issue VI, May, p. 20.

Elliot Major L. (1999) 'Who needs a broker', *Guardian Online*, 14 October, p. 10.

Emery D. (1999) 'The Mists and Fruitfulness of Electronic Commerce', *Innovation Through Electronic Commerce: 2nd International Conference IeC'99*, November, Manchester, p.8l.

Endlar L. and Davis D. (1999) 'Internet Gambling', *Bit World'99*, Cape Town, South Africa.

Esprit (1997) *ESPRIT and Acts projects related to Electronic Commerce*, http://www2.cordis.lu/esprit/src/ecomproj.htm.

Flight International (1999a) 'World Airline Directory: the Americas', *Flight International*, 17-23 March, pp.39–110.

Flight International (1999b) 'World Airline Directory: Europe and the CIS', *Flight International*, 24-30 March, pp.37–113.

Flight International (1999c) 'World Airline Directory: Africa, Asia and the Pacific', *Flight International*, 31 March – 6 April, pp. 47–116.

Freedman A. (1999) *The Computer Desktop Encyclopaedia* (2nd. ed.), Amacon, New York.

Graham A. and Hart M. (1999) *E-com Legal Guide (UK/EU)*, http://www. bakerinfo. com/apec/ukeuapec.htm.

Guttman R., Moukas A. and Maes P. (1998) 'Agent-mediated Electronic Commerce: a Survey', *Knowledge Engineering Review*, June 1998.

Handy C. (1999) 'E-flea Market', *Guardian Online*, 22 April, pp. 2–3.

Hamilton, S. (1991) 'Total Rethink', Computing, 3 October, pp. 24–27.

Henning P. (1997) 'Wie sicher ist "Sicher" ', *Bank und Market*, December.

Hersey (1999) *An Investigation into the commercial use of the Internet through the developent of a Web Assessment Model: A dissertation submitted to Manchester Metropolitan University as part fulfilment of the degree of Master of Science / Computing*, Department of Computing and Mathematics, September.

Hill R. (1997) 'Electronic Commerce, the World Wide Web, Minitel and EDI', *The Information Society*, Vol. 13, No. 1, pp. 33–42.

Hoffman D., Kalsbeck W. and Novak T. (1996) 'Internet and Web Use in the US', *Communication of the ACM*, December, Vol. 39, No. 12, pp. 36–46.

Hoffman P. (1995) *Netscape and the World Wide Web for Dummies*, IDG Books, Foster City, CA.

Holand C. and Lockett G. (1992) 'IT Strategy in Retailing: Organisational Change and Future Directions', *Journal of Strategic Information Systems*, Vol. 1, No. 3, pp. 134–42.

Hood K., Lawrenson M., Chen J. and Williams B. C. (1994) 'Information Technology Strategy in Retailing: a study of the impact of electronic data interchange on multiples and their suppliers', *World Congress of EDI Users – Research Forum*, Brighton, UK, June.

Jelassi T. (1994a) 'Binding the Customer through IT: Competing through Electronic Data Interchange at Papeteries Brun Passot, or Making Paper Passè', *European Case Book on Competing through Information Technology: Strategy and Implementation*, Prentice Hall, Hemel Hempstead, UK, pp. 84–106.

Jelassi T. and Loebbecke C. (1994b) 'Managing Strategic IT Adoption: EDI at Leroy-Merlin: A Standardised Success', *European Case Book on Competing through Information Technology: Strategy and Implementation*, Prentice Hall, Hemel Hempstead, UK, pp. 107–22.

Johnston H. R. and Vitale M. (1988) 'Creating Competitive Advantage with Interorganizational Information Systems', MIS Quarterly, June, pp. 153–65.

Katz (1999) 'Final Edition', Guardian Media, 13 December, pp. 2–3.

Keegan V. (1999) 'Is Britain a Virtual ElDorado', *The Guardian Online*, 15 July, pp. 2–3.

KPMG (1998) 'e-Christmas Achievements and Learning', *KPMG Home Page*, http://www.kpmg.co.uk.

KPMG (1999) Home Shopping - Retailers urged to experiment whilst matching customer needs, *KPMG Home Page*, http://www.kpmg.co.uk.

Krcmar H., Bjorn-Anderson N. and O'Callaghan R. (eds.) (1995) *EDI in Europe: How it Works in Practice*, Wiley, Chichester, UK.

Lawrence A. (1998) 'Front to Back', *Computer Business Review*, July.

Lee B. (1998) 'Payment for Goods and Services in an Information Age', in Romm C. and Sudweeks F. (eds), *Doing Business Electronically: A Global Perspective of Electronic Commerce*, Springer, London, pp. 163–73.

Loebbecke C. and Jelassi T. (1994) 'Innovating Service Delivery through IT: Home Banking: An IT-based Business Philosophy of a Complementary Distribution Channel? CORTEL 'versus' Crédit Commercial de France', *European Case Book on Competing through Information Technology: Strategy and Implemetation*, Prentice Hall, Hemel Hempstead, UK, pp. 244–66.

Lucas P. (1999) 'Internet Trading and its threat to the Traditional Stock Broker', *BIT World'99*, Cape Town, South Africa.

Lynch, R. (1997) *Corporate Strategy*, Pitman, London.

Malone T., Yates J. and Benjamin R. (1987) 'Electronic Markets and Electronic Hierarchies', *Communication of the ACM*, Vol. 30, No. 6, pp. 484–97.

Marr A. (1999) 'And the news is … electric', *Observer*, 17 October.

Metzgen (1990) *Killing the Paper Dragon: Electronic Data Interchange in Business*, Heinemann Newnes, Oxford.

McAfee R. P. and McMillan J. (1997) 'Electronic Markets', in Kalakota R. and Whinston A (eds.) *Readings in Electronic Commerce*, Addison Wesley, pp. 293–309.

McClennan J. (1999) 'Going, going strong', *Guardian Online*, p. 14, 28 October

McIntosh N. (1999) 'When crime is on the card', *Guardian Online*, 02 December, pp. 2–3.

Miers D. and Hutton G. (1999) *The Strategic Chalenges of Electronic Commerce*, http://www.enix.co.uk/electron.htm.

Miller K., Whiteley D. and Quick P. (1999) 'A trade cycle based view of evaluating e-Commerce', *Evaluation'99*, November, London.

Morgan (1999) 'Keep reading all about it', Guardian Media, 06 December, p. 10

Morrell P. (1998) 'Airline sales and distribution channels: the impact of new technology', *Tourism Economics*, Vol. 4, No. 1, pp. 5–19.

Morton R. and Chester M. (1997) *Transforming the Business: the IT contribution*, McGraw Hill, Maidenhead, UK.

Murthy G. and Jelassi T. (1994) 'Exploiting a Publicly Available IT Platform: Home Retailing Applications at CAMIF', *European Case Book on Competing through Information Technology: Strategy and Implementation*, Prentice Hall, Hemel Hempstead, UK, pp. 199–215.

Narendam P., Strom J. and Whiteley D. (1995) 'An Analysis of Electronic Markets in the context of SMEs', *3rd European Conference on Information Systems*, Athens.

Needle D. (1994) *Business in Context* (2nd ed.) International Thomson Business Press, London.

Negroponte N. (1995) *being digital*, Coronet, London.

Niederst J. (1999) *Web Design in a Nutshell*, O'Reilly, Sebastopol, CA.

Niemira M. (1996) 'Are Nonstore Sales a threat to Traditional Store Business?', *Chain Store Age*, 26 September.

Noll A. M. (1996) 'Cyber Network Technology: Issues and Uncertainties', *Communications of the ACM*, Vol. 39, No 12, pp. 27–31.

Palframan (1995) 'Concurrent Affairs', *Computing*, 02 June, p. 32.

Parfett, M (1992) *What is EDI? A guide to Electronic Data Interchange*, 2nd ed., NCC Blackwell, Manchester.

Porter M. E. (1980) *Competitive Strategy: Techniques for Analysing Industries and Competitors*, The Free Press, New York.

Porter M. E. (1985) *Competitive Advantage: Creating and Sustaining Superior Performance*, Free Press, New York.

Preston M. (1988) *What is EDI?*, NCC, Manchester.

Raman D. (1996) 'EDI: the backbone for business on the net', *Electronic Commerce and Communications*, Issue 4, March, pp. 18–21.

Rapaport I. and Jelassi T. (1994) 'Developing and Diffusing Strategic IT: The Technology of the Minitel System', *European Case Book on Competing through Information Technology: Strategy and Implementation*, Prentice Hall, Hemel Hempstead, UK, pp. 216–243.

Rebel T. and Koenig W. (1999) 'Ensuring Security and Trust in Electronic Commerce', in Romm C. and Sudweeks F. (eds), *Doing Business on the Internet: Opportunities and Pitfalls*, Springer, London, pp. 101–12.

Reekers N. and Smithson S. (1994) 'The Distribution of Benefits and Drawbacks of EDI Use in the European Automotive Industry', *5th World Congress of EDI Users: Research Forum*, Brighton

Revel P. (1997) 'Off your trolley', *The Guardian Online*, 02 July.

Rhodoes (1999) *Credit Cards and Web Site Usability*, html://www.webword.com/moving/creditcards.html.

Rowan W. (1999) *Net Benefit, Guaranteed Electronic Markets: The Ultimate Potential of Online Trade*, Macmillan, Basingstoke, UK.

Saxena and Wagenaar (1995) 'Critical Success Factors of EDI Technology Transfer: A Conceptual Framework' *3rd European Conference on Information Systems*, Athens.

Schaffer E. and Sorflaten J. (1998) 'Web Usability Illustrated: Breathing Easier with your Useable E-Commerce Site', *EDI Forum: The Journal of Electronic Commerce*, Vol. 11, Part 4, pp. 50–52, 57–64, 101.

Schmid B. and Lindemann M. (1998) 'Elements of a Reference Model Electronic Markets', *31st Annual Hawaii International Conference on Systems Science*, Hawaii.

Schofield J. (1997) 'The new seekers', *The Guardian Online*, 06 November, pp. 1–3.

Schofield J. (1999) 'Searching for the perfect engine', *Guardian Online*, 15 July, pp. 10–1.

Search Engine Watch (1999) *Search Engine Watch*, www.searchenginewatch.com

Seddon P. (1997) Defining Electronic Commerce, www.dis.unimelb.edu/staff/peter/InternetEra.html.

Seigel D. (1996) *Creating Killer Web Sites: The Art of Third-Generation Site Design*, Hayden Books, New York.

Selz and Schubert (1998) *WA - The Web Assessment Model*, http://www. businessmedia.org/businessmedia\businessmedia.nsf/pages/wa_model.html.

Shaw N. (1998) 'Leveraging Security Policy for Competitive Business Advantage in Electronic Commerce', in Romm C. and Sudweeks F. (eds.) *Doing Business Electronically*, Springer-Verlag, London.

Sokol P. (1989) *EDI: The Competitive Edge*, McGraw-Hill, New York.

Sokol P. (1995) *From EDI to Electronic Commerce: A Business Initiative*, McGraw-Hill, New York.

Swatman P. M. C. and Swatman P. A. (1993) 'Business Process Redesign Using EDI: An Australian Success Story', *Sixth International EDI Conference*, Bled, Slovenia.

Swatman P. M. C., Swatman P. A. and Fowler D. C. (1994) 'A model of EDI integration and strategic business reengineering', *Journal of Strategic Information Systems*, Vol. 13, No. 1, pp. 41–60.

Teather D. (1999) 'Blair puts finger on the e-problem', *Guardian*, 14 September, p. 23.

TEDIS (1992) *Trade EDI Systems Programme: TEDIS: Interim Report 1992*, Commission of the European Communities – DG XIII.

Tilson R., Dong J., Martin S. and Kieke E. (1998) *Factors and Principles Affecting the Usability of Four E-commerce Sites*, http://www.research.att.comm/conf/ hfweb/proceedings/tilson/index.html.

Toffler A. (1981) *The Third Wave*, Pan.

Waldman (1999) 'Internet revived the radio star', *Media Guardian*, 31 May, p. 7.

Webster J. (1994) 'EDI Standard Setters: Process, Politics and Power', *Technologie de l'information et Societe*.

Whiteley D. (1994) 'Hubs, Spokes and SMEs: Patterns of Electronic Trading and the participation of Small and Medium-sized Enterprises (SMEs) in EDI Networks': *World Congress of EDI Users - Research Forum*, June, Brighton.

Whiteley D (1995) 'EDI: Re-Engineering the Competitive Edge' *EDI-Edifact 95*, July, Moscow.

Whiteley D (1996) 'EDI Maturity and the Competitive Edge', *Logistics Information Management*, MCB University Press, Vol. 9, No. 4, pp. 11–7.

Whiteley D. (1998a) 'Would you buy an ice-cream cone over the Internet?', *Eleventh International Bled Electronic Commerce Conference*, June, Bled, Slovenia.

Whiteley D. (1998b) 'Merging Electronic Commerce Technologies for Competitive Advantage', *Association of Information Systems 1998 Americas Conference*, August, Baltimore, USA.

Whiteley D (1998c) 'EDI Maturity: A Business Opportunity', in Romm C. and Sudweeks F. (eds.) *Doing Business Electronically*, Springer-Verlag, London, pp. 139–149.

Whiteley D., Hersey I., Miller K. and Quick P. (1999a) 'Internet e-Commerce: buying the book and catching the plane', *BIT'99*, November, Manchester.

Whiteley D. (1999b) 'Learning to Drive e-Commerce', *Innovation Through Electronic Commerce: 2nd International Conference IeC'99*, November, Manchester, pp. 286–99.

Whiteley D. and Miller K. (1999c) 'e-Commerce: Flying in the Face of Competition', BIT World'99, June, Cape Town, South Africa.

Whiteley D (1999d) 'Internet Commerce - Hot Cakes and Dead Ducks', in Romm C. and Sudweeks F. (eds.) Doing Business on the Internet: Opportunities and Pitfalls, Springer-Verlag, London, pp. 9–20.

Wigland R. T. (1997) 'Electronic Commerce: Definition, Theory and Context' *The Inforation Society*, Vol. 13, No. 1, pp. 1–16.

Wilmot K (1995) 'Unwitting Users', *Electronic Trader*, Vol. V, Issue VI, pp. 18–20.

Wilson K. (1997) 'From tags to riches', *The Guardian Online*, 04 December, p. 8.

Windsor (1998) 'e-Commerce: Hit of Hype', Documents, June/July, pp. 36–42.

Ziariti R., Griffiths J., Bennett M. and Payne P. (1995) 'University of Central England – Rover Partnership' *Logistics Information Management*, Vol 8, No. 6, pp. 8–12.

Index